plastic cameras

Lo-fi photography in the digital age

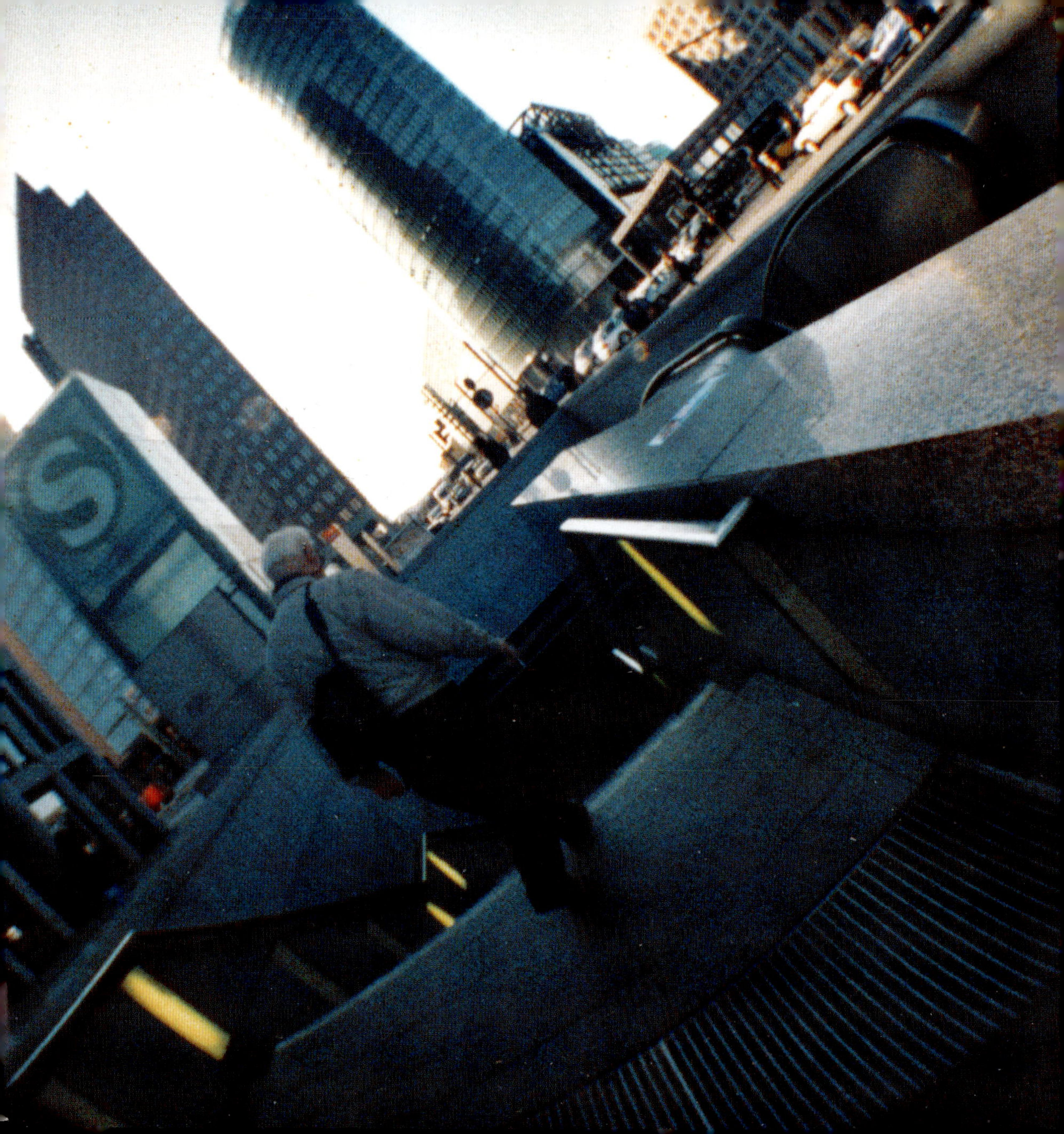

plastic
cameras

Lo-fi photography in the digital age

Chris Gatcum

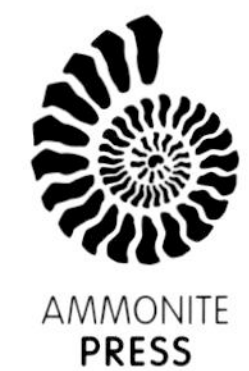

AMMONITE
PRESS

First published 2012 by
Ammonite Press
an imprint of AE Publications Ltd,
166 High Street, Lewes, East Sussex, BN7 1XU

ISBN 978-1-90770-840-4

British Cataloguing in Publication Data. A catalogue record of this book
is available from the British Library.

Editor: Richard Wiles
Design: Robin Shields

Colour reproduction by GMC Reprographics
Printed and bound in China by 1010 Printing International. Ltd

Page 2
CAMERA: Lomography
Fisheye No.1
FILM: Lomography Color
Negative 400
EXPOSURE: 1/100 sec. @ f/8

Berlin seen through a "new
eye" thanks to the Fisheye
No.1's 10mm lens.

Contents

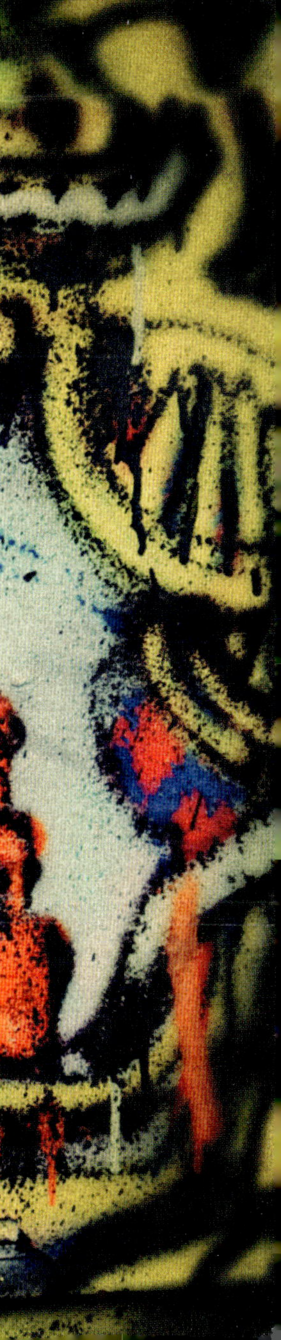

Introduction

Digital cameras have revolutionized photography in a way that has not been seen since George Eastman unveiled his Box Brownie at the start of the twentieth century. It may sound like an overstatement, but the impact that digital technology has had on the medium of photography should not be underestimated: from point-and-shoot compact cameras through to cell phones and high-end digital SLRs, it seems as if everyone has "gone digital." And who can blame them?

After all, digital capture frees the photographer from prohibitive film and processing costs, while ever-more sophisticated electronics endeavor to make certain that exposures and colors are "perfect" with each and every press of the shutter-release button. Images can be previewed and reviewed ad-nauseum, so you can be doubly sure that the image you commit to your memory card is the precise one that you want. That (in)decisive moment is then immediately ready to be sent around the globe as an email attachment or uploaded to the Internet, unleashing yet another series of 0s and 1s on an unsuspecting world.

But while digital photography is making it ever-easier to produce flawless shots with minimal fuss, it's arguably replacing freeform creativity with a stringent set of technical procedures—the technocrat's beloved "workflow." Only when the exposure is accurate to the n'th degree; the white balance fine-tuned to within a fraction of a Kelvin; and every pixel polished to perfection can a photograph be deemed "acceptable." Everything else should be deleted, and you certainly shouldn't share a technically deficient image with the rest of the world.

OK, so perhaps that's a slightly exaggerated view, but for many people—Average Joe included—photographs can be, and are, measured against a sliding scale of "right" and "wrong." The picture is sharp? That's great. The picture is blurred? Most definitely wrong! This is, of course, absolute hokum, and it is at this point that plastic cameras and the lo-fi aesthetic enter the discussion. As you will see in this book, the conjoined elements of camera and aesthetic—one physical, the other conceptual—are the antithesis to digital imaging's immediacy and its technologically augmented idea of the "perfect picture."

CAMERA: Lubitel 166B
FILM: Unknown
EXPOSURE: Not recorded

Multiple exposure can create striking abstract images. Shooting on film adds surprise and the "happy accident" to the equation.

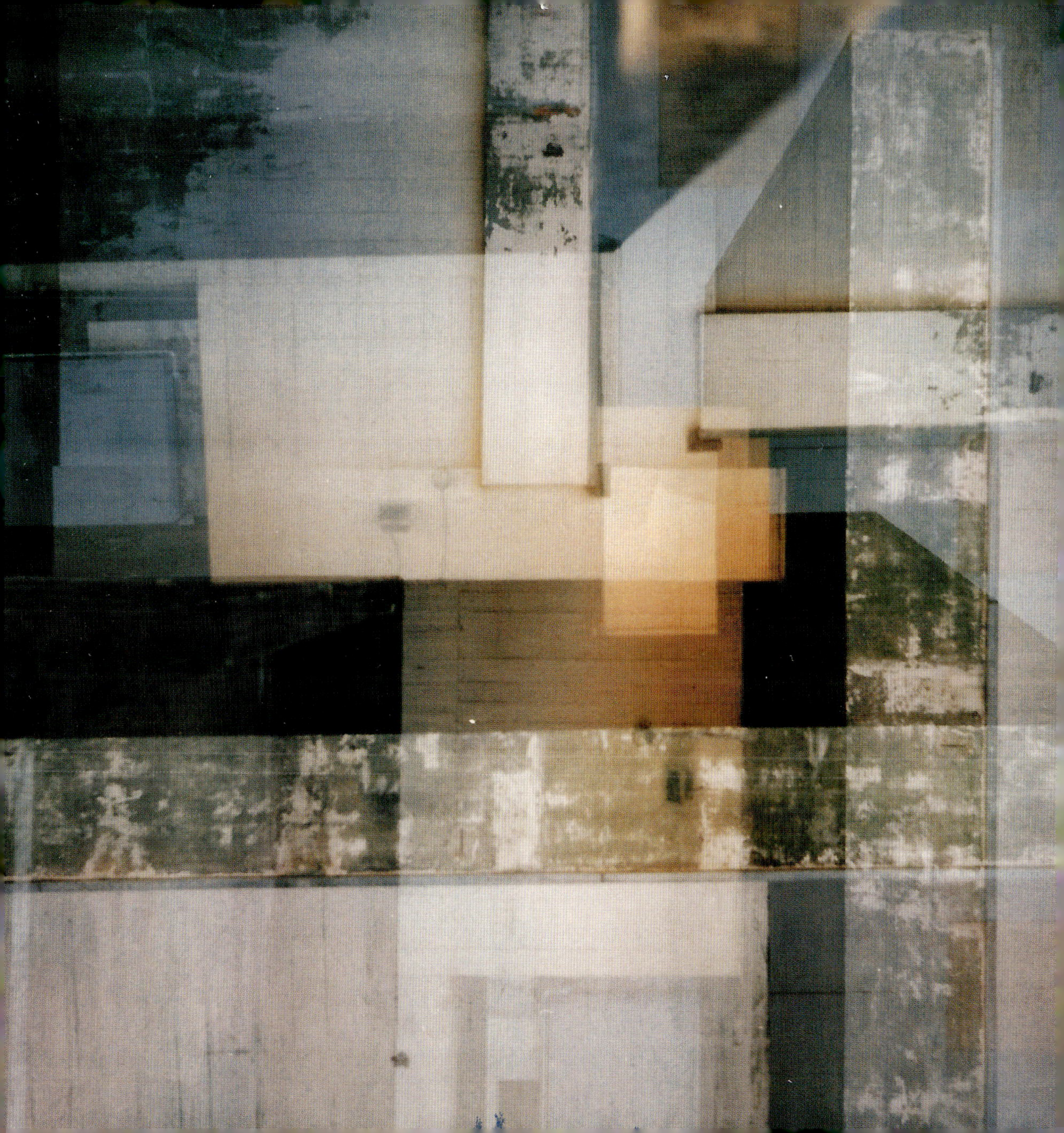

Plastic **pedigree**

The roots of plastic cameras can be traced back to the Bakelite cameras of almost a century ago, but it would be a step too far to describe these as the direct antecedents of the modern plastic camera. Antecedents, yes, but not direct antecedents. The reason I say this is simple: these pioneering cameras were built and designed using the technology, science, and resources available at the time. They were not constructed deliberately so that exposure or sharpness fell off toward the corners of the frame, or designed to produce high levels of lens flare and chromatic aberration. Instead, these "defects" were often the natural by-products of the optical systems used; optical systems that were often constrained by financial and technological considerations. Lens coating was not invented until the mid-1930s, for example, and it was a further 40 years before multicoating became widespread on camera lenses.

Conversely, contemporary plastic cameras intentionally use less sophisticated optical systems, and it is this intent that makes all the difference. None of the cameras featured in this book employs the latest optical technologies, and not one of them is aspiring to do so. Each and every one is deliberately relying on old-school science to produce their unique aesthetic, with a large number of the cameras employing nothing more sophisticated than a single-element plastic lens—the most basic lens design there is.

Even Lomography models such as the Diana F+ and Lubitel 166+ use the "dated" optical technology of their respective precursors to help create their images—they are certainly not incorporating new or cutting-edge optical designs, despite being "modern" cameras.

The camera is much more than a mere extension of the lens though, and the plastic body also plays a key role in the way in which the images are made. While the digital photographer has to work hard to master their camera of choice, the technology placed between the lo-fi analog photographer and their subject is far less demanding. Often, a plastic camera will contain a shutter that offers a single, fixed shutter

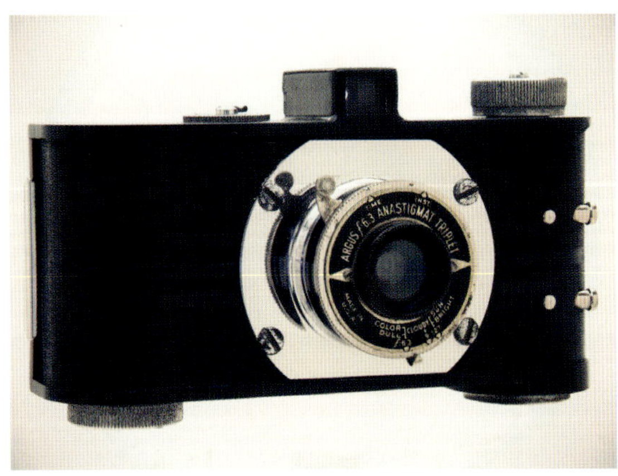

The Argus AA (1940–1942) is a Bakelite 35mm camera with a distinctly art deco vibe: in practical terms, however, it is considerably more sophisticated than many modern plastic cameras.

speed, for example, rather than the wide range of electronically-controlled speeds in a digital camera. The aperture may also have just one setting (or at least be severely restricted), and it can often be that the ISO of your chosen film becomes the only variable in the exposure process. Even this is fixed for the duration of the roll; start on a dull day with ISO 400 film and you may find your shots are overexposed when the sun comes out.

But this is entirely the point. Photography with a plastic camera is all about relinquishing control, accepting this isn't a "serious" photographic tool you're holding, and accepting fully the "happy accidents" that will result. By its very design the camera encourages a notion of spontaneity, which means that you are less beholden to technology: instead of agonizing over the exposure or white balance as you might with a digital camera, all you can do is point and shoot, perhaps not even with the luxury of a viewfinder to help you frame your shots. As a result, all of those things that are traditionally considered "wrong" in a photograph can be shamelessly celebrated when you're shooting with a plastic snapper—something that I shall refer to as the "lo-fi aesthetic."

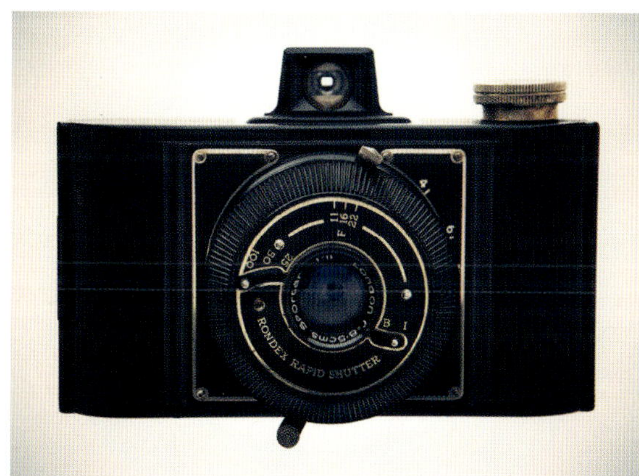

A medium format (6cm x 9cm) Bakelite Wembley Sports camera, introduced in 1950. With limited shutter speeds and aperture settings you're free to concentrate more fully on the subject than the camera technology.

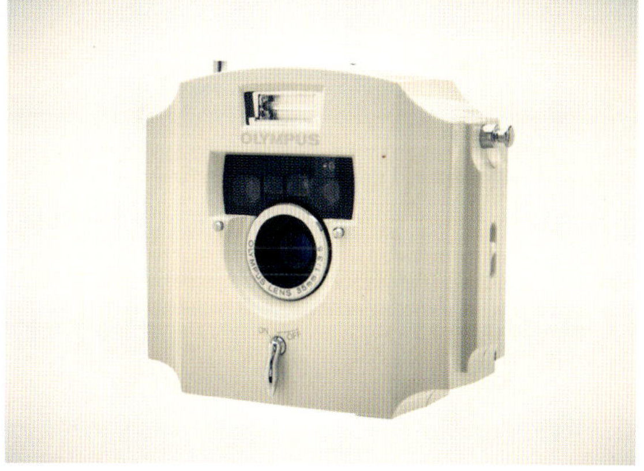

The limited edition Olympus Ecru (1991) has all the characteristics of a plastic camera with one key exception: it aims to minimize anything in an image that might be considered a "defect."

The lo-fi aesthetic

As well as requiring a different technological approach when compared to digital photography, using a plastic camera demands a fresh mindset. A greater emphasis has to be placed on what is in front of the lens and, by extension, the photographer's eye. This is encouraged by the fact that every exposure you make on film costs money, while a digital snap does not.

Choosing the "best" subject is only part of the story. When it comes to shooting with a plastic camera, be prepared to embrace the inherent "failings" of the technology. So what if your shots are over- or underexposed—does it really matter? Is the world going to end if the focus drifts off toward the edges of your image, or your photo suffers from heavy vignetting? Of course not! Some people might say that these are crimes against photography, but just direct them to the pioneers of the medium: soft focus, vignetting, and uneven exposures are the basis upon which photography was built, so why not celebrate that?

You should learn to revel in extreme lens flare, overlapping frames, exposure and focus that falls off deliciously at the corners of the frame, and, of course, light leaks: nothing says "lo-fi" in quite the same way as light that has seeped in through the seams of a Holga, Oktomat, or Recesky TLR to bleach the film inside.

This is what I describe as the "lo-fi aesthetic"—a distinct set of image characteristics that provide an overarching "visual signature" that is shared by virtually all of the cameras featured in this book. With this in mind, if your only concern is the optimum aperture of your lenses; or the pitch of your pixels; or you find yourself trying to memorize hyperfocal distance tables; or you aim to consistently get your exposures accurate to within 1/3-stop, stop reading now—this book is not for you. If, however, you can embrace chance, find beauty in the flawed, and accept imperfection, it's time to turn the page.

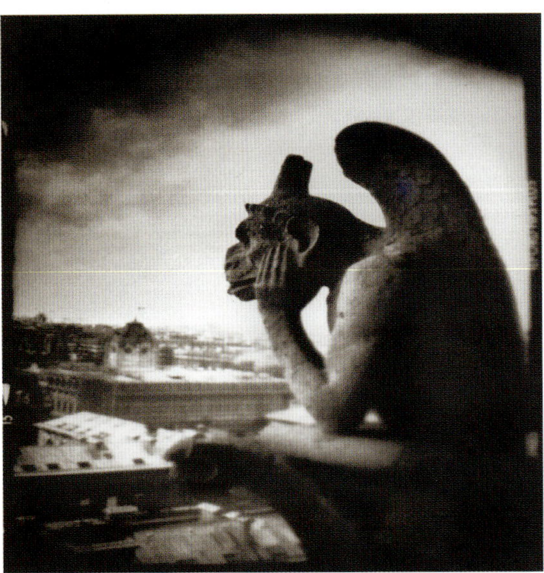

Learn to celebrate the inherent flaws that result from lo-fi photography and discover the happy accidents that make an image unique.

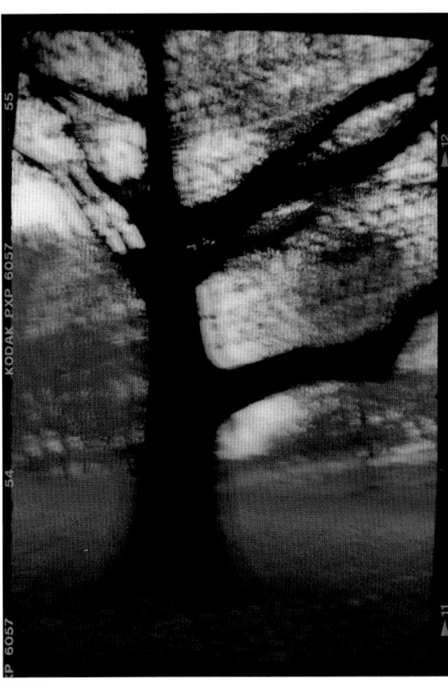

Falcon Model 4
Kodak Plus X
Multiple exposures, each
approx. 1/100 sec. @ f/16

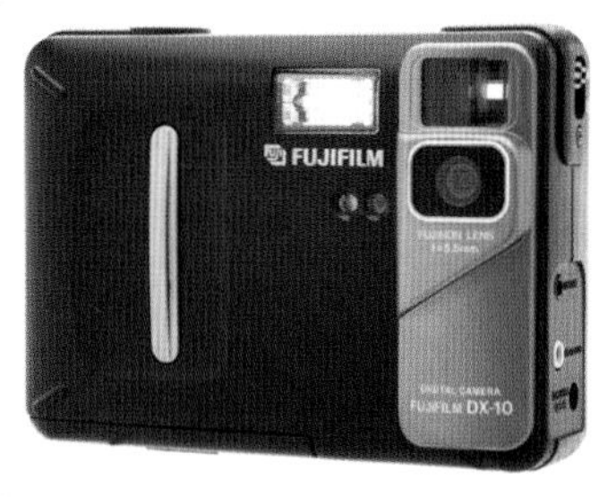

The Fuji DX-10 was cutting-edge when it was launched in 1999, but its 0.8 megapixel resolution and fixed lens mean it is nothing more than a lo-fi digital "toy" today.

Digital lo-fi dilemma

Some manufacturers have begun to market certain digital cameras as plastic "toy cameras," in an attempt to benefit from the popularity of lo-fi imaging. However, these digital offerings should not be considered in the same context as analog plastic cameras: fitting a digital camera with a low resolution sensor and a "cheap" lens (which is, essentially, all that is being done in most cases) creates nothing more than a "bad" digital camera that produces poor results. A digital camera cannot create light leaks in the same way that a film-based camera can, and a low-resolution sensor will only deliver low quality results that cannot be enlarged by any great amount.

You may say the same is true of plastic film cameras—that they also deliver "poor" results—but consider this: the original Diana, despite all its faults, uses medium format film that is equally suited to high quality professional work. Even 35mm film technology can produce an A4-sized enlargement with little trouble. So, while plastic cameras produce lo-fi images, they do so on a high-quality medium: the same can't be said of a digital camera fitted with a 2–3 megapixel sensor.

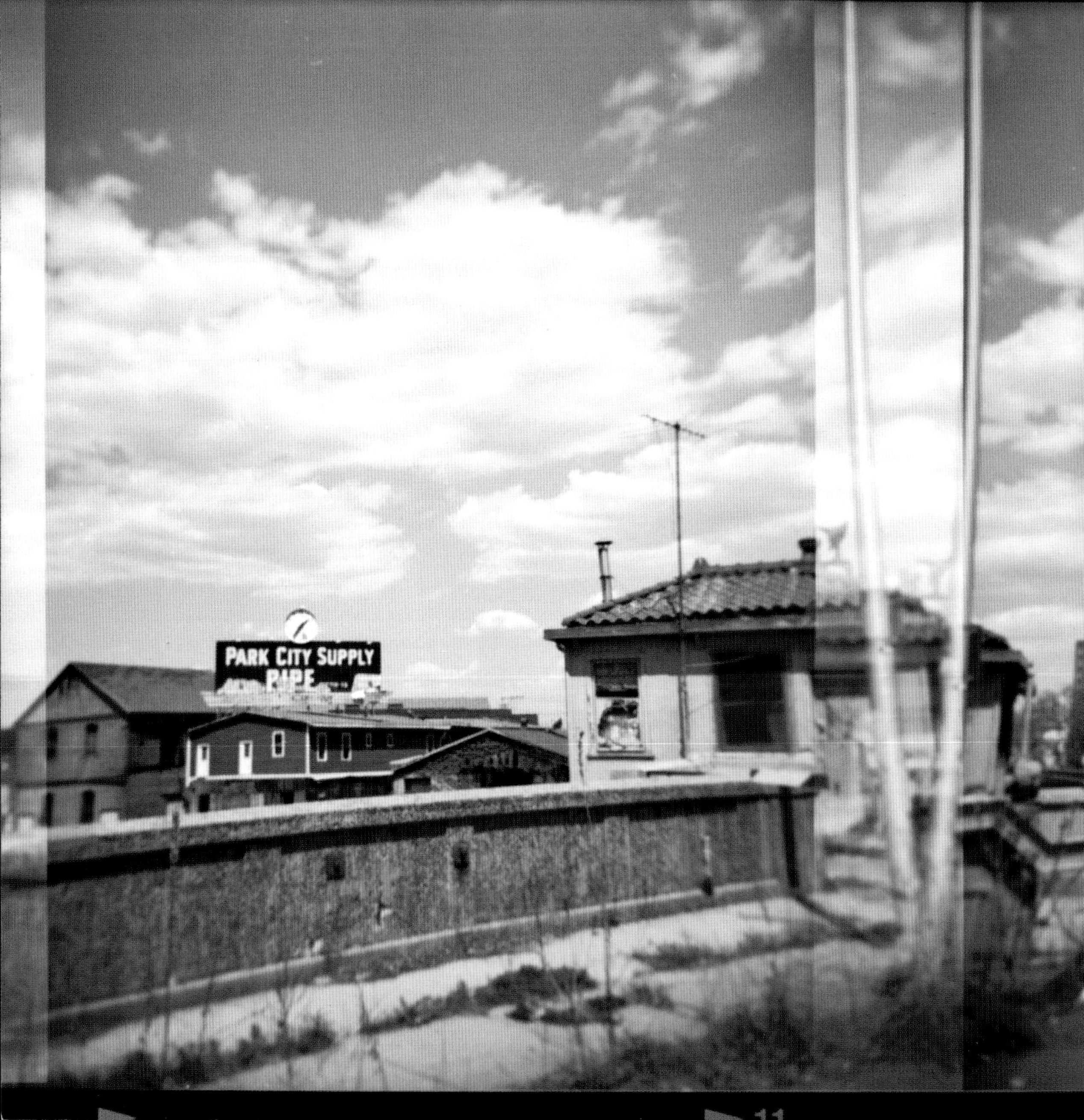

PARK CITY SUPPLY
PIPE

Chapter 1:
MEDIUM FORMAT LEGACY

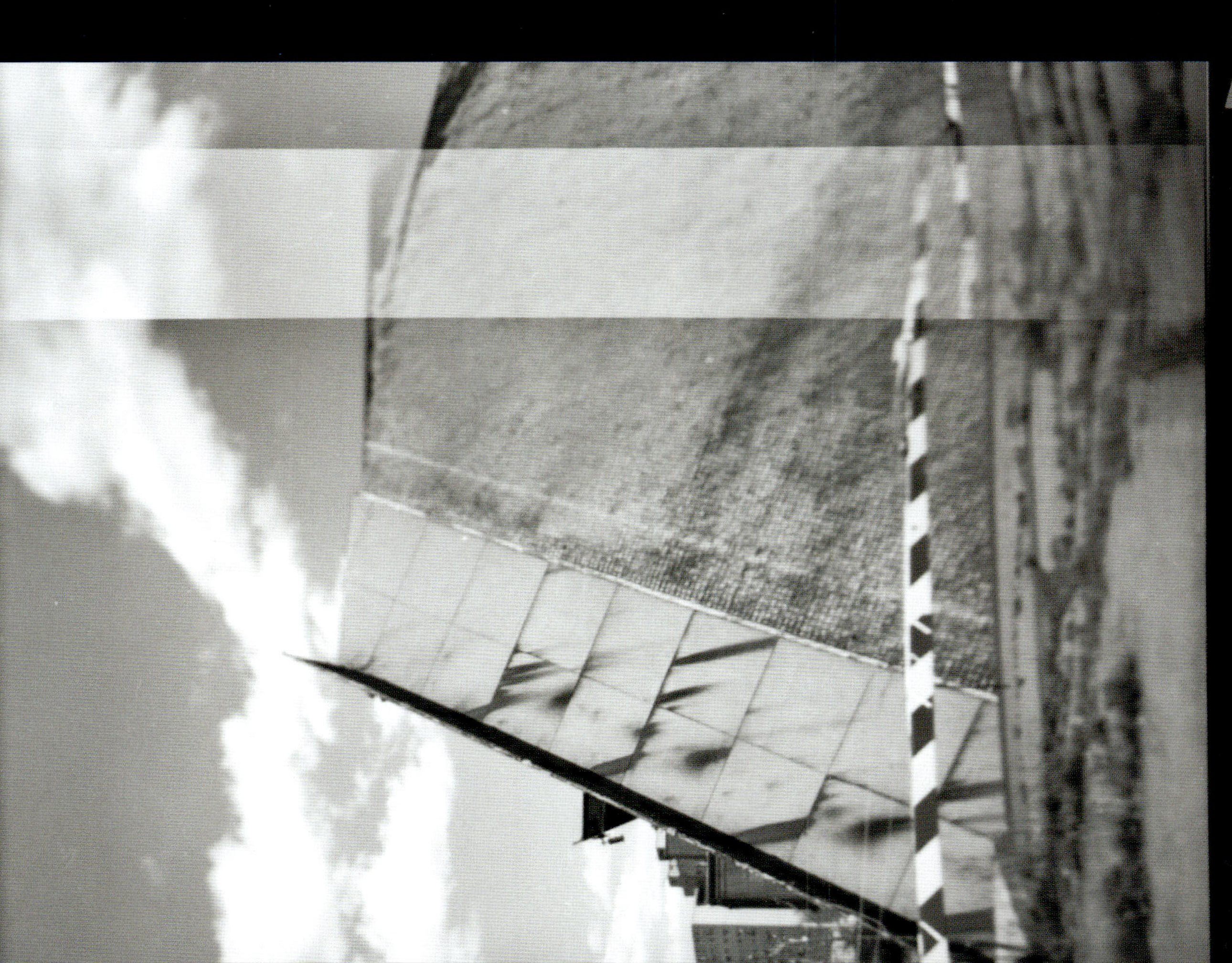

Cameras for the **people**

Although modern plastic cameras share a relative simplicity (to a greater or lesser extent) with early Bakelite models, and utilize a common material in their construction (or at least a very similar one), their true origins do not lie so far in the past.

Instead, to find the first direct descendent of today's medium format plastic cameras we need to travel to post-war Russia, and the elaborately named Leningradskoye Optiko Mechanichesckoye Obyedinenie—or LOMO as it is better-known. Using technology plundered from the defeated Germans, LOMO unveiled its original Bakelite Lubitel in 1949, and more than 60 years later the Lubitel name remains in use (albeit under new ownership).

However, it was not until the company launched its (plastic) 166 series in 1976 that we see a clear link to today's plastic cameras. Even then, the Lubitel 166 models are not closely associated with the lo-fi aesthetic: multiple aperture and shutter speed settings, and a reasonable triplet lens mean that most Lubitels are actually "usable" in the traditional photographic sense. In fact, some might go as far as saying that they can produce "good" results, and certainly not always "lo-fi" ones.

To discover the camera that is widely regarded as the cornerstone of the modern lo-fi movement, you instead have to turn the clock back to the 1960s, and head to Kowloon, China, where the Great Wall Plastic Factory was producing its medium format Diana camera. Ironically, this camera was produced primarily as a novelty item, which was more likely to be given away as a promotional gift than used as a "serious" photographic tool. Yet today, some 50 years on, the name endures (thanks to Lomography), as does the aesthetic propogated by the Diana's plastic lens and camera body.

Proto-plastic

The roots of today's plastic cameras—at least in the context of this book—can be traced back to the Bakelite cameras of the 1930s. At this time, manufacturers around the world, including legendary brands such as Argus and Kodak, used the early plastic material to produce cameras ranging from the simple to the complex.

First seen in the 1960s, the Diana is widely considered to be the "original" plastic camera and is arguably responsible for the lo-fi aesthetic that we love. However, cameras such as LOMO's Lubitel 166B also have a place in plastic camera history, and remain usable today.

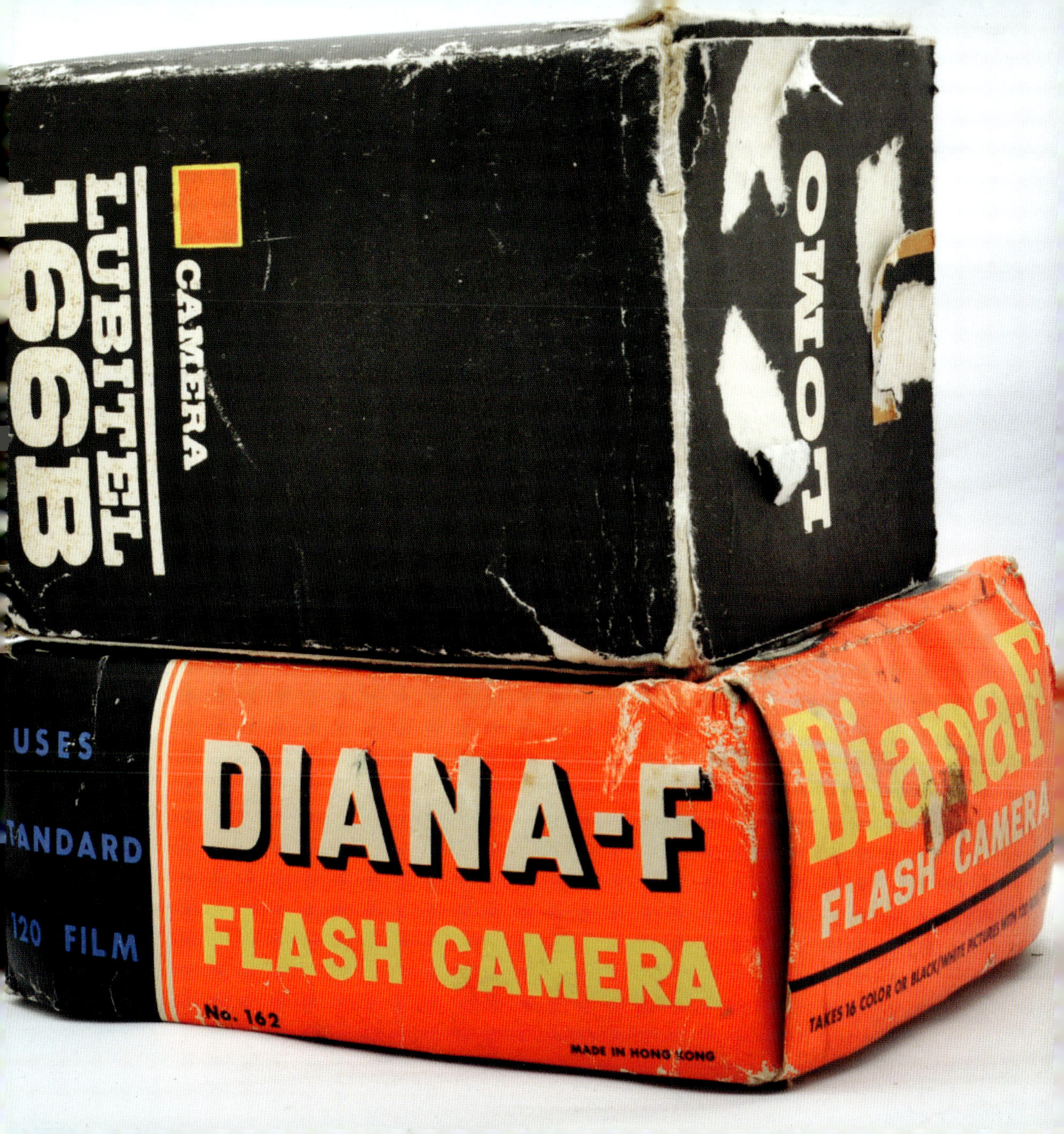

LUBITEL 166B

CAMERA

LOMO

USES
STANDARD
120 FILM

DIANA-F
FLASH CAMERA

No. 162

MADE IN HONG KONG

Diana-F
FLASH CAMERA

TAKES 16 COLOR OR BLACK/WHITE PICTURES WITH YOU

Medium format **exposed**

In this chapter, oversized plastic camera bodies and (mostly) plastic lenses engage in a debauched coupling that's almost certain to produce light leaks, vignetting, chromatic aberration, overlapping frames, multiple exposures, and more besides—everything, in fact, that should be celebrated in the lo-fi aesthetic.

Medium format photography isn't for everyone. For a start, you're typically looking at 12, maybe 16, shots per film, and if you're also a trigger-happy digital snapper, this can prove expensive unless you can curb your shutter-finger.

There are also issues regarding accessibility. Medium format film was once widely available thanks to its prolific use by pro photographers shooting with Hasselblads, Pentax 67s, and Mamiya RBs and RZs. With the mass exodus from film to digital, the demand for medium format roll film has nose-dived in recent years, with Kodak perhaps suffering in the most dramatic fashion. But no matter what the naysayers tell you, it hasn't gone for good, and is unlikely to disappear any time soon (if at all).

Sure, Kodak (and Agfa before them) may have fallen by the wayside, but manufacturers such as Fujifilm, Maco (under the Rollei brand), and China Lucky Film Corp. continue to supply traditional color and black-and-white emulsions that are perfect for your medium-format machinations. On top of this you have Ilford and Foma catering exclusively for the monochrome market, and if you want something a little less "ordinary" then that's OK too—Lomography's X-Pro and Redscale films are both worth exploring.

A word of caution though; it's a good idea to establish somewhere that will process your film for you before you begin, as processing labs—like the film itself—are becoming less widespread. Most photo stores should be able to point you in the right direction, but if you're shooting black and white there's no reason why you shouldn't learn to process it yourself. It really isn't that difficult!

CAMERA: Diana F
FILM: Fuji Velvia 100 (expired)
EXPOSURE: Unrecorded

A plastic camera and expired film that is cross processed is a combination that is almost guaranteed to produce striking lo-fi results such as this.

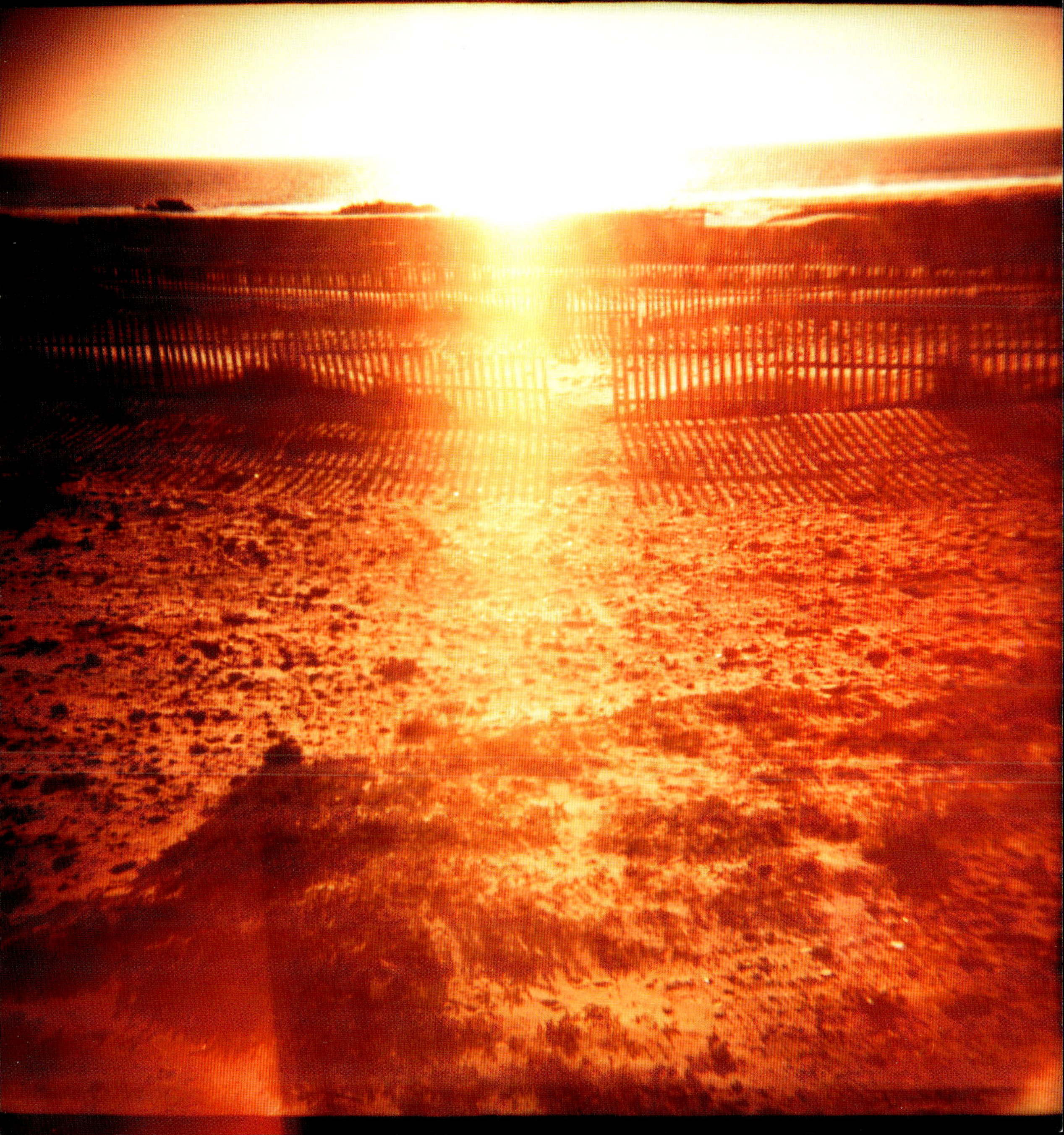

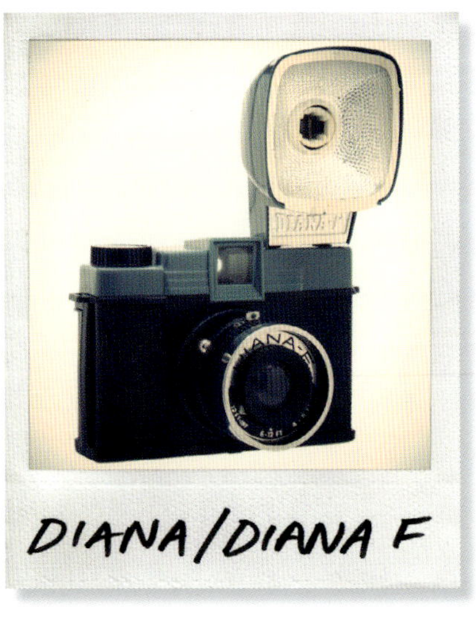

CAMERA: Diana & Diana F
MANUFACTURER: Great Wall Plastic Factory
FILM TYPE: 120 roll film
IMAGE FORMATS: 4.5cm x 4.5cm (16 shots)
LENS: 75mm
FOCUS: Three preset distances
(4ft–6ft, 6ft–12ft, 12ft–Infinity)
APERTURES: f/11, f/13, f/19
SHUTTER SPEEDS: N (around 1/50–1/100 sec.), B (Bulb)
OTHER FEATURES: Diana F has two pin flash socket

CAMERA: Diana F
FILM: Fuji Velvia 100 (expired)
EXPOSURE: Unrecorded

Light leaks and heavy corner shading are classic Diana traits that should be celebrated for their beauty.

Not long after it first appeared in the early 1960s, artists and photography students alike began to exploit the medium format Diana's creative potential. The San Francisco Art Institute reportedly went as far as making its photography students use this "novelty" camera in an attempt to (rightly) demonstrate that photography is about the photographer's vision, rather than their equipment.

Certainly the Diana can be seen as a great leveler in terms of technology. Unlike most other cameras, which are "built for purpose," the plastic-bodied Diana suffers from (or should that be benefits from?) light leaks, heavy vignetting, and a plastic lens that is soft in terms of both focus and contrast, and produces heavy flare and chromatic aberrations. It is also limited in terms of its controls, with a single "automatic" shutter speed (which varies from camera to camera, but is nominally around 1/50–1/100 sec.), three vague aperture settings, and slightly wayward focusing. But this doesn't stop it from producing some stunning results.

Production of the Diana (and the flash-enabled Diana F) was short-lived though, as just a year after it was launched, Kodak released the first of its Instamatic models. These—and cameras like them—began to dominate the global photography market, replacing Average Joe's dependency on roll film with more convenient, easy-load 126 format film cartridges. By the 1970s, more than 50 million Instamatics had been produced, and a decade after it first appeared the Diana slid silently into the history archive. And that would have been the end of the Diana story, were it not for Lomography...

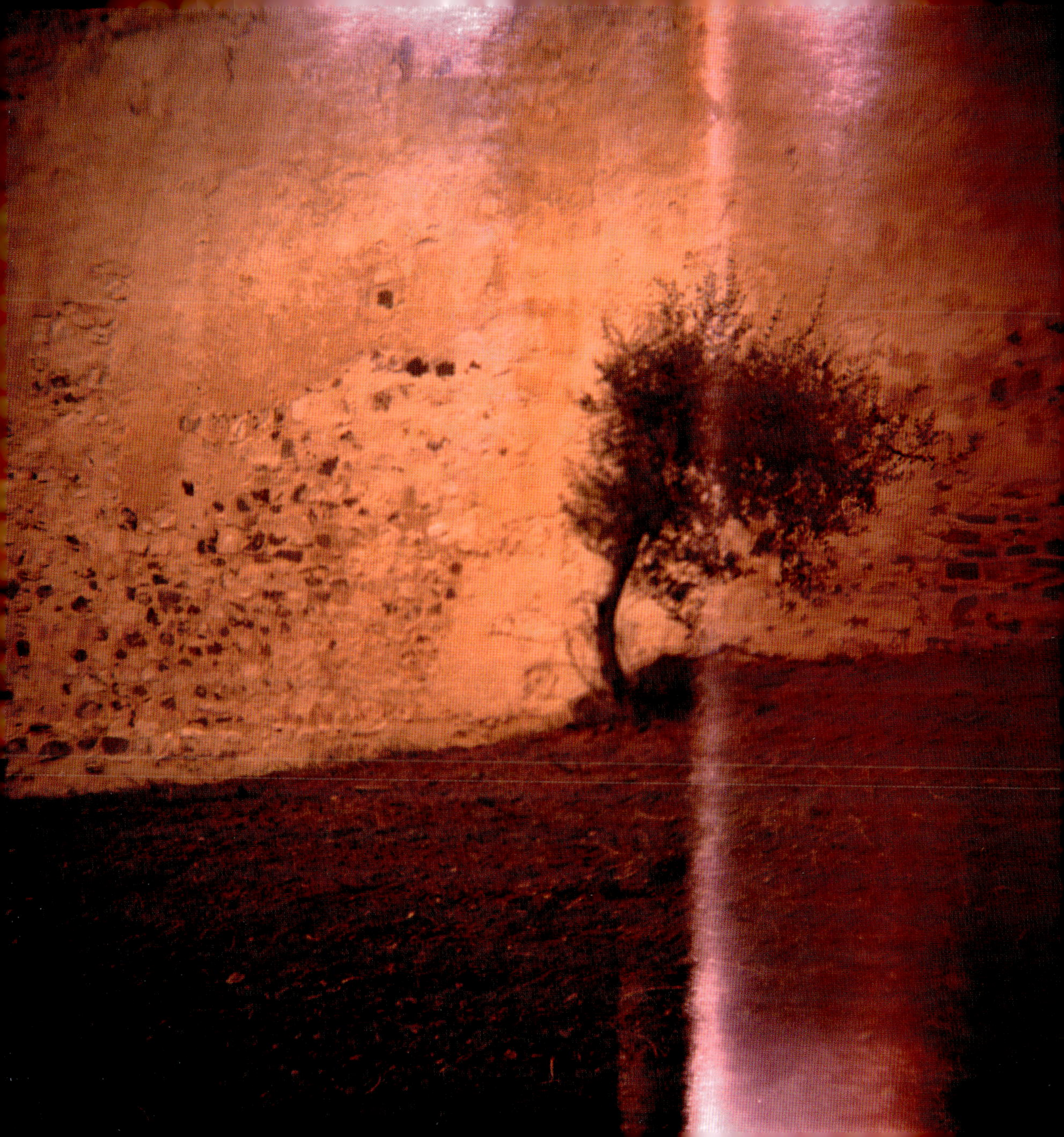

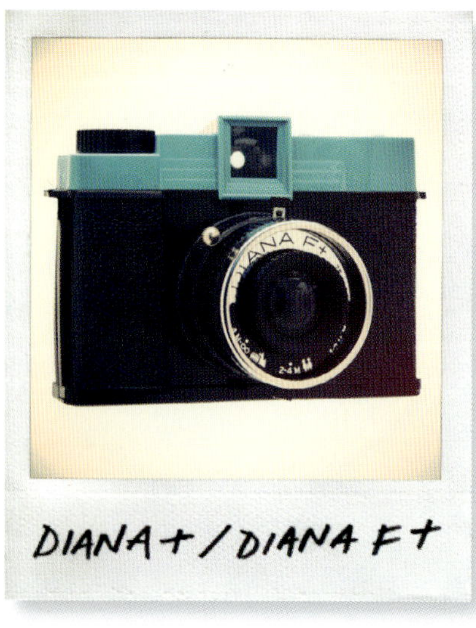

CAMERA:	Diana+ & Diana F+
MANUFACTURER:	Lomography
FILM TYPE:	120 roll film
IMAGE FORMATS:	5.2cm x 5.2cm (12 shots)
	4.2cm x 4.2cm (16 shots)
	4.6cm x 4.6cm (endless panorama)
LENS:	75mm (interchangeable)
FOCUS:	Three preset distances
	(1m–2m, 2m–4m, 4m–Infinity)
APERTURES:	Cloudy (f/11), Partial cloud (f/16),
	Sunny (f/22), Pinhole (f/150)
SHUTTER SPEEDS:	N (1/60 sec.), B (Bulb)
OTHER FEATURES:	Manual shutter lock exposures
	Interchangeable lenses
	Tripod mount
	Compatible with new Diana flash

In 2007, the Diana was reborn in the form of Lomography's Diana+ and Diana F+. Externally, the cameras appear almost identical to their 1960s counterparts, but Lomography took the opportunity to perform an internal overhaul. The aperture settings changed from f/11, f/13, and f/19, to a more conventional f/11, f/16, and f/22, and the instant shutter speed is more consistently around 1/60 sec. There's also a shutter locking mechanism for longer Bulb exposures, although in reality this amounts to a small piece of plastic that you stick in the lens to physically prevent the shutter lever from returning to the closed position: functional, but by no means elegant.

What is more interesting is Lomography's development of the Diana from a standalone plastic camera to what can be described as a plastic camera "system." Just like an SLR camera, the plastic lens on the Diana+ is now interchangeable, allowing you to fit wider or longer focal length lenses, or you can remove it entirely and shoot pinhole photographs. The camera's back is also removable, with instant "Polaroid" backs and 35mm film backs on offer if you want to shoot something other than medium format film.

CAMERA: Diana+
FILM: Kodak Portra 160NC
EXPOSURE: 1/60 sec. @ f/22

There is something about circuses and fairgrounds that begs to be captured with a plastic camera. The hanging sign in this photo seems custom made to "pop" against the blue sky.

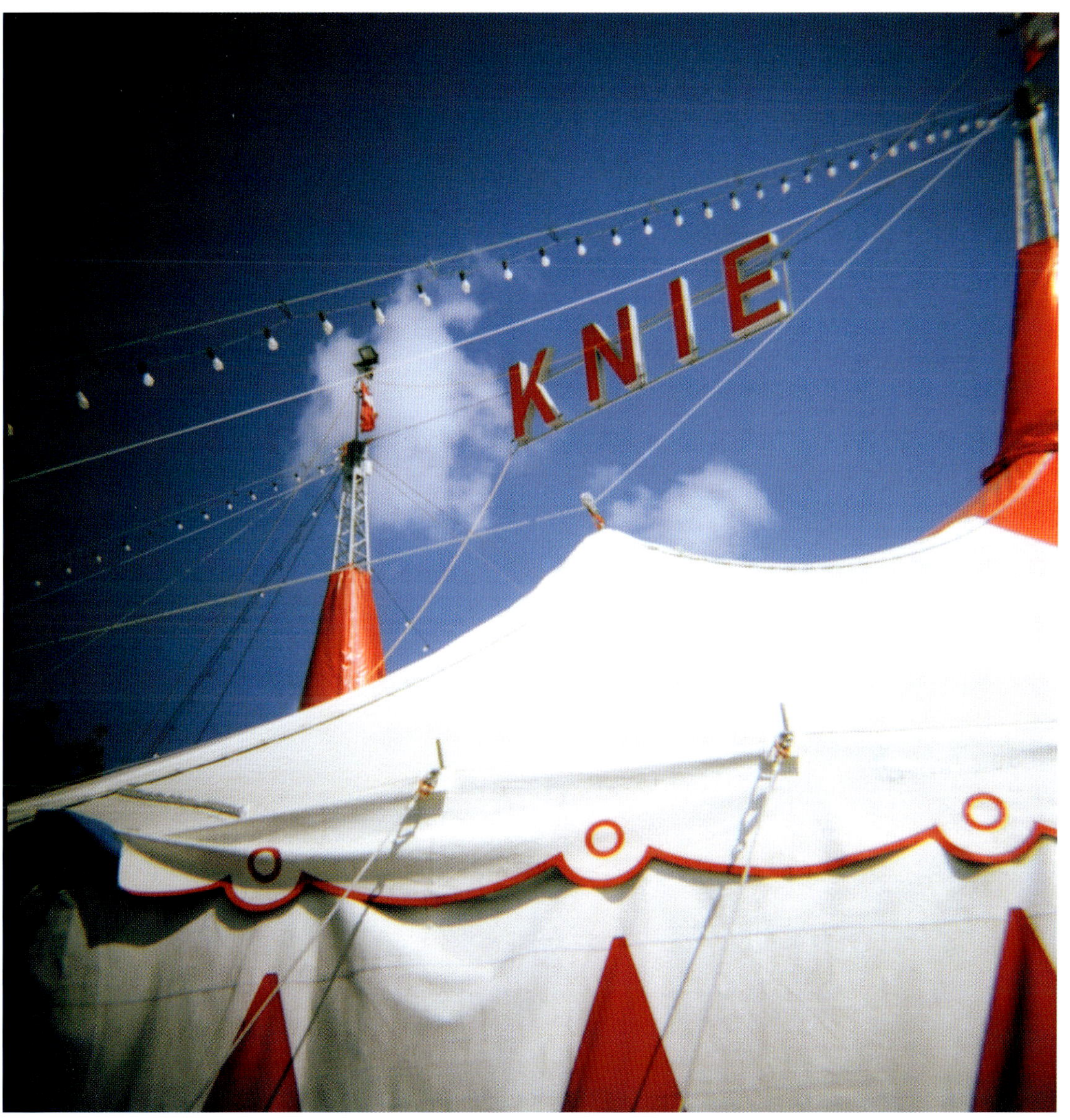
KNIE

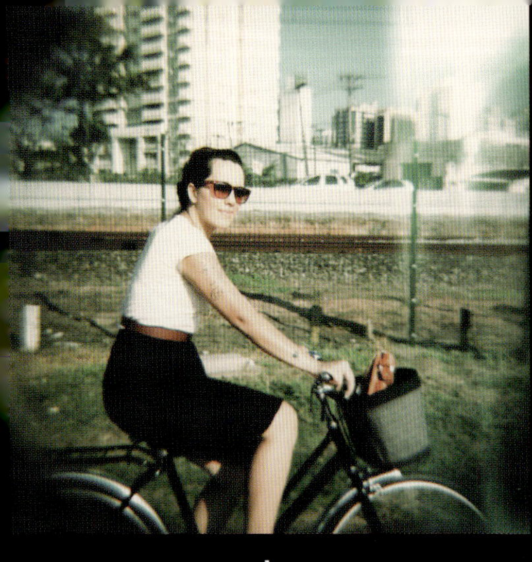

1

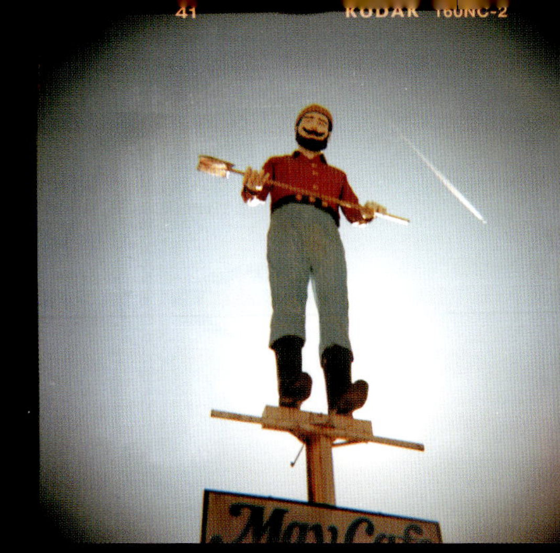

2

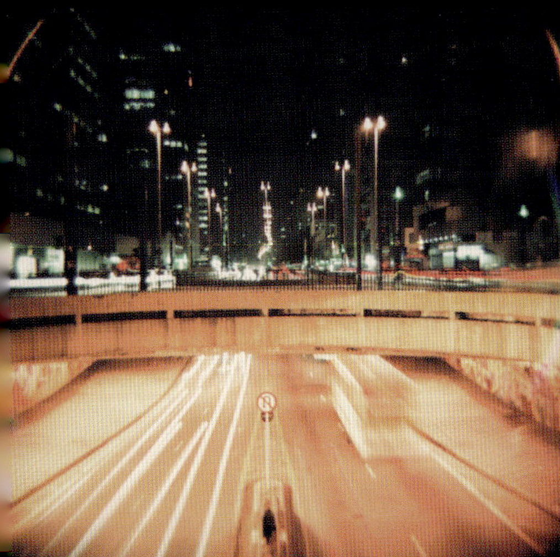

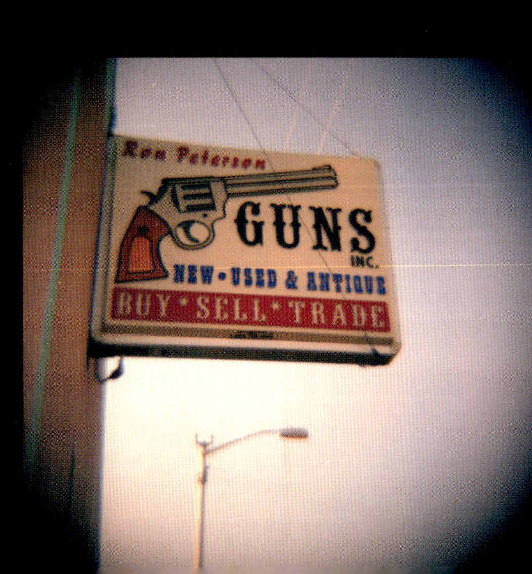

3

However, even if you decide to stick with medium format, there are now several shooting options to choose from. As with the original camera, there is a "small square" format that allows 16 shots to be recorded on a roll of film, but this has been joined by a 12-shot, 5.2cm x 5.2cm image size, which maximizes the vignetting and focus fall off. There is also as an "endless panorama" option that enables you to shoot a virtually seamless sequence of images with little or no gap between frames.

Endless panoramas

Shooting an endless panorama requires you to do two things: fit your Diana+ with the larger (4.6cm x 4.6cm) mask and set the frame counter window to 16. And that's all there is to it! Just shoot as normal, and wind on using the numbers on the film as a guide—the mask will ensure that each frame sits almost perfectly beside the next, with a negligible overlap or gap. Although you can shoot

1	2
CAMERA: Diana F+	**CAMERA:** Diana+
FILM: Fuji Pro 160S	**FILM:** Kodak Portra 160NC
EXPOSURE: 1/60 sec. @ f/11	**EXPOSURE:** 1/60 sec. @ f/16

3	4
CAMERA: Diana+	**CAMERA:** Diana F+
FILM: Fuji Velvia 100	**FILM:** Fuji Pro 160S
EXPOSURE: Unrecorded	**EXPOSURE:** Unrecorded

5	6
CAMERA: Diana+	**CAMERA:** Diana F+
FILM: Kodak Portra 160NC	**FILM:** Fuji 400H
EXPOSURE: 1/60 sec. @ f/16	**EXPOSURE:** 1/60 sec. @ f/16

a whole roll of film in this way, to create an "über-panorama," you will find it is much easier to store and scan panoramas that are made up of no more than four exposures in a row: more than this and you may find that you will have to scan your panoramic image in two or more stages.

Diana flash

The original Diana F uses what is today regarded as a nonstandard flash connector: a two-pin socket on the top of the camera instead of the more familiar hotshoe or PC flash sync socket.

In its modern retelling of the Diana story, Lomography has produced a revamped version of the Diana flash that it describes as a "faithful reproduction of the classic 1960s design." This includes the original two-pin connector. While you are restricted to using just this one flash unit with the Diana F+, you can at least use the flash on a different camera, as it ships with an adapter that enables it to be used in a standard hotshoe.

Diana+ lenses

Interchangeable lenses are perhaps one of the main reasons why you might choose a Diana+ over the original Diana, and there are currently five lenses available, including the "standard" 75mm lens. Your options are:

20mm Fisheye: Provides a 180-degree angle of view and the circular image of a "true" fisheye lens.

38mm Superwide: Delivers an angle of view that's roughly equivalent to a 24mm focal length on a 35mm camera.

55mm Wide and Close-up: Used as a wide-angle lens, this will deliver an angle of view that is similar to a 34mm focal length in 35mm camera terms, but slip on the close-up adapter and your Diana's focus is set at approximately 6 inches (15cm).

75mm: The standard lens for the Diana+ is based on the original plastic lens from the 1960s.

110mm Soft Telephoto: Gives you a mild telephoto effect (roughly the equivalent of a 75mm focal length in 35mm terms), with a slight soft-focus appearance.

In keeping with the original, all of these supplementary lenses are plastic. It's simply a case of twisting the lens on the camera counterclockwise by 30-degrees to remove it, and then reversing the process with your new lens: a crude "bayonet" mount. To help you compose your shots, rather than guessing what you're photographing, each lens also comes with a supplementary viewfinder (or viewfinder adapter in the case of the 110mm lens).

Diana+ pinhole

In addition to interchangeable lenses, removing the lens entirely on a Diana+ and setting the aperture to "P" will swing a pinhole lens into action. This effectively gives you an aperture of

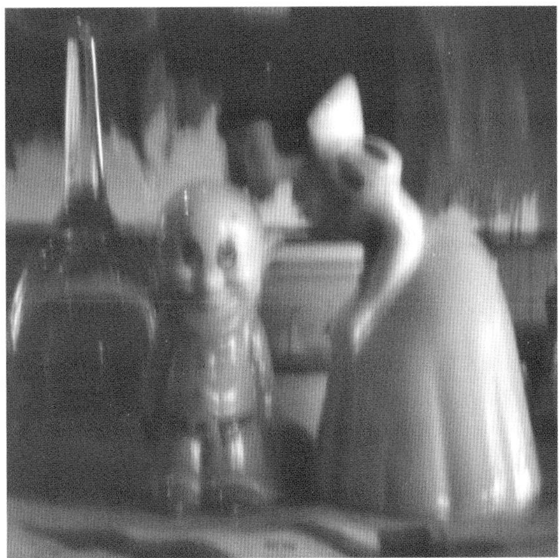

CAMERA: Diana+
FILM: Ilford Delta 100
EXPOSURE: 30 sec. (pinhole)

By removing the lens from your Diana+ you will convert it into a pinhole camera that has an effective aperture of f/122 and so produces some fascinating results.

CAMERA: Diana+
FILM: Ilford Pan F
EXPOSURE: 6 minutes (pinhole)

Atmospheric light streaks were created as the sun moved through the trees for the remaining seconds of a long pinhole exposure.

f/122, guaranteeing ultra-long exposures that make the use of the Bulb setting and shutter lock essential. However, by doing away with the Diana's plastic lens you will sacrifice the vignetting and focus fall-off that typifies the camera's images, although the low contrast and light leaks will remain. It is up to you whether this is a worthwhile trade or not.

Diana Multi-Pinhole Operator

The latest camera to bear the Diana name is the Diana Multi-Pinhole Operator, although the shape of the camera is the only real link between the two. Instead of a lens, you use one, two, or three pinhole lenses to produce an image—in conjunction with colored gels if you want. However, employing more than one pinhole (and gels) can easily result in a barely decipherable mess that even the most ardent lo-fi fan would struggle to redeem. Not a highlight in the history of plastic cameras.

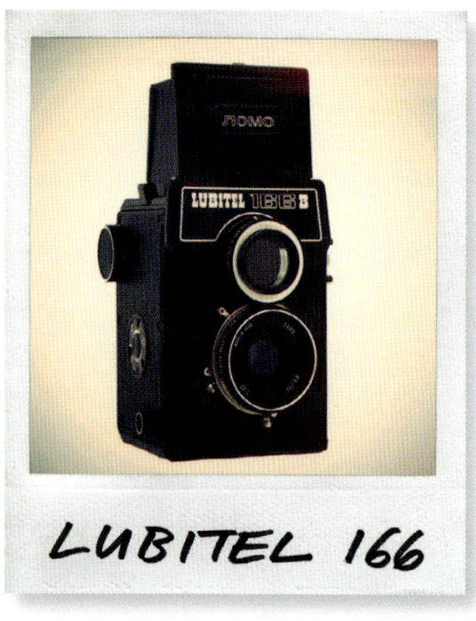

LUBITEL 166

CAMERA: Lubitel 166B
MANUFACTURER: Lomography
FILM TYPE: 120 roll film
IMAGE FORMATS: 6cm x 6cm (12 shots)
LENS: 75mm
FOCUS: 1.4m–Infinity
APERTURES: f/4.5, f/5.6, f/8, f/11, f/16, f/22
SHUTTER SPEEDS: 1/250–1/15 sec., B (Bulb)
OTHER FEATURES: Self timer (7–12 sec. delay)
PC flash sync socket
Tripod socket

Although the first Lubitels rolled off the LOMO production line in 1949, it was not until 1976 that Bakelite bodies were replaced with plastic and the Lubitel 166 bloodline began. The first model was simply named the Lubitel 166, and it combined the 75mm f/4.5 lens used by its Bakelite predecessor (the Lubitel 2) with a film counter and coupled film advance that also readied the shutter for another exposure.

This more practical model was joined in 1980 by the Lubitel 166B, which is by far the most prolific of the Lubitel 166 incarnations. Although ostensibly similar to the original 166 (all Lubitels rely on the same lens), the 166B was "dumbed down" in certain areas to make it simpler to operate and, one would assume, cheaper to manufacture. To this end the built-in frame counter was downgraded to a red-filtered window on the back of the camera (cue light leaks!) and the coupled film advance was "uncoupled," so that winding on the film and cocking the shutter became two separate actions again—ideal for both accidental and deliberate multiple exposures!

Despite being a simpler camera, production of the 166B flourished, with over 900,000 units produced in a ten-year period from 1980–1990. During this time very little changed apart from the camera's markings, which differed depending on whether the camera was intended for the domestic market or for export.

Only three years into its production, the 166B was joined by the 166U, or 166 Universal. This was fundamentally the same camera, with the headline addition of a mask that enabled it to shoot 6cm x 4.5cm format images in addition to the 6cm x 6cm images recorded by its predecessors. Production of the 166U survived into the mid 1990s, spanning the fragmentation of the Soviet block. As a result, earlier cameras bear the legend "Made in USSR," while later models declare themselves "Made in Russia."

However, despite their differences, all Lubitel 166 cameras share the same core elements of a low-cost, lightweight plastic body and a glass lens based on the Cooke triplet design. Although crude by modern standards (and unrefined when measured against premium TLR cameras), Lubitels are far more sophisticated than the majority of the cameras in this book. Indeed, couple a Lubitel with a handheld lightmeter and a roll of slide film and you're arguably in a very strong position to start learning the fundamentals of photography.

Of course, a certain amount of vignetting and light leaks are to be expected with all three 166 models, but these are definitely not as pronounced as they are with a Diana or standard Holga. The glass lens is also capable of delivering genuinely sharp pictures, which is ideal if you're looking for "proper" results from a plastic camera (but clearly less inspiring for photographers who want to exploit the lo-fi aesthetic).

When it comes to choosing a used Lubitel, the original 166 is something of a rarity, so can be expensive, leaving the 166B or 166U as the "best" buys. Of these, the 166B is by far the

easiest to find, and therefore the cheapest, but the 166U has the added appeal of dual-format shooting if that's important to you. Alternatively, there's Lomography's 166+ Universal—the modern pretender to the Lubitel throne.

CAMERA: Lubitel 166
FILM: Lomography X-Pro Slide 200
EXPOSURE: Unrecorded

A handheld lightmeter is almost essential if you want to get the best from your Lubitel 166.

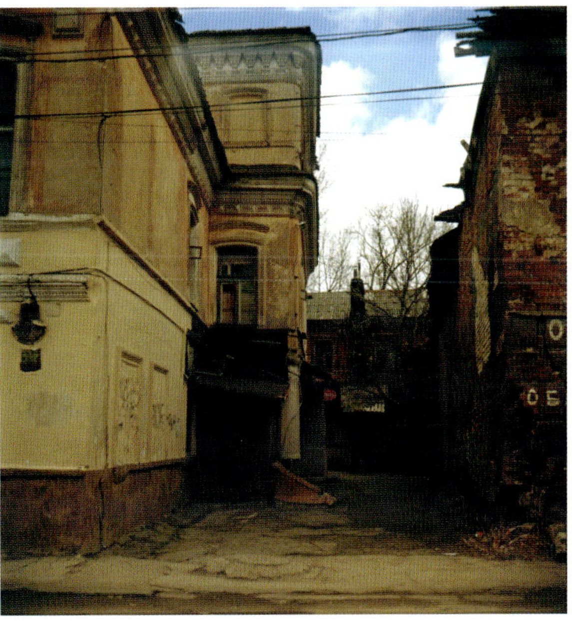

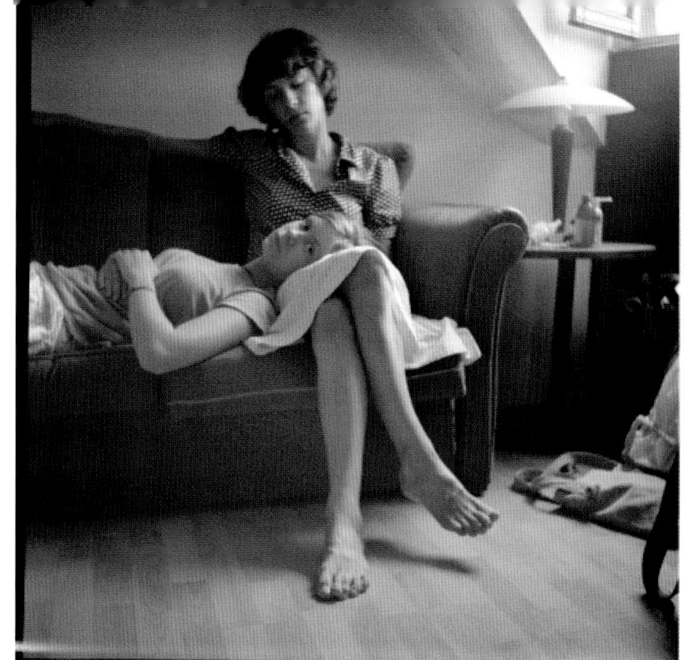

CAMERA: Lubitel II
FILM: Ilford HP5+ (rated
at ISO 1600)
EXPOSURE: 1/60 sec.
@ f/4.5

The Lubitel II is the
forerunner to both the
Lubitel 166 and 166+
Univeral, and shares the
same LOMO T-22 lens.

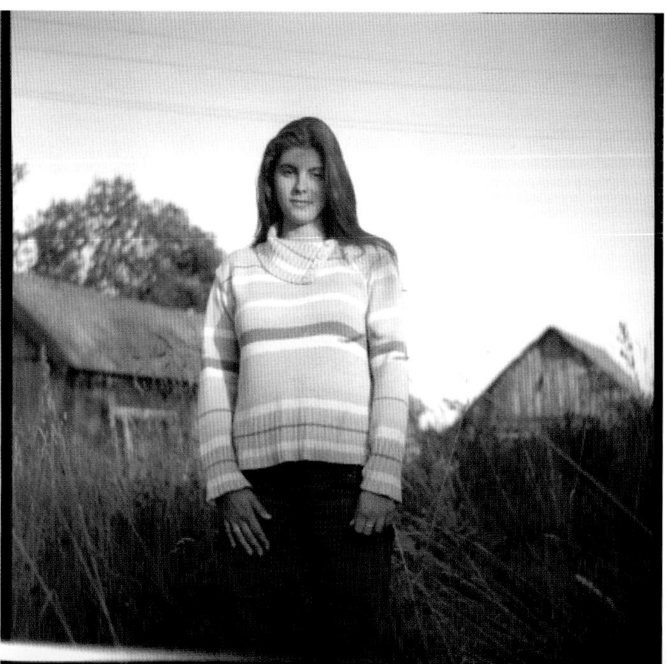

CAMERA: Lubitel II
FILM: Ilford HP5+
EXPOSURE: Unrecorded

The Lubitel's 75mm lens
uses a classic triplet
design, which is what
helps give the images
their distinctive look.

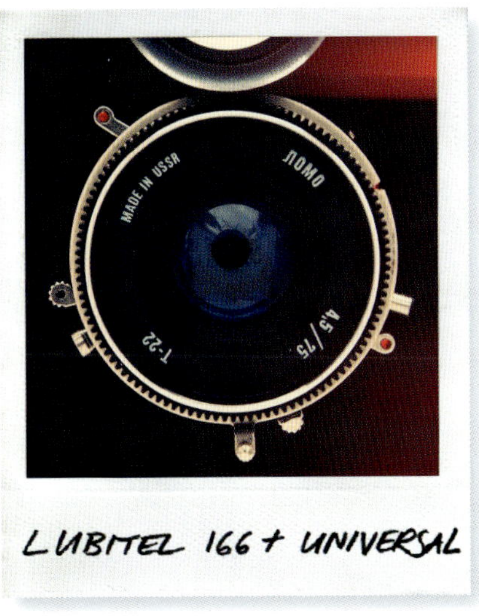

LUBITEL 166 + UNIVERSAL

CAMERA: Lubitel 166+ Universal
MANUFACTURER: Lomography
FILM TYPE: 120 roll film or 35mm
IMAGE FORMATS: 6cm x 6cm (12 shots on 120 roll film)
6cm x 4.5cm (16 shots on 120 roll film)
58mm x 33mm (on 35mm film)
LENS: 75mm
FOCUS: 0.8m–Infinity)
APERTURES: f/4.5, f/5.6, f/8, f/11, f/16, f/22
SHUTTER SPEEDS: 1/15–1/250 sec., B (Bulb)
OTHER FEATURES: Panoramic (35mm) format includes
sprocket holes in image area
Rewind facility for 120 film
"Endless panorama" 120 mode
Removable, interchangeable back
and viewfinder
Hotshoe
Cable release socket
Tripod mount

2008's Lubitel 166+ Universal is a Lomography-designed reinvention of the original Lubitel 166U, with twists and additions intended to drag it kicking and screaming into the twenty-first century. Key changes include the addition of a "live" hotshoe (rather than a flash sync socket), an improved viewfinder offering 100% coverage and a brighter outlook on your subjects, and the ability to focus slightly closer (albeit with increased parallax issues).

There is also a change to the image formats you can shoot, with the classic 6cm x 6cm square and more economical 6cm x 4.5cm rectangle of the original Universal joined by an endless panorama option and a 35mm panoramic setting that produces 58mm x 33mm images (including sprockets!) on 35mm film. You can also rewind 120 roll film—useful for multiple exposures.

Finally, there's the option to remove the back and viewfinder, which Lomography cites as an "investment in the future." It's worth noting that there's no sign of alternative backs or 'finders; some critics are asking if this is marketing hype.

What is more contentious is the price of the Lubitel 166+ Universal, which would set you back almost £300 (approx. $475) from Lomography in the UK. Admittedly, prices vary around the world, and you could say this is reasonable when you compare it to the cost of a used Rolleiflex TLR (an argument that some people use). However, remember that an original Lubitel 166U is likely to cost around 1/3 of this amount, while a 166B will be less again. If you don't feel you will benefit from the features added by Lomography you may find that an original Lubitel is better suited to both your photography and your pocket.

Technique: Multiple exposures

It doesn't matter if you're shooting with a Diana, a Lubitel, or a Holga—all of the medium format cameras in this chapter are simplicity incarnate when it comes to making stunning multiple exposures. The reason for this is none of them have linked shutter and winding mechanisms, so setting/firing the shutter and winding the film on are two separate acts. If you want to make a multiple exposure, this means you simply don't wind the film on before shooting again, and it's for this very reason that "accidental" multiple exposures are often quite common. However, while the process is straightforward, you do need to put in a little bit of mental effort when it comes to deciding on your multiple subjects, because when you start overlapping images it's easy to end up with a photographic mess rather than a masterpiece.

Start by loading up with a slow-ish film (ISO 100 or 200 is good for this), because every time you fire the shutter you are adding to the overall exposure, making the final image brighter. Next, decide on your subject(s). If you've never shot multiple exposures before then consider keeping things ultra-simple to start with: photograph something relatively plain for one exposure (grass, the street, a brick wall, or some other fairly repetitive texture or pattern) and something more detailed for your second (a person, a building, or whatever else

it is that you're into). This will give you a basic multiple exposure (although not necessarily an "exciting" one), which will help you familiarize yourself with the process.

From there, you can think about becoming more adventurous, perhaps by combining a couple of slightly more detailed elements. Large, graphic, abstract shapes work particularly well when combined, and sometimes you only need to turn your camera 90 degrees between shots to get a great result. This can also avoid any issues with clashing colors. Remember, there are no rules to say you have to have two totally disparate subjects, and it's impossible to say what will and will not work. You don't even have to limit yourself to just two frames: if you want to have more, don't wind on and just keep shooting!

It's easy to produce multiple exposures with any camera that has separate shutter and winding mechanisms: simply shoot without winding the film on.

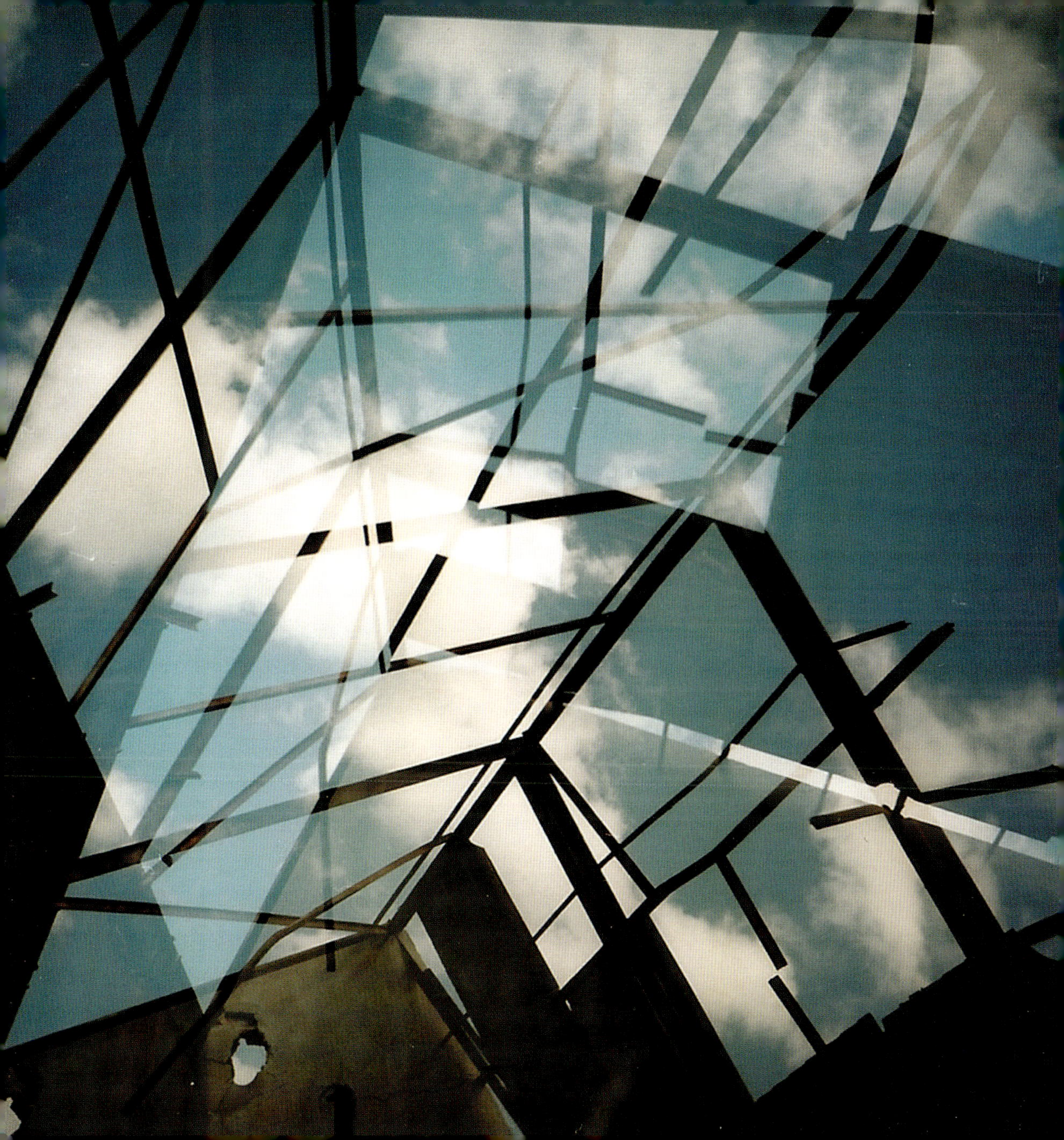

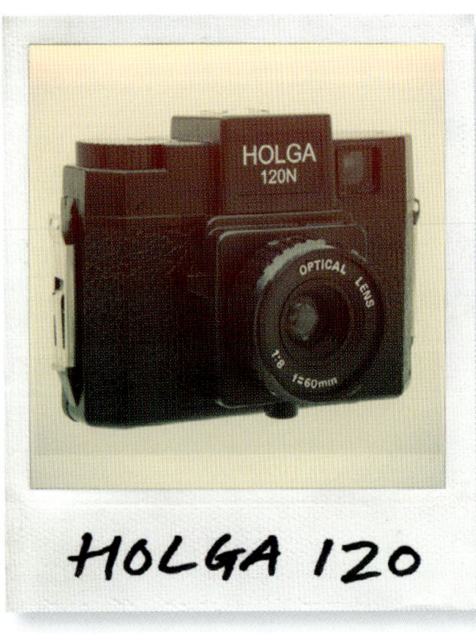

HOLGA 120

CAMERA:	Holga 120N/120GN
MANUFACTURER:	Holga
FILM TYPE:	120 roll film
IMAGE FORMATS:	6cm x 6cm (12 shots)
	6cm x 4.5cm (16 shots)
LENS:	60mm (glass)
FOCUS:	4 preset distance settings
	(approx. 1m, 2m, 6m, Infinity)
APERTURES:	Cloudy (f/8), Sunny (f/11)
SHUTTER SPEEDS:	N (1/100 sec.), B (Bulb)
OTHER FEATURES:	Tripod mount
	Standard hotshoe
	Plastic lens (120N) or
	glass lens (120GN)

Although the Diana and Lubitel predate it by at least two decades, the Holga is perhaps the epitome of plastic cameras. It is also the most enduring as Holga production has not ceased since Mr Lee introduced it in the early 1980s, so it has not required "reinventing" in the same way as the current batch of Lubitel and Diana models. As such, I make no excuses for devoting more space to this humble Chinese plastic.

It is perhaps surprising that of the three medium format "originals" it's the Holga that has weathered the passing of time better than the rest. Compared to the Diana it was clearly last in line when looks were handed out, and it is far less capable than a Lubitel when it comes to picture taking. But perhaps that's why it is so pervasive. The basic medium format Holga has a primitive, unrefined charm that is impossible to manufacture intentionally. It is the beautiful by-product of flawed design, low-cost materials, and a quality control department that just doesn't seem to turn up to the factory that often—which I mean in the nicest possible way!

If the design was refined, and manufacturing tolerances tightened, a Holga just wouldn't be a Holga any more—it would be a soulless piece of plastic designed to appeal to the "completist" collector. But as it stands, a classic medium

CAMERA: Holga 120N
FILM: Fuji Provia 100 (cross processed)
EXPOSURE: 1/100 sec. @ f/8

This was shot as part of an outdoor series capturing friends and an elusive summer youthful feeling. The color and feel of the image is eternally nostalgic.

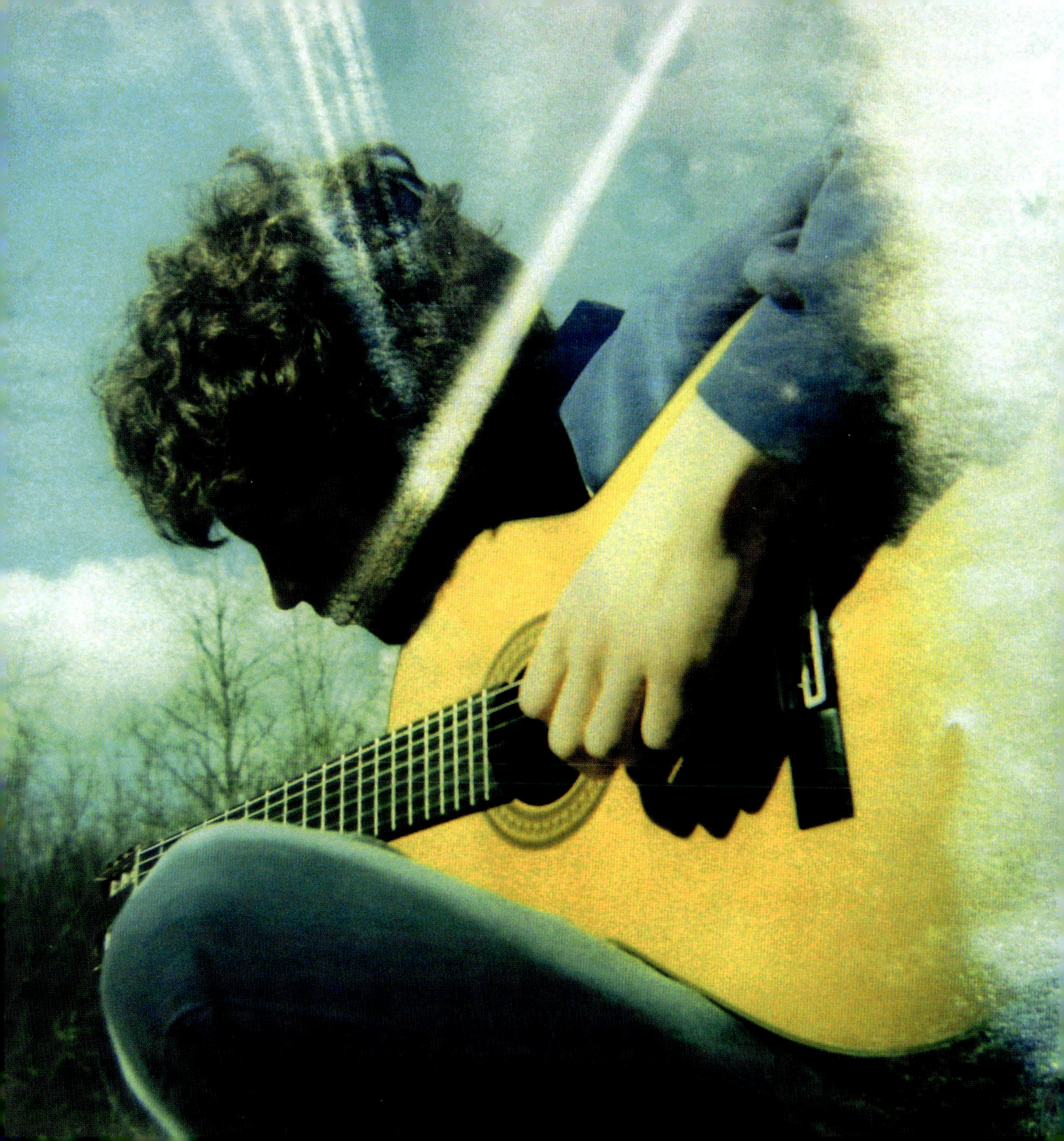

format Holga is an essential addition to any enthusiast's arsenal. There are plenty to choose from, and the basic premise is simple: all of the "standard" Holgas take 120 roll film and shoot 6cm x 6cm or 6cm x 4.5cm format images, producing 12 or 16 shots per film respectively. A 60mm focal length lens provides a mild wide-angle view of the world (with the viewfinder showing only around ¾ of that), with a choice of two aperture settings and either a 1/100 sec. shutter speed or a manual, Bulb exposure.

Beyond this basic specification you have the choice of a plastic or a glass lens, but despite claims that the glass lens is sharper, in real terms it's debatable that there's any significant difference between the two. With either option you can choose a camera with a hotshoe or one with a built-in flash, but note that you can't change the batteries of a built-in flash model if you have a film loaded—the design means that the film covers the cells. Ultra-creative types might want to pick a color flash variant, which allows you to "dial" a colored filter in front of the built-in flash to color the light.

Regardless of which option you go for, stick with the 6cm x 6cm square format for maximum vignetting and focus fall off. Don't get hung up by light leaks, overlapping frames, and "dodgy" exposures—revel in them and accept that your Holga is perfect just the way it is. As you will see on the following pages, you could expand its abilities, or add a different Holga to the mix.

Standard Holga **models**

The Holga range has expanded over the years, from a single camera in the early 1980s to a line-up that now incorporates more than 20 different models. This "at-a-glance" grid, which includes the original 120S and 120SF models, will help you find the medium format model that's right for you:

Model	120S	120SF	120N	120FN	120CFN	120GN	120GFN	120GCFN
Film type	120 roll film							
Format masks	6cm x 4.5cm	6cm x 4.5cm	6cm x 4.5cm 6cm x 6cm	6cm x 4.5cm 6cm x 6cm	6cm x 4.5cm 6cm x 6cm	6cm x 4.5cm 6cm x 6cm	6cm x 4.5cm 6cm x 6cm	6cm x 4.5cm 6cm x 6cm
Lens	Plastic	Plastic	Plastic	Plastic	Plastic	Glass	Glass	Glass
Focal length	60mm							
Focus	4 distance settings (approx. 1m, 2m, 6m, Infinity)							
Apertures	Cloudy (f/8), Sunny (f/11)							
Shutter speeds	N (1/100 sec.)	N (1/100 sec.)	N (1/100 sec.) B (Bulb)	N (1/100 sec.) B (Bulb)	N (1/100 sec.) B (Bulb)	N (1/100 sec.) B (Bulb)	N (1/100 sec.) B (Bulb)	N (1/100 sec.) B (Bulb)
Flash	Hotshoe	Built-in	Hotshoe	Built-in	Built-in (color flash)	Hotshoe	Built-in	Built-in (color flash)
Tripod mount	No	No	Yes	Yes	Yes	Yes	Yes	Yes

What's in a **name?**

We are surrounded by camera model numbers that are largely meaningless. The numbers and letters in the model names of the Holgas featured in this book are far more useful, as they describe the physical characteristics of the camera. The following list refers to all Holga cameras, although some of the entries apply only to the 35mm cameras discussed in the following chapter.

120: Refers to the film format. If 120 is in the model name, you're looking at a medium format Holga.

135: Refers to the film format—in this case 135, or 35mm, film.

3D: This means the Holga has two lenses that will enable you to create stereoscopic pairs of images for a 3D effect.

BC: Short for Black Corners (also referred to as Bent Corners), indicating a camera with deliberately enhanced vignetting. Only applies to 35mm models.

CF: The camera has a built-in Color Flash, which features a "dial in" system of colored filters that can be used to color the light.

F: The camera has a standard (daylight balanced), built-in Flash.

G: Indicates that the camera has a Glass lens.

N: The Holga 120N is an updated version of the original 120S and the most basic model in the current lineup. Perhaps N stands for "Normal"?

PC: Stands for Pinhole Camera, so there's no lens on this one, just a tiny hole.

S: The Holga 120S is the original Holga model, complete with a plastic lens. As far as can be determined, the S is meaningless—perhaps it's short for "Standard"?

TIM: Twin Image Maker. A dual lens system currently found on just one 35mm camera. Allows you to shoot half-frame images or create a 3D effect with close-up subjects.

TLR: Indicates the camera has a Twin Lens Reflex viewing system.

W: Wide. Relates to the image format rather than the focal length of the lens, so indicates a panoramic camera.

Once you know what all of these acronyms mean you can determine precisely what to expect from a specific Holga model, without actually seeing it. The 120CFN is a basic medium format Holga with a color flash, for example, while the 120WPC is a pinhole camera that creates panoramic shots on medium format roll film. The 135BC TLR in the next chapter is… well, you work it out.

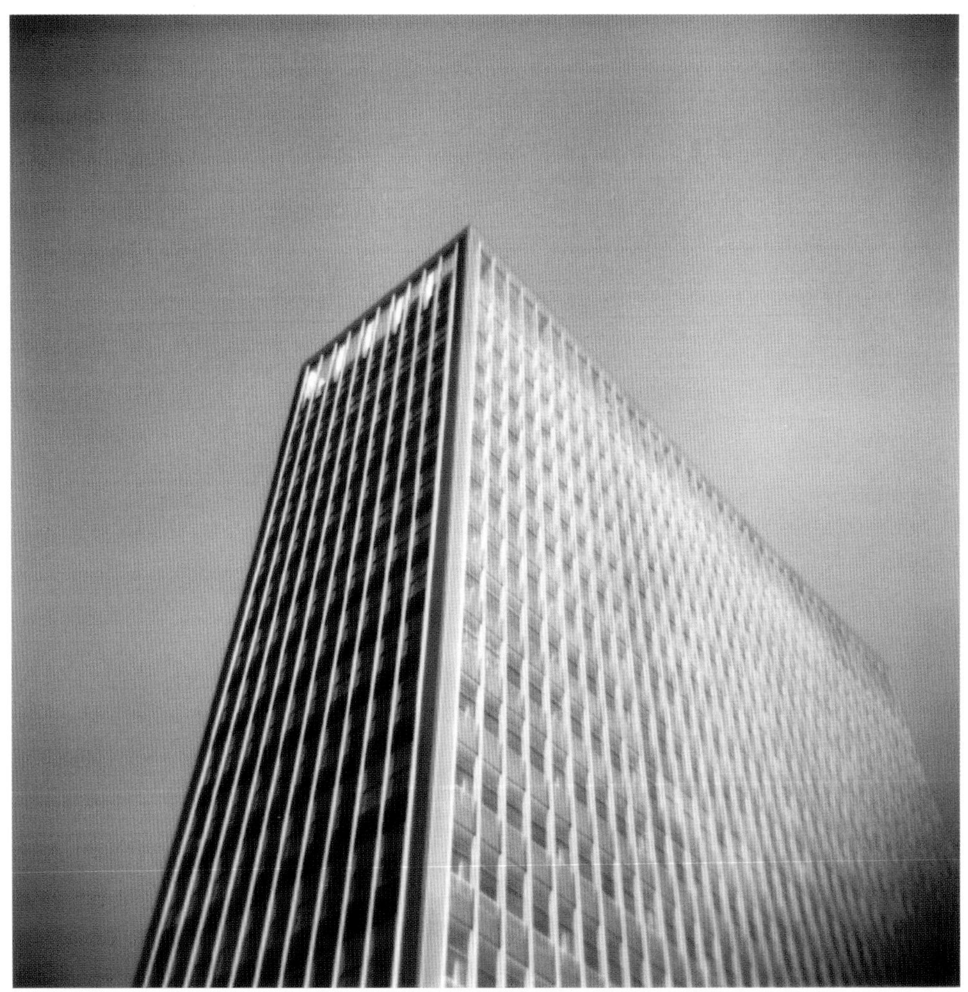

CAMERA: Holga 120FN
FILM: Ilford HP5+
EXPOSURE: Unrecorded

Shooting 6cm x 6cm format
images guarantees corner
shading since the Holga's
lens struggles to expose the
entire frame evenly.

CAMERA: Holga 120FN
FILM: Ilford HP5+
EXPOSURE: 1/100 sec. @ f/11

Fast film is generally
recommended for shooting
with a Holga, and ISO 400
makes a good starting point.

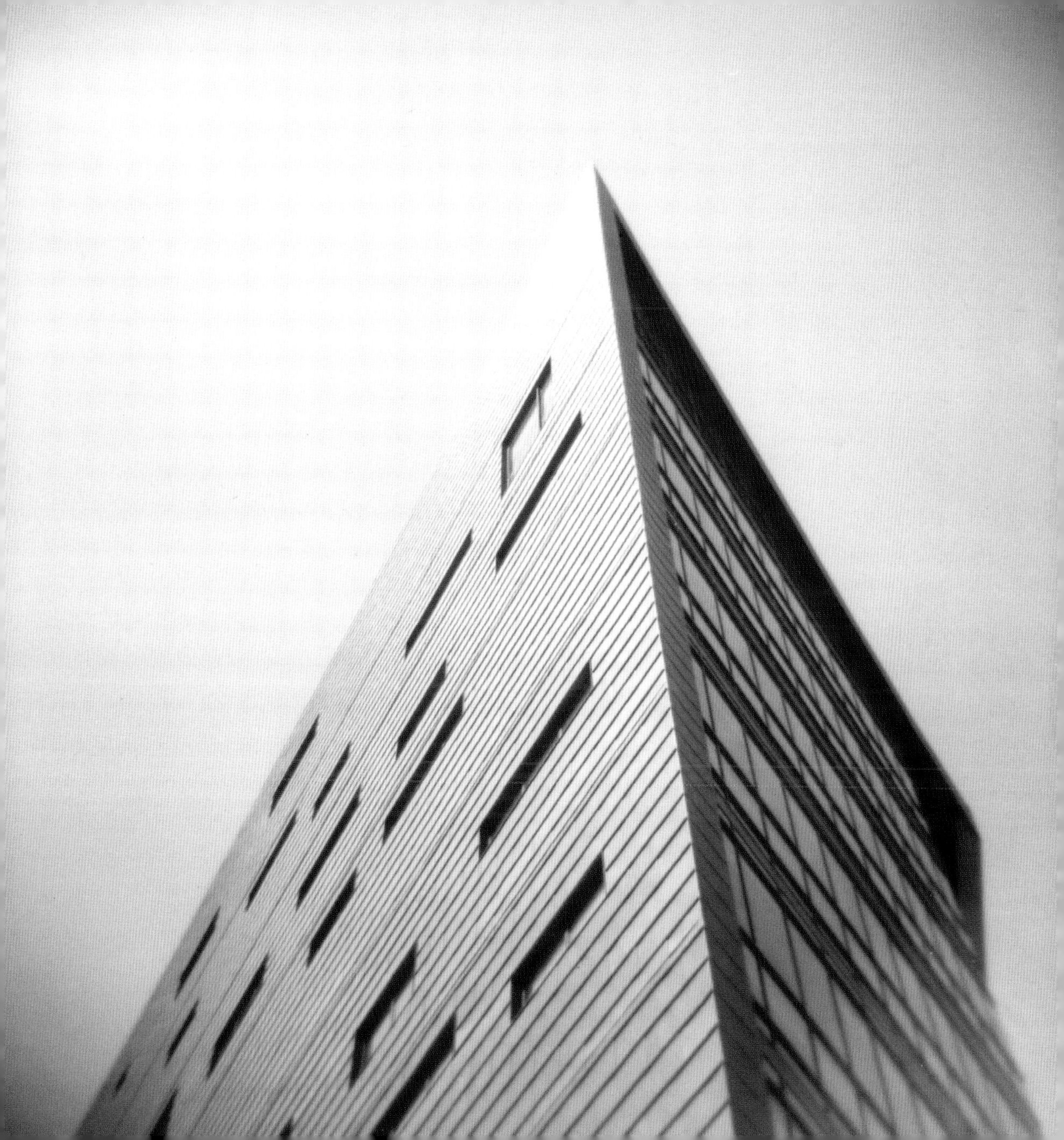

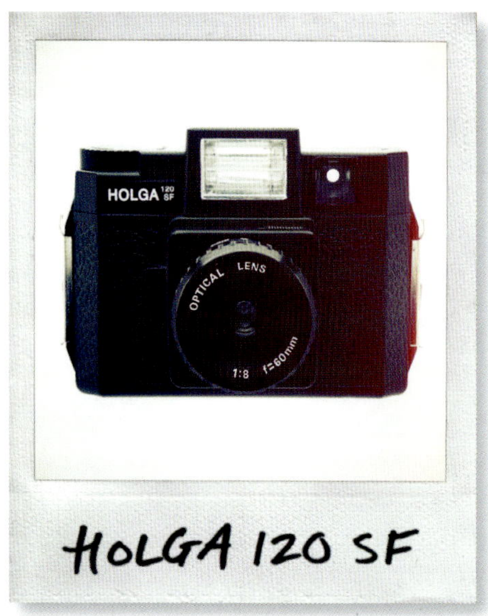

HOLGA 120 SF

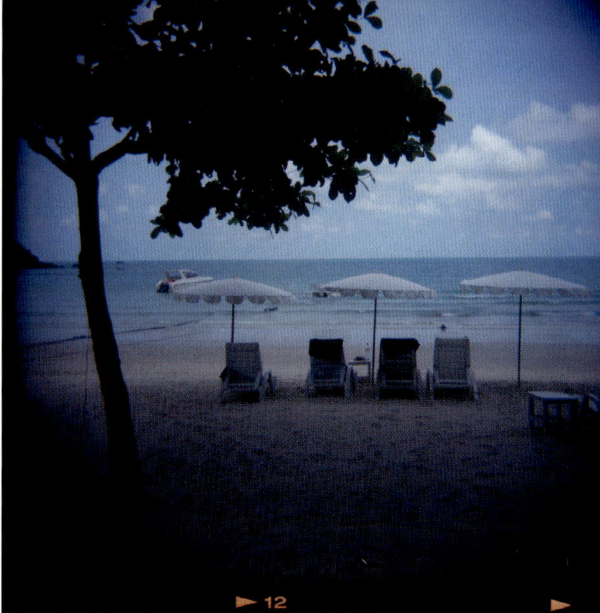

CAMERA: Holga 120SF
FILM: Kodak Portra 160NC
EXPOSURE: 1/100 sec. @ f/11

The original Holga's 60mm plastic lens displays pronounced vignetting.

Original **plastic**

The original Holga 120S from the early 1980s, and the 120SF that was released shortly after, are the Holgas that epitomize the spirit of plastic cameras. Unlike their successors (the 120N/120FN respectively) they do not have a mask for 6cm x 6cm format images; they lack a B setting for manual exposures; and neither camera is fitted with a tripod mount.

As if this wasn't enough, a design issue means that these models don't even have two working aperture settings. Although the Sunny and Cloudy settings appear to work, the actual apertures in the lens sit behind a slightly smaller hole, so it is this hole that determines how much light passes through the lens.

It is this inherent quirkiness and the limitations imposed by low-cost production that make the 120S and 120SF so much fun—it is not about what they can do, but about what you can do with them. This ethos extends far beyond picture taking, and for some years these cameras supported a small industry of "fixers," who—for a fee—would add a tripod mount to your Holga, fix the aperture, add a B setting, and so on. Sadly, this came to an end when the 120S/120SF were replaced by the 120N/120FN, which came with these things factory-fitted.

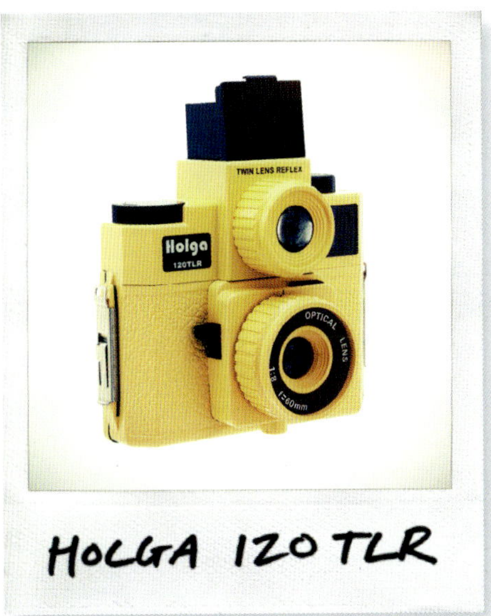

HOLGA 120 TLR

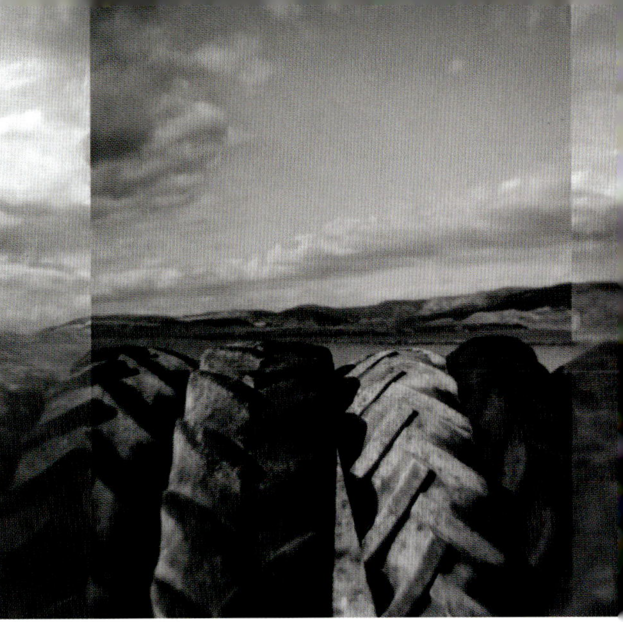

CAMERA: Holga 120N
FILM: Ilford HP5+
EXPOSURE: 1/100 sec. @ f/11

The results you get from a Holga TLR will be identical to those you would expect from a "standard" Holga—only the viewing system is different.

Twin lens **Holgas**

Available with a plastic lens (120TLR) or a glass lens (120GTLR) Holga's medium format TLR cameras are identical to the 120CFN and 120GCFN in terms of their specification and performance. The only notable difference is the viewing system: the TLR (as its name suggests) employs a waist-level viewfinder and viewing lens to display a reversed view of the subject.

In all other respects—including image quality—the cameras are the same, so choosing one over the other is a purely personal decision. It is worth noting that the TLR viewing system is more accurate when it comes to seeing what will be recorded on the film—the "direct" viewfinder of a standard Holga is woefully inept by comparison.

A splash of color

Like Henry Ford's original Model T automobile, Holgas were traditionally available in any color you wanted, just so long as it was black. Now, however, there are myriad different color schemes for some (but not all) camera models, including plain colors, camouflage, and multicolored options.

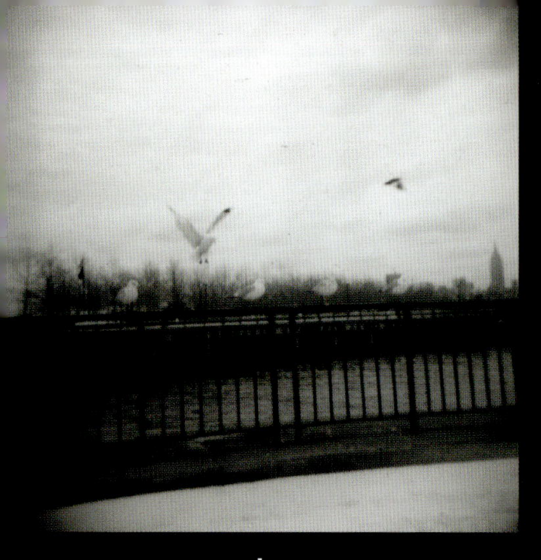

1

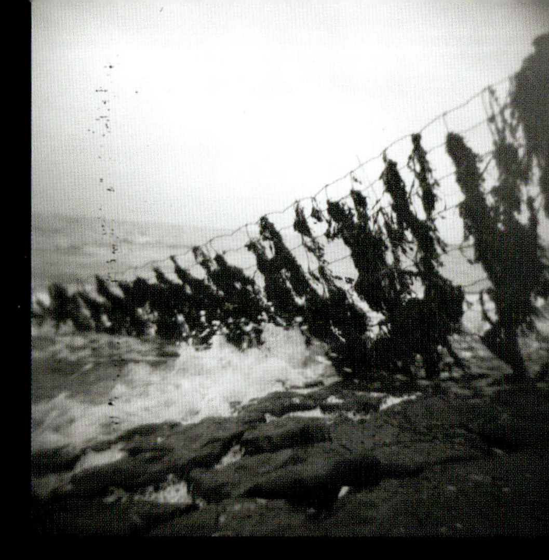

2

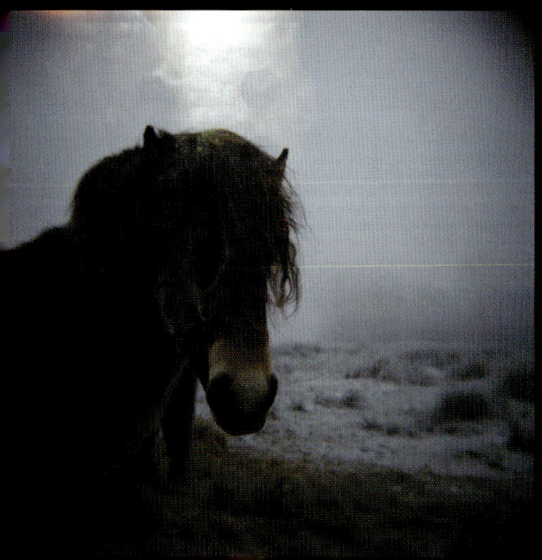

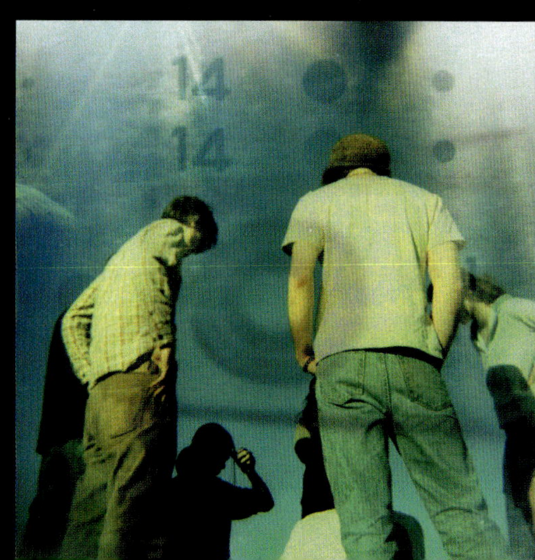

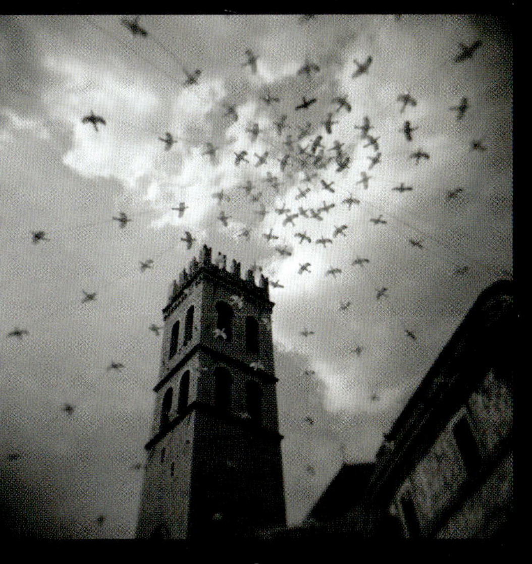

3

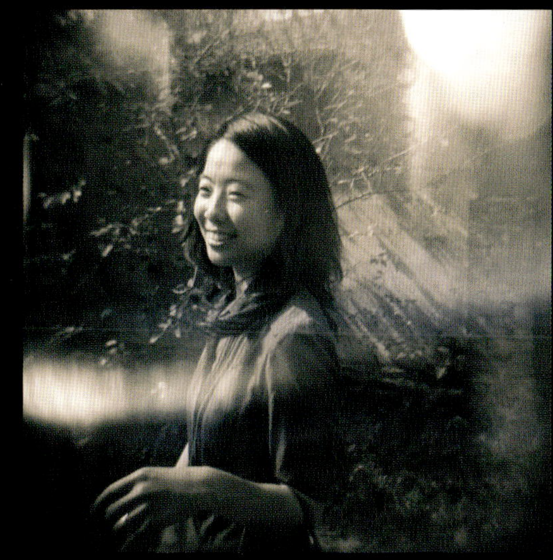

4

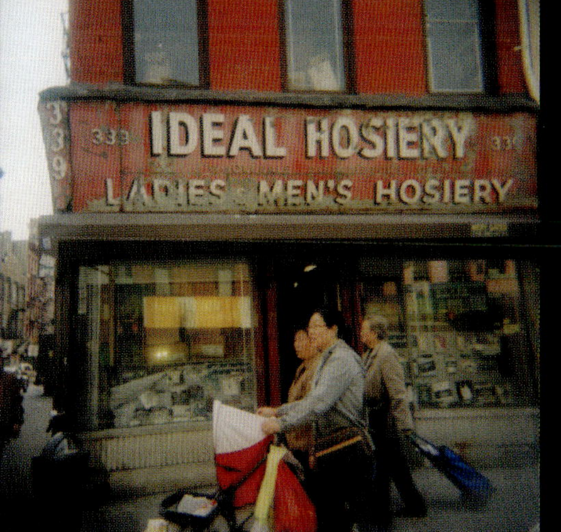

1
CAMERA: Holga 120CFN
FILM: Unknown
EXPOSURE: Unrecorded

2
CAMERA: Holga 120GN
FILM: Kodak Tri-X 400
EXPOSURE: Unrecorded

3
CAMERA: Holga 120GFN
FILM: Ilford HP5+
EXPOSURE: Unrecorded

4
CAMERA: Holga 120N
FILM: Kodak Plus-X
EXPOSURE: Unrecorded

5
CAMERA: Holga 120GN
FILM: Fuji Pro 400H
EXPOSURE: Unrecorded

6
CAMERA: Holga 120N
FILM: Fuji Provia 100
(cross processed)
EXPOSURE: 1/100 sec.
@ f/8

7
CAMERA: Holga 120CFN
FILM: Unknown
EXPOSURE: Unrecorded

Lenses

The 60mm lens on a Holga may not be interchangeable in the same way as the lens on a Diana F+, but that doesn't mean you are stuck with its slightly-wider-than-standard focal length. Both telephoto and fisheye lens adapters are available that slide over the Holga's lens: the telephoto lens increases the focal length by 2.5x (to 150mm) and the fisheye lens provides you with an ultra-wide 170° angle of view (similar to the 35mm Fisheye cameras on page 94–95).

However, working with both lenses is hit-and-miss, as the viewfinder on your Holga doesn't change. The built-in 'finder might be vague at the best of times, but when you change the focal length of the lens entirely it becomes redundant, leaving you to guess what the camera will capture.

In addition to its supplementary lenses, Holga also produces a slide-on filter holder, allowing you to use filters on your camera. The filters designed to accompany the filter holder include plain colored filters, soft surround (for increased softness around the edges of your frame), and split image, which is the sort of filter you are likely to use just once...

Flash

If your Holga's got a hotshoe, then chances are you might want to get yourself a flash. The obvious choice would be one of Holga's flashes, but like the built-in flash units, these tend to be small and weak, so are only going to help you when your subject is close to the camera.

Luckily, the Holga uses a standard hotshoe, so you can use pretty much any flash you like: Ebay is a great source for low-cost, manual, hotshoe flashes.

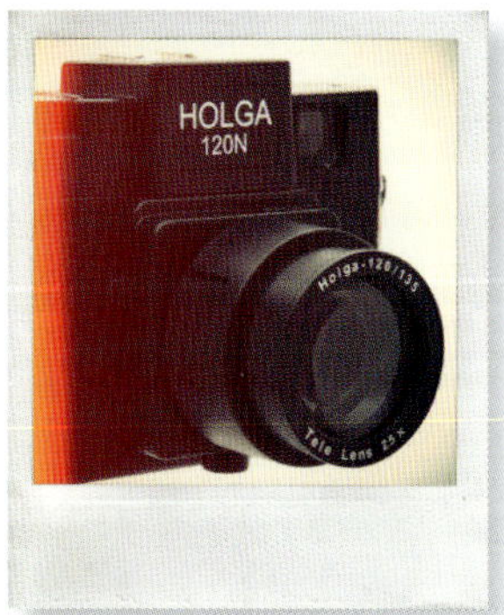

Add a telephoto lens adapter to the standard 60mm lens to increase focal length by 2.5x (150mm).

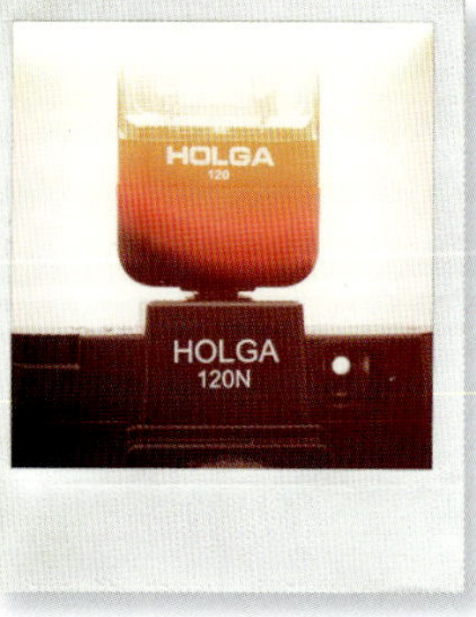

A Holga with a hotshoe gives you more options when it comes to choosing a flash unit.

35mm film **adapter**

Shooting 35mm film in a medium format camera is a great way to produce fantastic "sprocket shots." There are several adapters available to convert a Holga to use 35mm film, but save your money and spend it on film instead: later in this chapter you'll see that all you need is a few bits of sponge, a rubber band, and some tape.

CAMERA: Holga 120N
FILM: Fuji Superia 400 (35mm)
EXPOSURE: 1/100 sec. @ f/8

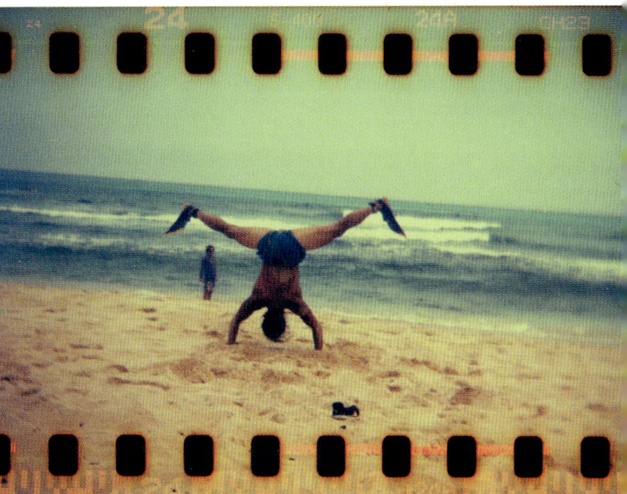

Sprocket holes are a great way to frame your shots. If you have a medium format Holga or Diana you can buy an adapter and load it with 35mm film.

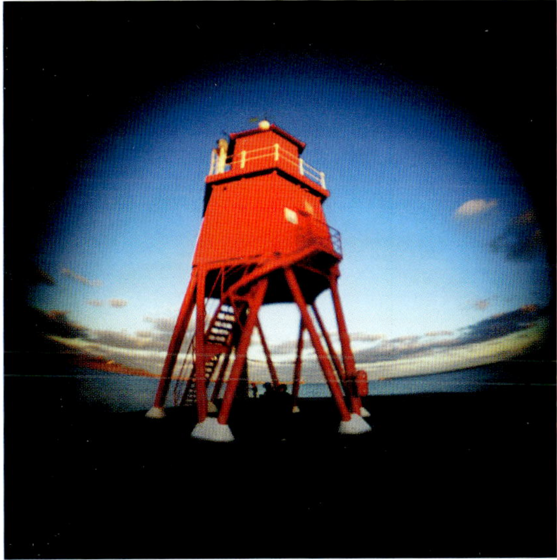

CAMERA: Holga 120CFN with Fisheye lens
FILM: Fuji Superia 100
EXPOSURE: 1/100 sec @ f/11

Holga's fisheye adapter gives an ultra-wide view and creates a heavily distorted, circular image.

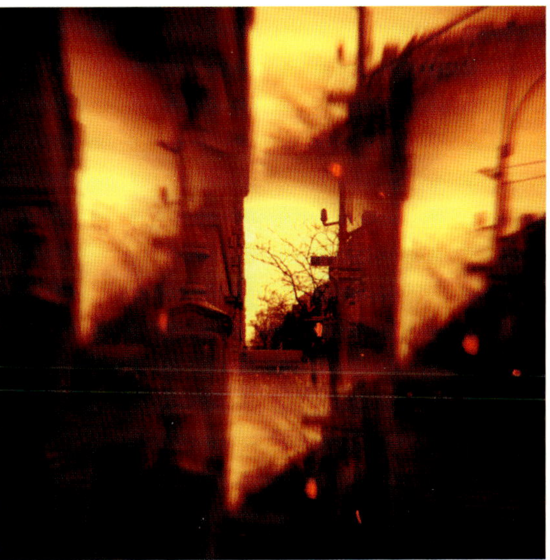

CAMERA: Holga 120CFN with Holga kaleidoscopic filter.
FILM: Redscale (hand rolled)
EXPOSURE: Unrecorded

It's certainly not a "must have" accessory, but Holga's kaleidoscopic filter can produce some great shots.

Holgaroid

A "Holgaroid" is simply a Holga camera fitted with an instant film (Polaroid) back. The camera's regular film back is removed, and a Polaroid back attached in its place, held on with the standard metal clips. The idea is a simple (if somewhat expensive) one, yet it has been plagued by misfortune.

The earliest Holgaroid backs were produced by Polaroid itself, around 2002. They used square, Type 80 Polaroid film, which was ideal for the square-shooting Holga—at least it was until Polaroid discontinued Type 80 film in 2006.

Despite this setback, a new wave of Holgaroid backs emerged a year later, manufactured by A-Power and designed to use Type 100 film. Yet only a year later tragedy struck again, with the loss of the entire Polaroid Corporation. In an instant, Polaroid's Type 100 film range was discontinued, leaving only Fujifilm's less expansive range of instant films to fill the void.

This has not deterred hardcore Holgaroiders, though, and with Type 100 film having been introduced recently by The Impossible Project, things are looking up once again. However, given the Holgaroid's turbulent history, it is anyone's guess how long this will last.

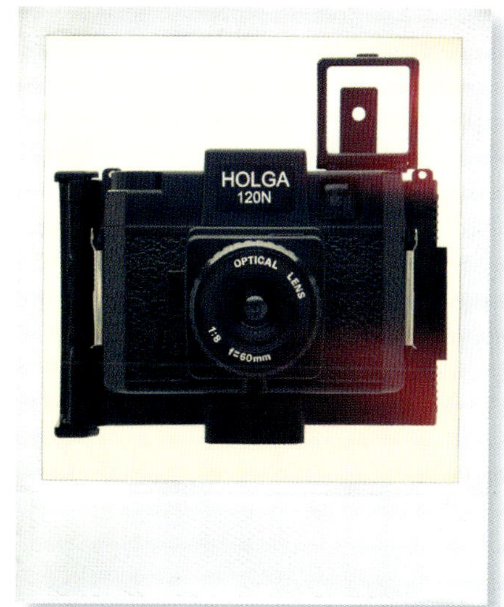

CAMERA: Holga 120N with Polaroid back
FILM: Polaroid Viva Type 80 (expired)
EXPOSURE: Unrecorded

Frustration and experimentation typifies the first few weeks with a Holga and Polaroid back.

CAMERA: Holga 120N with Polaroid back
FILM: Polaroid Type 80
EXPOSURE: Unrecorded

The original Type 80 Polaroid was perfect for shooting on a Holga as the square film matched the camera format.

Uneven spacing and overlapping frames are a common phenomenon when you shoot with a Holga, and are a part of the "happy accident" ethos. They generally occur either because the film "slips" slightly as you wind it on (due to a lack of tension), or you just don't wind it on by the exact same amount each time. But you can also overlap your frames intentionally to create striking panoramic images, or "Holgaramas."

In fairness, the term Holgarama is misleading, as this technique can be employed using any camera that has separate winding and shutter mechanisms, such as a Diana. You can even shoot panoramas with a Lubitel, although the way the film passes through the camera would mean they would have to be vertical panoramas—useful for cityscapes. However, the technique is best known (and used) among Holga users, simply because the design of the standard 120 cameras makes it so easy. In fact, shooting a Holgarama is not that much more difficult than taking a "straight" shot.

Facing page, top
CAMERA: Holga 120GN
FILM: Ilford HP5+
EXPOSURE: Unrecorded

The viewfinder on the Holga is somewhat misleading, but with practice you can learn to predict how much more of a scene will end up on the negative.

Facing page, bottom
CAMERA: Holga 120GN
FILM: Kodak BW400CN
EXPOSURE: Unrecorded

The easiest way to get consistent spacing and overlap is to shoot at 6cm x 6cm, but advance as if your are shooting 6cm x 4.5cm images.

Winding on

Because intentionally overlapped frames are the order of the day for a stunning Holgarama, you'll need to modify your winding-on process. If you're shooting 6cm x 6cm format images, the easiest way of doing this is to set the red frame-counter window at the back of the camera to "16" (as you would for 6cm x 4.5cm shots). You can then wind on using the numbers on the film's backing paper, which will result in a fairly consistent overlap between frames.

Alternatively, you can use the "Wind One" technique: just turn the winding wheel one full turn between shots. The overlaps between your frames will be less consistent, but this can enhance the "handcrafted" look of your Holgaramas.

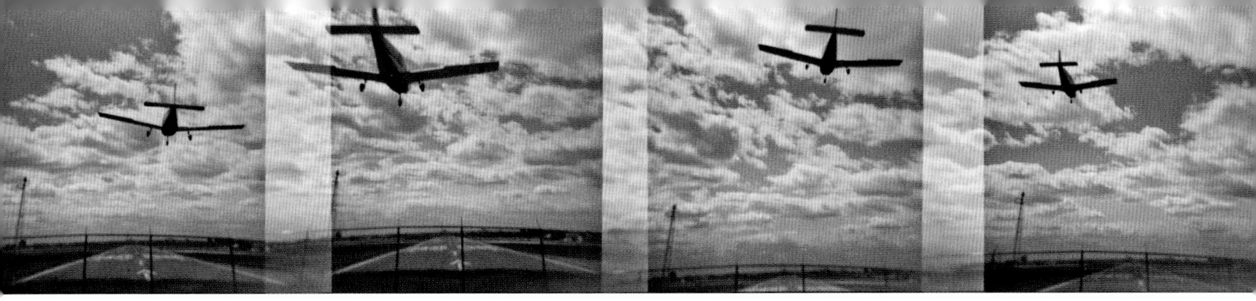

The Holgarama **process**

1. Before you start, check that your camera is set to shoot 6cm x 6cm format images. This isn't mandatory, but it makes it much easier to overlap your frames consistently.

2. The next step is to decide how you want to shoot your panorama. There are two options here: you can either stand in the same spot or turn the camera, or you can physically move sideways to take your shots. Which one you go for will largely come down to the subject distance—turning on the spot is the better option for distant subjects, "crabbing" sideways is better for close subjects.

3. Aim your camera at the left edge of your scene (or stand so you are targeting the left side of the shot you want to take) and make your first exposure. It doesn't matter whether you use N or B, or Sunny or Cloudy—just match the exposure to the subject as you would for a single shot.

4. Wind your film on using either one of the methods outlined opposite.

5. Turn the camera (or move) to the right to line up the next frame. Use the viewfinder as a guide if you have to, but remember that it's not very accurate. If you're turning on the spot, you want to turn the camera by about 45–50 degrees to avoid gaps appearing in the photographed scene or heavy overlaps.

6. Take your second shot, wind on again, and turn/move to set up your third shot. Repeat this process until you reach the right side of the scene you wanted to cover and that's your Holgarama finished.

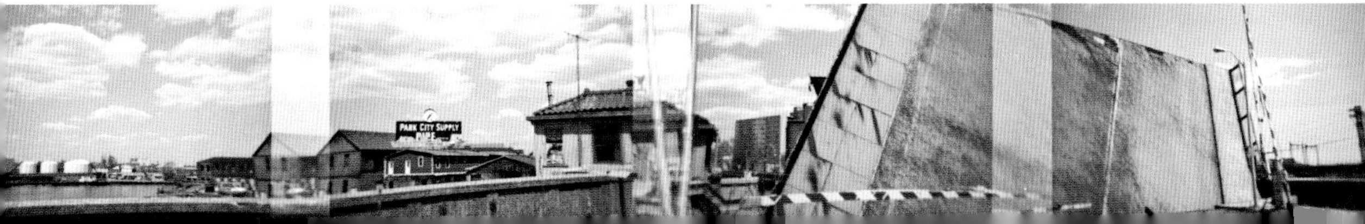

Holga **hacks**

A Holga is a beautifully imperfect picture-making machine, and each camera is seemingly different to the next. For some people this is what gives them their unique "personality"— like fingerprints or DNA. It is also the unique blend of light leaks, vignetting, and other "deficiencies" that makes one camera good and another one great.

However, there are photographers who revel in refining their Holga, by modifying or "hacking" it to suit their preferred vision. The "standard" medium format Holga models are ripe for customization, and some of the early 120S and 120SF cameras almost demand some type of modification if you want to get the most out of them.

Hack #1: Taping

Holgas leak light. Period. But not all Holgas leak the same amount of light in the same places, and even one specific camera can produce wildly different results on consecutive films. If this bugs you, or you simply want to shoot a roll of film with minimal light leaks, then taping up the seams is definitely the way to go.

After you've loaded a film, use PVC electrical tape to seal all of the seams on the back of the camera—I've used green tape here so it's easy to see where it is, but black tape is the more conventional option. Start by taping around all four sides of the camera back, where the film door joins the camera body, paying careful attention to the metal "locks" at each side. Be sure to tape up the frame counter window as well, or tape a piece of card over it as shown here: although it's got a "safe" red filter over it, it's common for light to sneak round the edges. You will need to remove the window tape when you want to wind your film on, but keeping its exposure to the light to a minimum will help prevent leaks.

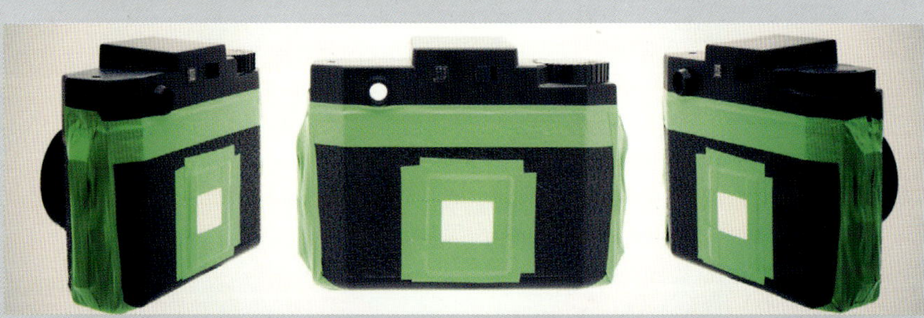

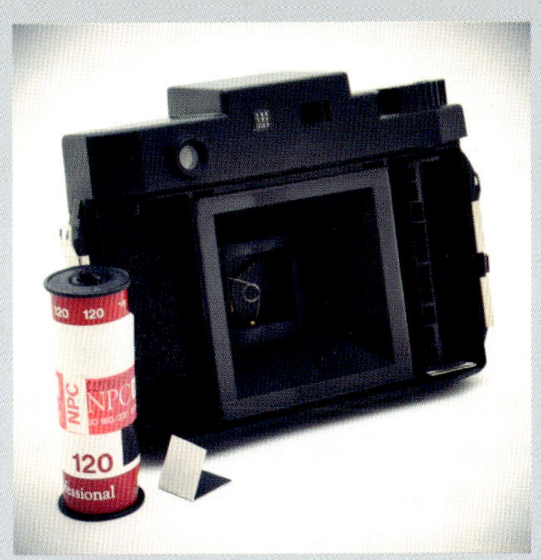

Hack #2: Spool tensioners

Frames that overlap slightly are a common Holga phenomenon, and can sometimes create really interesting results. However, there's a big difference between overlapping your frames intentionally and discovering that the camera has done it without your knowledge.

The answer is simple: cut two small pieces of relatively heavy card stock and fold them in half. Slip one of these under each of the film spools when you load the camera and the natural "spring" of the card trying to open will help hold your fresh film spool and take-up spool in place, preventing them from slipping accidentally as you wind the film on. Remember to take a few spare tensioners with you when you're out shooting—if you need to reload there's every chance you will lose one of them.

Hack #3: Flocking

A "flocked" Holga is designed to minimize internal reflections. Although they often go unnoticed, there are times when strong light coming through the lens can reflect off the shiny internals of the camera, producing internal flare.

To alleviate this risk, remove the back of your Holga and mask off the inside of the lens, shutter, film spool "compartments," and battery posts (if your camera has them), as shown here. Then, spray paint the inside of the camera flat black. Voilà—no more internal reflections!

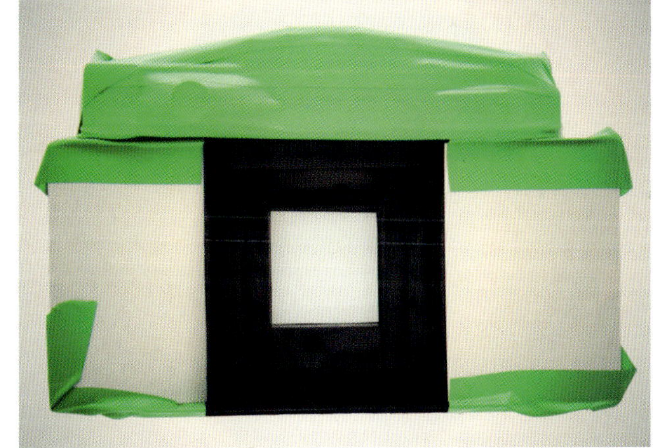

Hack #4: Internal taping

Most new Holgas come with masks for both 6cm x 6cm and 6cm x 4.5cm format images. These masks not only determine the shape of your frames, but they also hold the batteries in (on cameras with a built-in flash), as well as providing the film with a smooth surface to glide over, reducing the chance of it getting scratched.

However, the Holga 120S and 120SF only has the smaller 6cm x 4.5cm mask, which has to be removed for 6cm x 6cm shots. This reveals a hard-edged plastic frame that loves nothing more than to scratch your film as it's dragged across it. With the 120SF you also risk the batteries falling out (and they will!), and it's impossible to refit them if you have film loaded in the camera.

To avoid all of this, use PVC electrical tape to tape along the edges of the frame inside the camera and provide your film with a smooth surface to pass over. While you're at it, use a couple of strips of tape to secure the batteries as well.

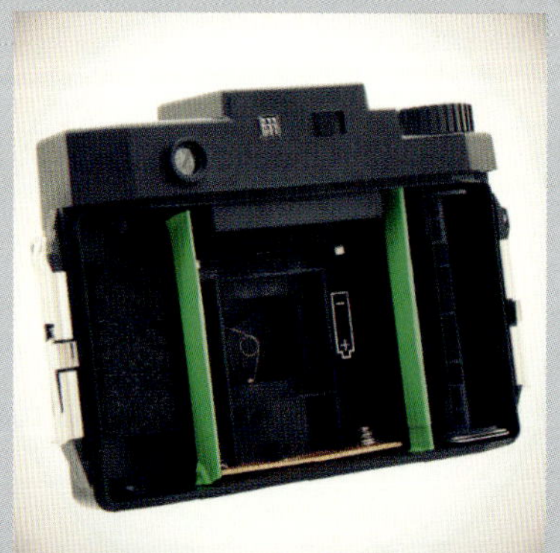

Hack #5: Filters

Holga produces a lens filter holder and a selection of filters for your creative endeavors, but if you already own a few filters (for your SLR perhaps), then there is a cheaper option.

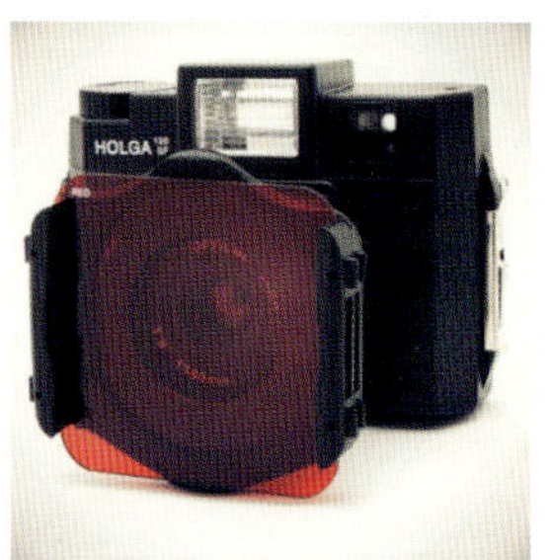

The standard Holga lens has a 46mm internal diameter, but it doesn't have a filter thread (not like your "proper" lens). No problem! The plastic rim around the front of the lens isn't as hard as it looks, so you can "cut" a thread into it with a step-up ring.

Select a step-up ring from 46mm to the diameter of the filters you already have (46mm–49mm, or 46mm–52mm, for example) and simply screw it into the plastic at the front of your Holga's lens (top left). Make sure that you screw it straight, and you will have your own permanent filter thread. You could also use the step-up ring to attach a lens hood, or even a filter holder for slot-in "system" filters (bottom left).

Hack #6: Close focus

The minimum focus distance of a standard Holga is approximately 3 feet (1 meter), but you can decrease this distance in two simple steps for even closer focusing:

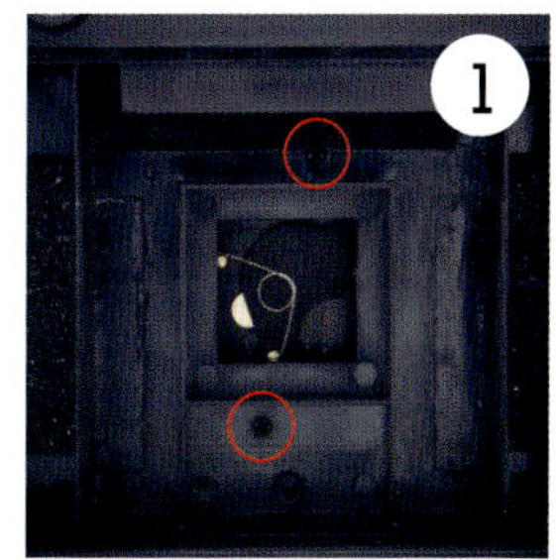

1. Open the back of your Holga and remove the mask (if fitted). Use a small cross-head screwdriver to undo the two screws indicated. This will free the front lens panel, leaving it held on by the pair of wires that activate the hotshoe/built-in flash.
2. Identify the deeply recessed screw indicated in the accompanying illustration and loosen it by a couple of full turns. This screw acts as a "stop," which prevents the lens from turning past the 3ft/1m mark. Without the stop in place the lens can focus much closer (or be removed), although you will have to guess the distance—there's no focus confirmation on a Holga!

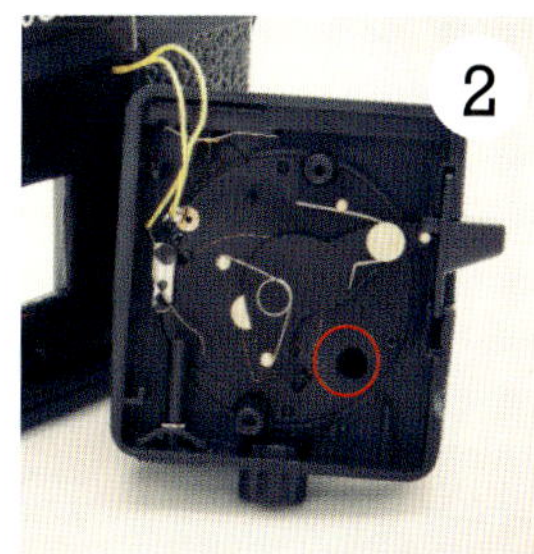

Hack #7: Tripod socket

All current Holgas have a tripod socket, so unless you've picked up a 120S or 120SF, this mod won't be necessary. Unless you convert your 120S/SF to a Time Machine (see Hack #8) it's unlikely that a tripod will help you—the shutter speed is fast enough to avoid camera shake and the viewfinder too vague to allow precise composition. However, if you must have one, there are several ways to add a tripod socket.

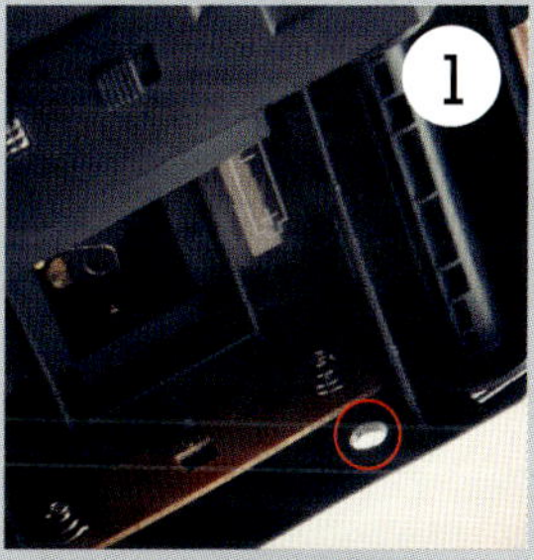

The first, and simplest option is to use epoxy resin to attach a suitable nut to the bottom of your camera. Pick up a ¼-inch nut (20 threads per inch) from your local hardware store, and just stick it on! The result won't be pretty—or permanent—but it just might do everything you want it to. Until it falls off that is...

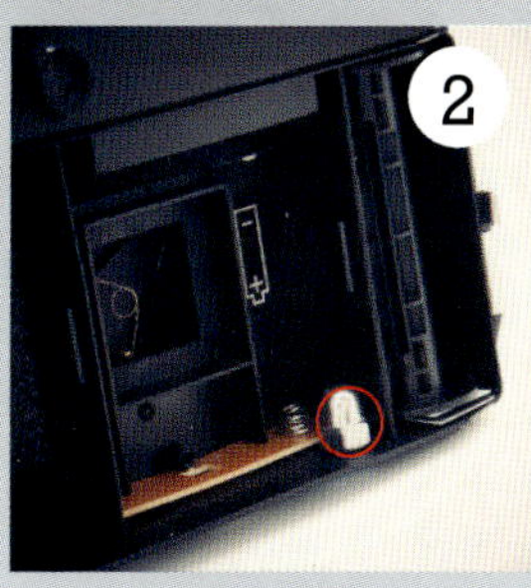

For a slightly more "professional" solution, drill a ¼-inch hole in the bottom of your Holga (1) and glue a ¼"x20 dome nut on the inside of the camera, in a corner so it can't twist free (2). Once the glue is dry, seal around the nut and paint it black to avoid internal light reflections.

Hack #8: Time Machine

Unlike the modern Holgas, the original 120S/120SF only had one shutter speed—1/100 sec. However, if you're willing to sacrifice this modest exposure time you can convert these early Holgas into a "Time Machine" that's perfect for recording dreamily blurred shots of time passing by. It's important to note that there might not be any going back once you've hacked your 120S/120SF in this way, so if you want the option of shooting 1/100 sec. snaps, as well as long, manual exposures, you should buy a newer Holga instead.

Assuming that you do want a Time Machine, you need to do just one thing: lock the rotating disk in the shutter mechanism so it is permanently in the "open" position. In doing so, you will disable the 1/100 sec. shutter speed, so any exposure will last for as long as the shutter-release button is held down, effectively giving you a Bulb mode. Here's how it's done:

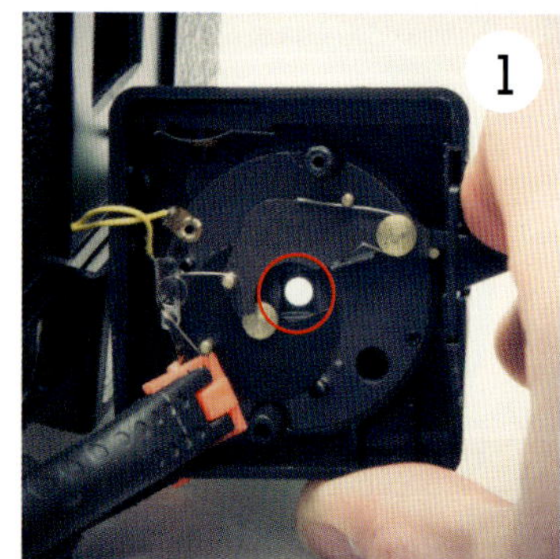

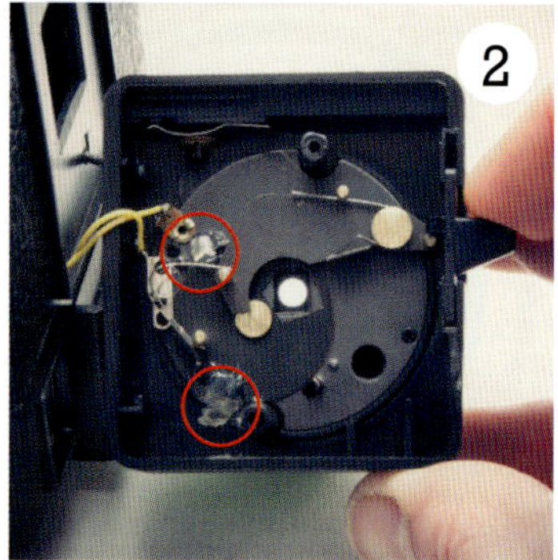

1. Remove the two screws that hold the front lens panel (as described previously) so you can see the rotating disk that is responsible for the 1/100 sec. shutter speed. Press down gently on the shutter-release button with one index finger, while applying light pressure to the rotating disk with your other index finger. The aim is to trap the disk when it is "open," revealing the lens—I'm using a clamp to hold it open here.

2. With the disk held in its "open" position, glue it in place so it cannot shut. Use epoxy, "chemical metal," or a hot glue gun to hold the disk in place, taking care not to get glue in the way of the shutter arm. Once the glue is dry, refit the lens panel.

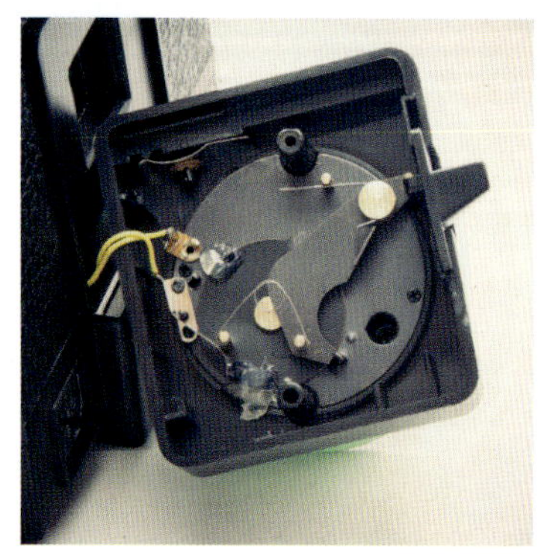

TIPS:

Because the rotating disk is open behind the lens at all times, only the Holga's shutter is preventing light from getting through to your film. To avoid light leaks via the lens, fit a lens cap between shots to prevent light getting in.

To make sure that your Time Machine requires the longest possible shutter speeds, load with ISO 100 film and add a couple of 2- or 3-stop neutral density filters to the front of the lens. The more filters and/or the stronger they are, the longer your exposures will need to be.

Hack #9: Pinholga

If a Time Machine conversion isn't giving you the long exposures you crave for, or you simply want to experiment with lens-less photography, then how about creating a Pinholga?

Pinhole lenses can be bought commercially, or you can make one yourself—there isn't space here to explain how, but the Internet has plenty of options. I'm using a commercial pinhole lens that's been fitted in several DIY pinhole cameras over the years—now it's time for this f/180 gem to go to work in a Holga!

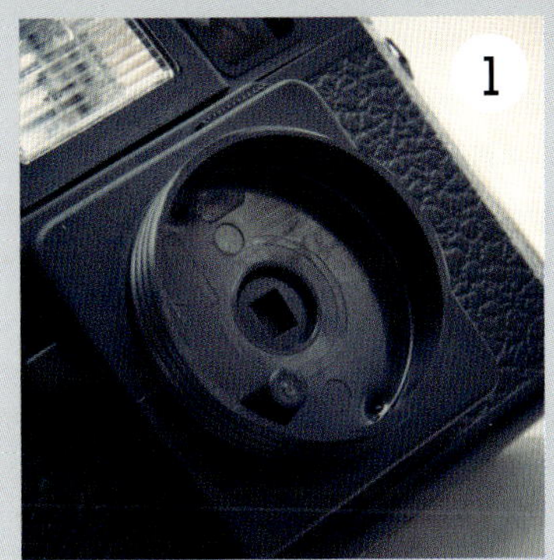

1. Start by removing the front lens assembly as described previously, then loosen the lens stop screw and unscrew the lens. Reattach the shutter assembly (but not the lens!). It should be quite obvious where you will be mounting your pinhole lens.
2. If you are making the pinhole yourself, make sure the metal you make it in is big enough to cover the hole in the front of the Holga's shutter and then epoxy it on. If you are using a commercial pinhole you may need to mount it on a larger plate—a tap washer or similar is ideal—before epoxying it to the camera. I lucked in here: my commercial lens is a perfect fit!

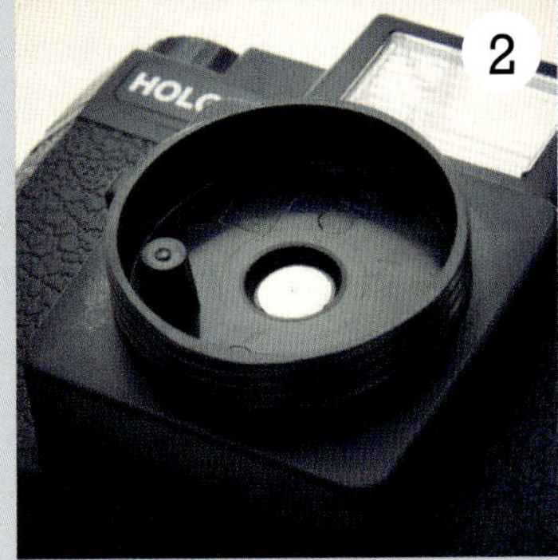

3. If you're using a Holga that has a B (Bulb) setting, all you need to do is fit the lens cap and your Pinholga is good to go—just remove the cap and fire the camera using B to take a shot.

However, if you're using a Holga 120S or 120SF you will need to perform a Time Machine conversion so you can hold the shutter open indefinitely. You will probably want to add a tripod socket as well.

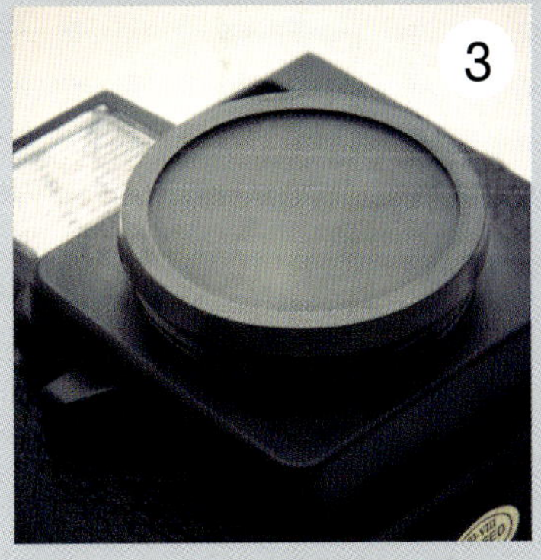

If this all seems like too much effort to convert a Holga to lensless capture, you might want to consider buying a ready-made Holga 120PC instead. But where's the fun in that?

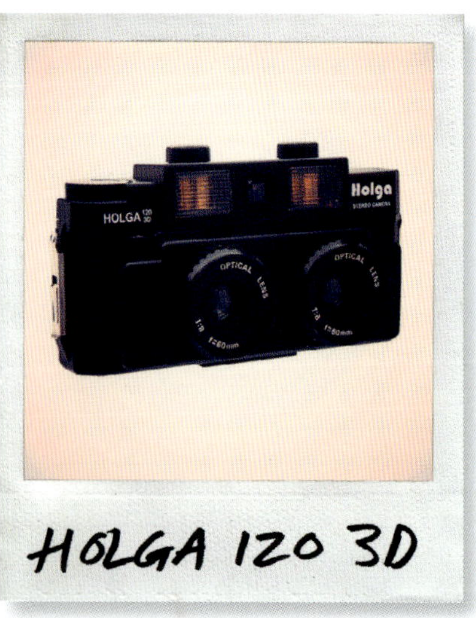

HOLGA 120 3D

CAMERA: Holga:	120 3D
MANUFACTURER:	Holga
FILM TYPE:	120 roll film
IMAGE FORMAT:	Pair of images, 6cm x 6cm
LENS:	60mm
FOCUS:	4 distance settings (approx. 1m, 2m, 6m, Infinity)
APERTURE:	f/8
SHUTTER SPEEDS:	N (1/100 sec.), B (Bulb)
OTHER FEATURES:	2 x built-in color flashes Tripod mount Cable release socket

There's no escaping it: 3D is BIG business. Movies such as Star Wars received digital 3D revamps, and countless films and TV shows are being filmed in 3D, with scant consideration to whether the process adds anything or not. The technology is seeping into our homes as well, with 3D televisions and Blu-Ray players set to become the "must have" devices.

Against this backdrop of high-end digital trickery and shameless commercialism, Holga's 120 3D camera is pure lo-fi magic. It's hard to imagine what was going on in Holga HQ when the idea of producing a 3D camera was first mentioned, but the outcome is obvious: two Holga 120 cameras were forced together to create a striking twin-lens monster that is reminiscent of the wooden turn-of-the-century stereoscopic cameras of the late 1800s. Only in plastic, naturally.

The appearance of the Holga 120 3D is fully indicative of its performance: it looks like the mating of two standard 120CFN Holgas because that is almost precisely what it is, right down to its dual color flashes and choice of N and B shutter speeds. Differences do exist though: both lenses are triggered by a single shutter-release button and the aperture is fixed at f/8. In addition (and unlike other Holga cameras), it is recommended that the 120 3D is used with slide film. This is because it is easier to "see" the 3D effect when you view positive images in the optional Holga slide viewer (120-3DV).

However, using slide film is a problem with the Holga 120 3D. Exposures are far more critical with slide film than they are with print film, and Holgas are not known for their super-precise exposures, or indeed their exposure control:

the 120 3D's single aperture setting isn't going to help you when you (ideally) want to get an exposure that is accurate to within ±1/2 stop. So, while the promise is there, you may struggle to produce well-exposed images. One answer is to use print film: it's not impossible to use it with the 120 3D, simply less convenient as you will need to make positive images from your negatives, either by scanning the film and/or having prints made.

You will need to make sure that the exposures and size are a near-perfect match for each pair—any major differences between them will ruin the 3D effect.

The Holga 120 3D records two images that approximate the view we see through our eyes.

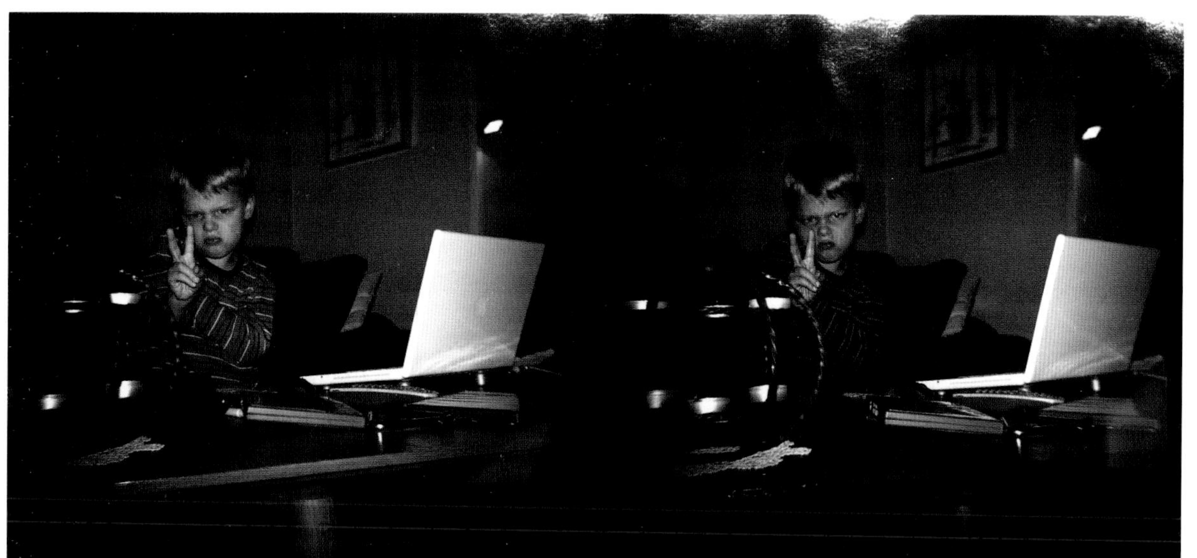

How stereo photography works

At its simplest, stereo imaging attempts to recreate the way in which we see the world around us. This process starts with the use of two lenses. Ideally, these should be roughly the same distance apart as our eyes so that they see two slightly different views of the same thing—just like our eyes. When a picture is taken, both lenses fire at the same time to produce a "stereo pair." This pair of images is viewed using a stereoscopic viewer and your brain merges them to create a 3D effect. You can also view stereo pairs using a "cross-eyed" viewing method, although this doesn't work for everyone.

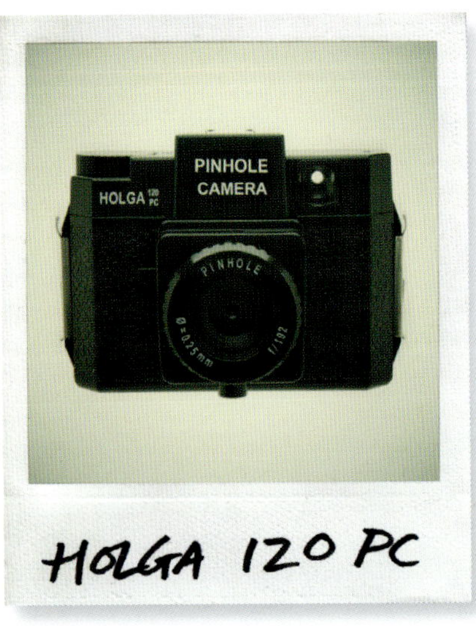

HOLGA 120 PC

CAMERA: Holga 120PC
MANUFACTURER: Holga
FILM TYPE: 120 roll film
IMAGE FORMAT: 6cm x 6cm (12 shots)
LENS: Pinhole
FOCUS: N/A
APERTURE: f/192 (approx.)
SHUTTER SPEED: B (Bulb)
OTHER FEATURES: Tripod mount

CAMERA: Holga 120PC
FILM: Kodak Ektar 100
EXPOSURE: Unrecorded

Shooting into the sun with a pinhole camera results in a different type of flare to a glass (or plastic) lens.

Can a Holga have a pinhole lens? This might sound like a slightly strange question considering there's a pinhole camera with a Holga badge on this very page, but think about it—one of the fundamental characteristics of a Holga is its lens. And if you want to be really pedantic, its plastic lens. That plastic lens is what Holgas were born with back in 1982, and it is that lens that has helped define what we know and love about Holgas today.

With that in mind, the lens-less 120PC will never hold quite the same cachet as its lens-based stablemates, despite sharing the same plastic body. Indeed, there's an underlying feeling that minimal effort went into creating the pinhole variant: the shutter speed selector has been glued in the B position, rather than being removed, and a crude plastic blanking plate has been stuck in place of the aperture switch. The lack of a cable release socket does it no favors either, leaving you to physically hold the shutter-release button down for the duration of your exposure (guaranteeing additional blur through camera shake), or investing in an optional cable release adapter (an unwelcome additional expense). Holga or not, there are better pinhole cameras out there.

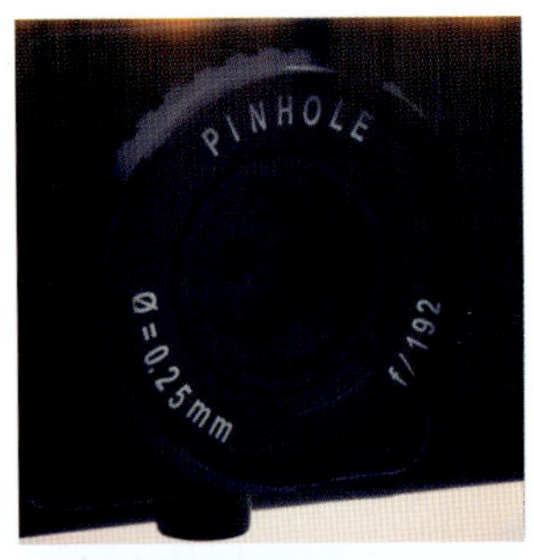

The 120PC's 0.25mm pinhole lens gives an effective aperture of f/192, which guarantees long exposure times.

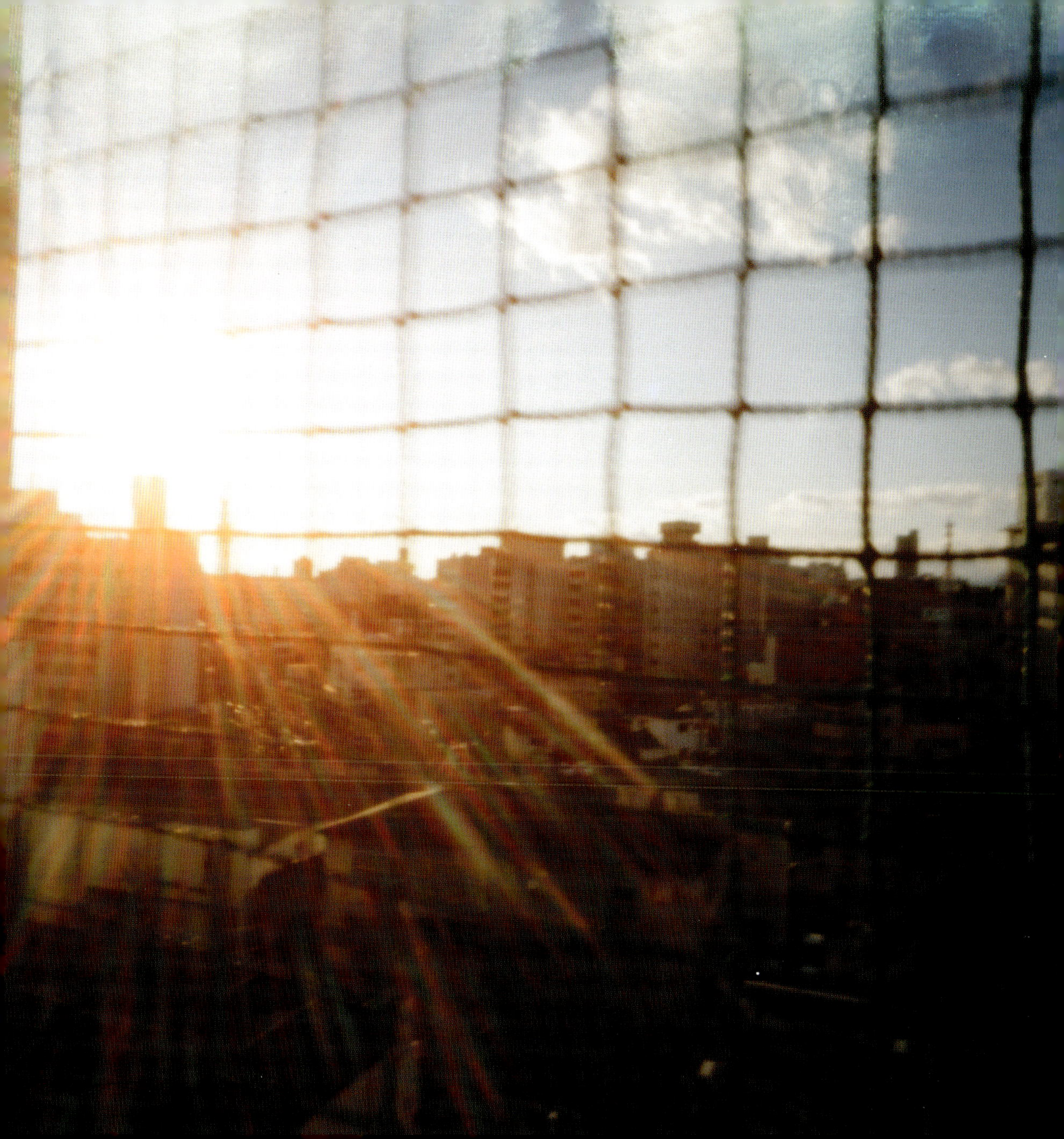

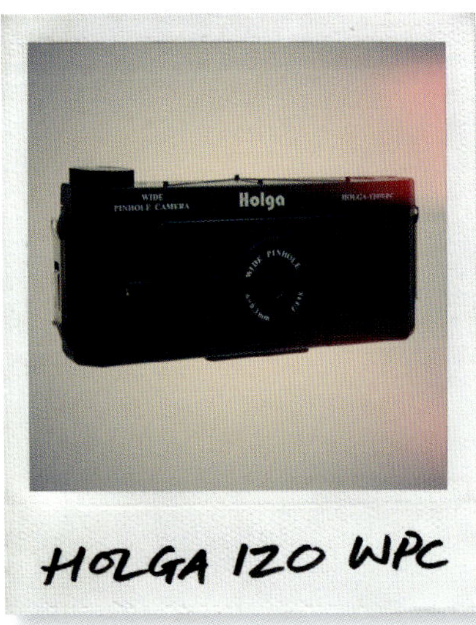

HOLGA 120 WPC

CAMERA: Holga 120WPC
MANUFACTURER: Holga
FILM TYPE: 120 roll film
IMAGE FORMATS: 6cm x 9cm (8 shots)
6cm x 12cm (6 shots)
LENS: Pinhole
FOCUS: N/A
APERTURE: f/135 (approx.)
SHUTTER SPEED: B (Bulb)
OTHER FEATURES: Tripod mount
Cable release socket

While the 120PC is something of a nonentity in terms of both pinhole cameras and Holgas, the same can't be said about the Holga 120WPC: if you want a pinhole Holga this one is worth a go.

The 120WPC doesn't shoot conventional Holga-sized 6cm x 6cm images. Instead you get masks for 6cm x 9cm shots, or stunningly wide 6cm x 12cm panoramas. Also, unlike the 120PC it has a threaded shutter-release button, so you can use a cable release without having to buy an adapter. The entire shutter mechanism has been redesigned, and while it bears no relation to the standard Holga 120 cameras, it is all the better for it.

To help you aim the camera, a pin-based sighting system is moulded into the top, which will let you determine the left and right edges of the (6cm x 12cm) frame. Although it isn't a refined system, it does a reasonable job, and for landscape shots it's more than adequate. The top-mounted spirit level will help you make sure that your elongated horizons are kept level.

With a handy (albeit rough-and-ready) exposure guide on the back of the camera (below) the 120WPC offers all you need to start enjoying pinhole photography, plus genuine Holga-style vignetting if you stick to the 6 x12 format.

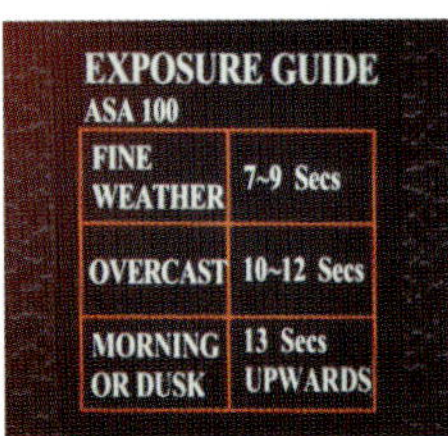

CAMERA: Holga 120WPC
FILM: Unknown
EXPOSURE: Unrecorded

The 120WPC's panoramic format is ideally suited to landscape subjects.

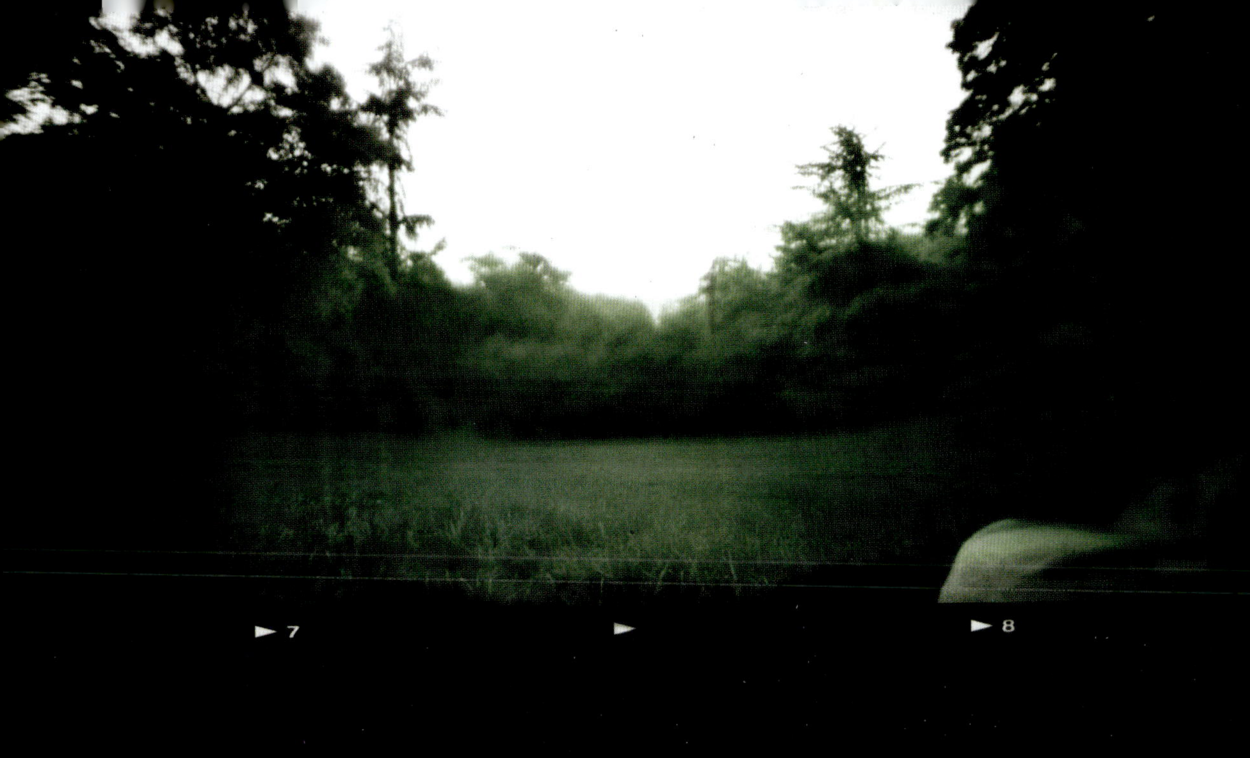
7
8

Just because you've decided that you want a medium format camera, doesn't mean that you have to turn your back on 35mm film entirely. In fact, quite the opposite applies when it comes to plastic cameras and the lo-fi aesthetic: the sprocket holes in a 35mm film deserve to be celebrated, not hidden!

This area of the film is usually "lost" as it performs the pragmatic behind-the-scenes task of transporting the emulsion through a standard 35mm camera. However, with "sprocket shots" this is not the case—the image covers the entire film, including the area usually reserved for the manufacturer's name, frame numbers, and, of course, the sprocket holes. This results in slightly panoramic images measuring roughly 60mm wide in a 6cm x 6cm camera (so about 50% wider than a regular 35mm frame). Depending on the camera you will also benefit from any edge defects such as soft focus and light fall off.

You will need to be a little "creative" and employ lateral thought when loading 35mm film into a camera that wasn't designed to accept it, and the process will vary depending on the camera— loading 35mm film into a Lubitel isn't the same as loading it into a Holga. That said, the steps that follow will get you close to a workable solution and stunning sprocket shots, no matter which medium format camera you choose.

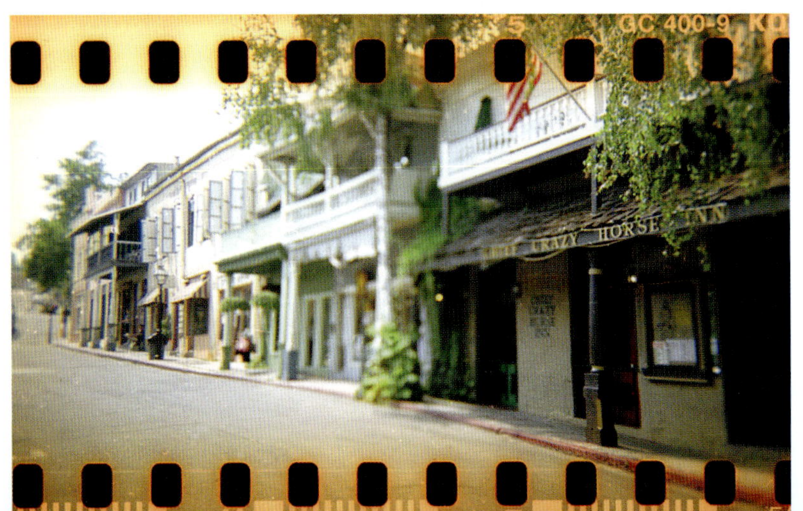

CAMERA: Holga 120N
FILM: Kodak Gold Ultra 400
EXPOSURE: 1/100 sec. f/11

If your 35mm film isn't held flat in the back of the camera the focus can vary across the frame, but this invariably adds to the lo-fi effect.

Loading

Loading 35mm film into most medium format cameras is a straightforward process: the 35mm cassette will simply sit where a 120 film roll would be, and you will wind on to a standard 120 spool (as you would when shooting medium format film).

However, there are a few considerations. First of all, you want to make sure that your 35mm film cassette doesn't rattle around inside the camera. The easiest, and most common way of securing a 35mm film cassette is to simply push a pieces of sponge above and below it in the film chamber. If you want to, you can use a thin piece of sponge bewtween the film and the camera back as well, so that when you close the back of the camera it gently compresses against the film cassette, preventing it from rattling backward and forward.

With the film cassette securely in place, the next thing you want to do is to make sure that the film winds relatively straight onto the take up spool, which involves a very simple modification to a standard 120 film spool. Take a spool and wrap rubber bands or hair bands around the top and bottom of it, leaving a gap that is the same height as your 35mm film. Put the spool in the camera and when you load your 35mm film, use a small piece of tape to hold it on the spool. Gently wind the film around the spool a couple of times to be sure that it's on (as you would when loading medium format film) and close the camera back.

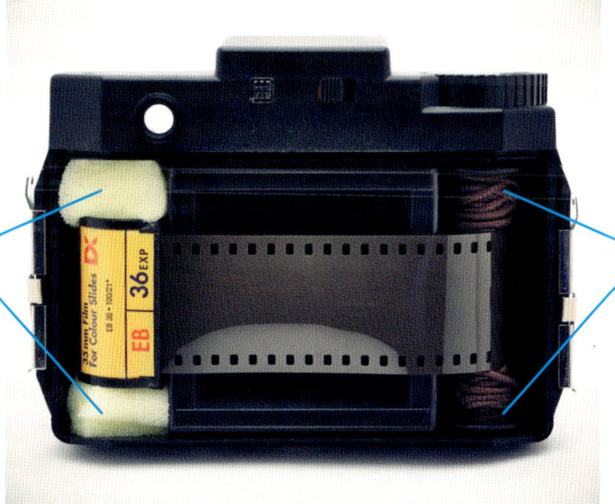

35mm film cassette
Use sponge to pack the top and bottom of the camera and hold your 35mm film cassette in place.

Take-up spool
Use a rubber band or hair bands to narrow down a standard medium format spool so your 35mm film will wind onto it straight.

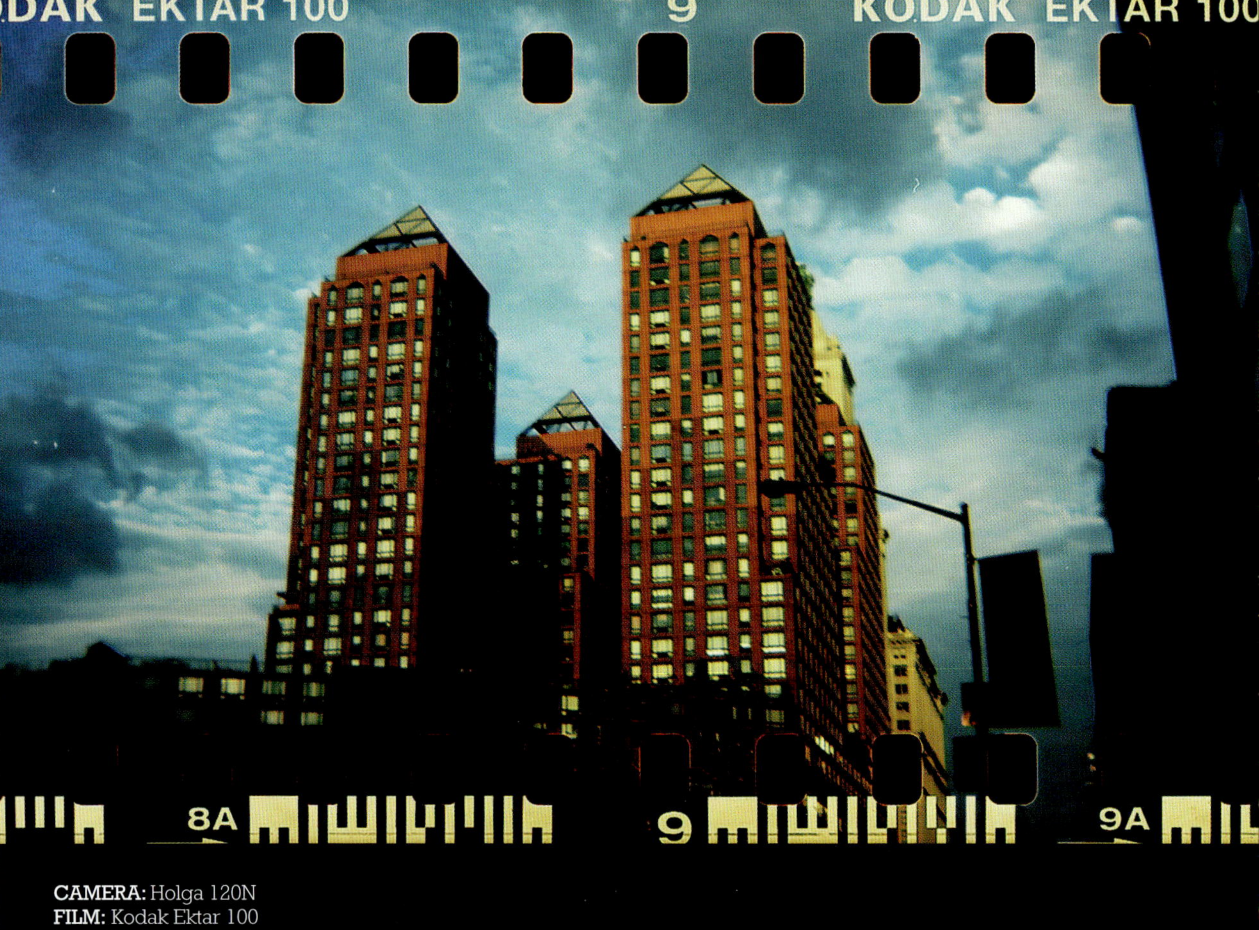

CAMERA: Holga 120N
FILM: Kodak Ektar 100
EXPOSURE: Unrecorded

Loading 35mm film into a medium format camera isn't
difficult and the edges of the film can add to your shots.

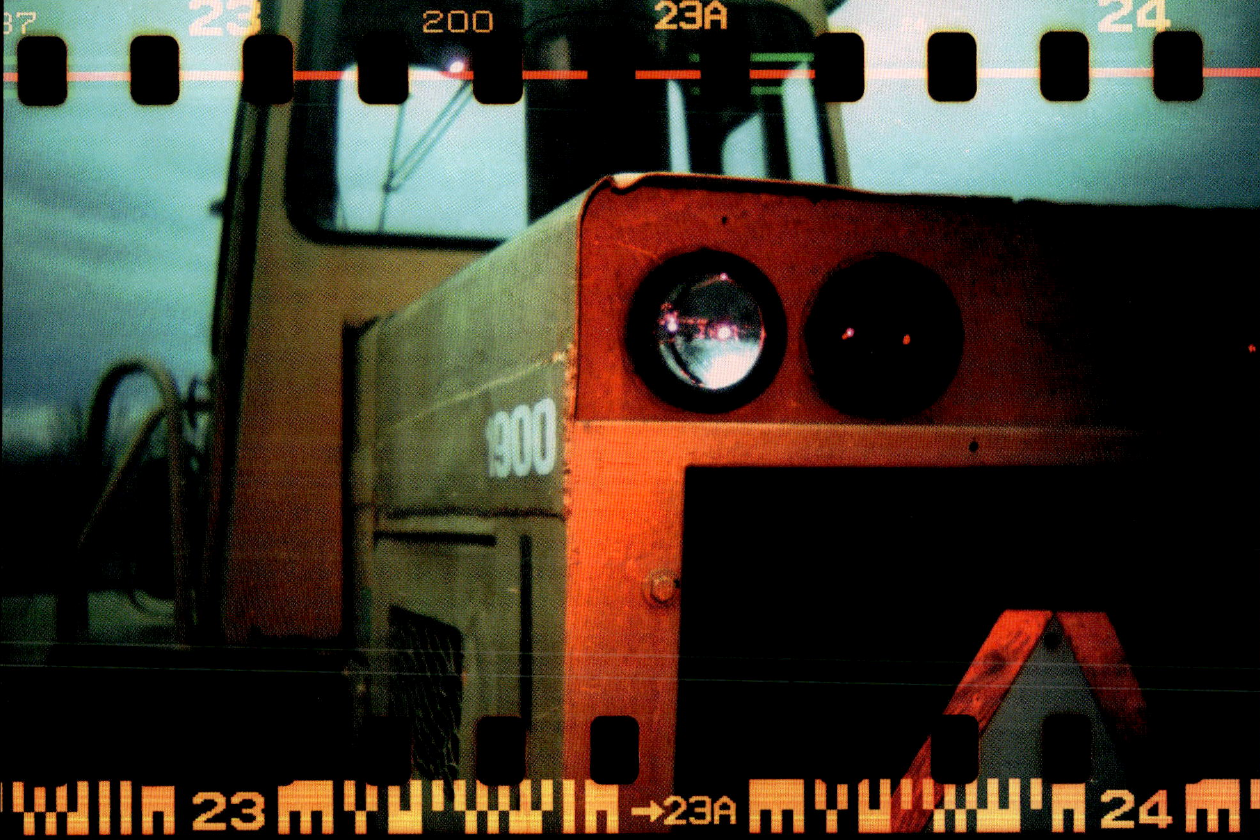

CAMERA: Holga 120N
FILM: Fuji Superia 200
EXPOSURE: Unrecorded

Because your 35mm film covers the full width of the Holga's 6cm x 6cm
frame, you can expect the exposure and focus to fall off at the edges.

Shooting

It doesn't matter what camera you're using, or whether you've loaded it with 35mm or 120 film; you should take your shots in the exact same way. However, once you've taken a shot things get a little more convoluted, as there's no frame counter to help you wind on to the next frame. This means you're going to have to work out how far to wind on to avoid under-winding (which will result in overlapping frames), or overwinding (which will leave big gaps between your frames and waste film).

The easiest way to do this is to scrap a roll of 35mm film. Yes, you'll waste the roll, but you will only have to do this once. Load your film into the camera as described previously and, with the back open, roughly mark the image area (this is between the edges of the 6cm x 6cm mask in the case of the Holga camera shown here).

Wind the film on so that the left edge of the marked frame becomes the right edge of the next frame, noting how far you have to turn the winding dial to do this. Mark the new frame and repeat the process, again noting far you need to turn the winding wheel. After a few frames you should start to get an idea of how far you need to wind on between frames. Once you're confident, the next step is to load up and shoot for real.

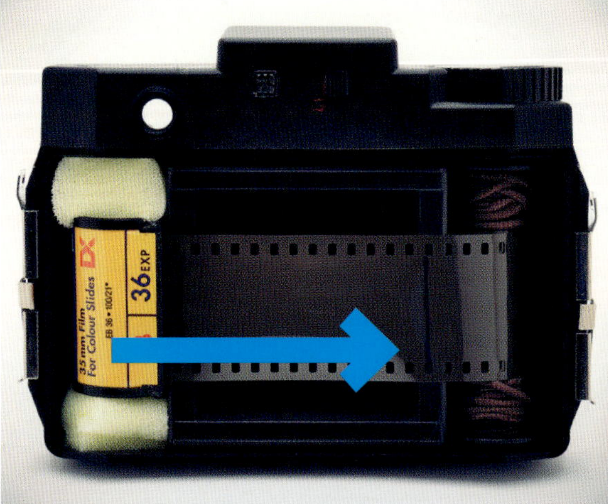

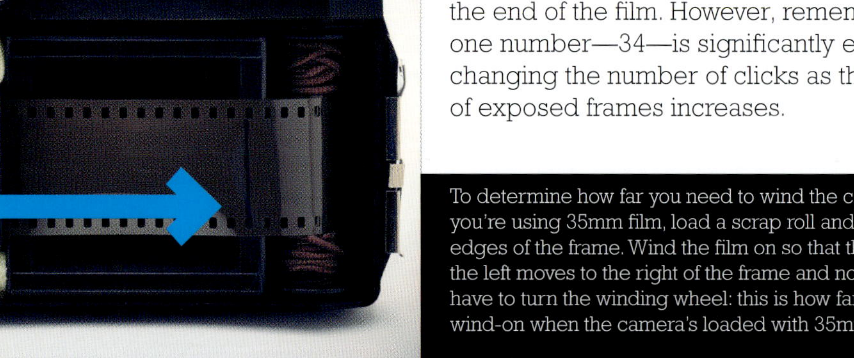

TIP: Winding a Holga

A standard 120 Holga "clicks" when you wind the film on, and you can use the number of clicks to determine how far you wind your 35mm film. Most people use 34 clicks as the optimum number to wind on by, but this doesn't give consistent results—the gaps between your frames will increase toward the end of the film. However, remembering one number—34—is significantly easier than changing the number of clicks as the number of exposed frames increases.

To determine how far you need to wind the camera when you're using 35mm film, load a scrap roll and mark the edges of the frame. Wind the film on so that the mark on the left moves to the right of the frame and note how far you have to turn the winding wheel: this is how far you'll need to wind-on when the camera's loaded with 35mm film.

Unloading

One of the major drawbacks of shooting 35mm in a medium format camera is the lack of a rewind crank. Whereas 120 roll film passes from one spool to the other, with backing paper keeping it protected from the light when you load and unload it, 35mm film is "naked." This means you need to take your film out in total darkness and rewind it manually back into its cassette before you can take it into the light.

This is undoubtedly the biggest inconvenience with this technique, because every time you finish a film you will need to head to a darkroom to open your camera, or try and unload it in a changing bag. Neither of these is ideal, especially if you're out shooting and want to change films because you've finished a roll. Because of this, it's actually more convenient to have two (or more) "sprocket shooters" already loaded, and just swap one camera for another, rather than trying to unload your film on location.

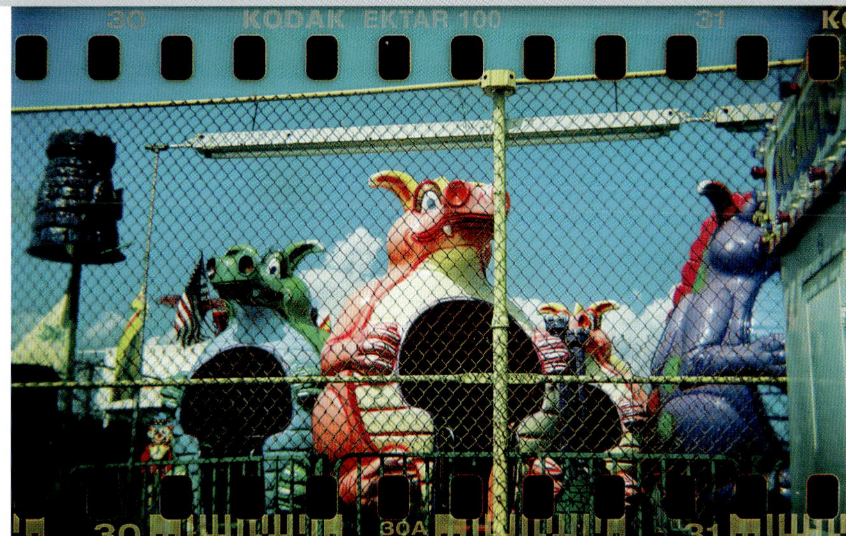

CAMERA: Holga 120N
FILM: Kodak Extar 100
EXPOSURE: Unrecorded

You need to be sure to tape up your Holga when you're using it with 35mm film.

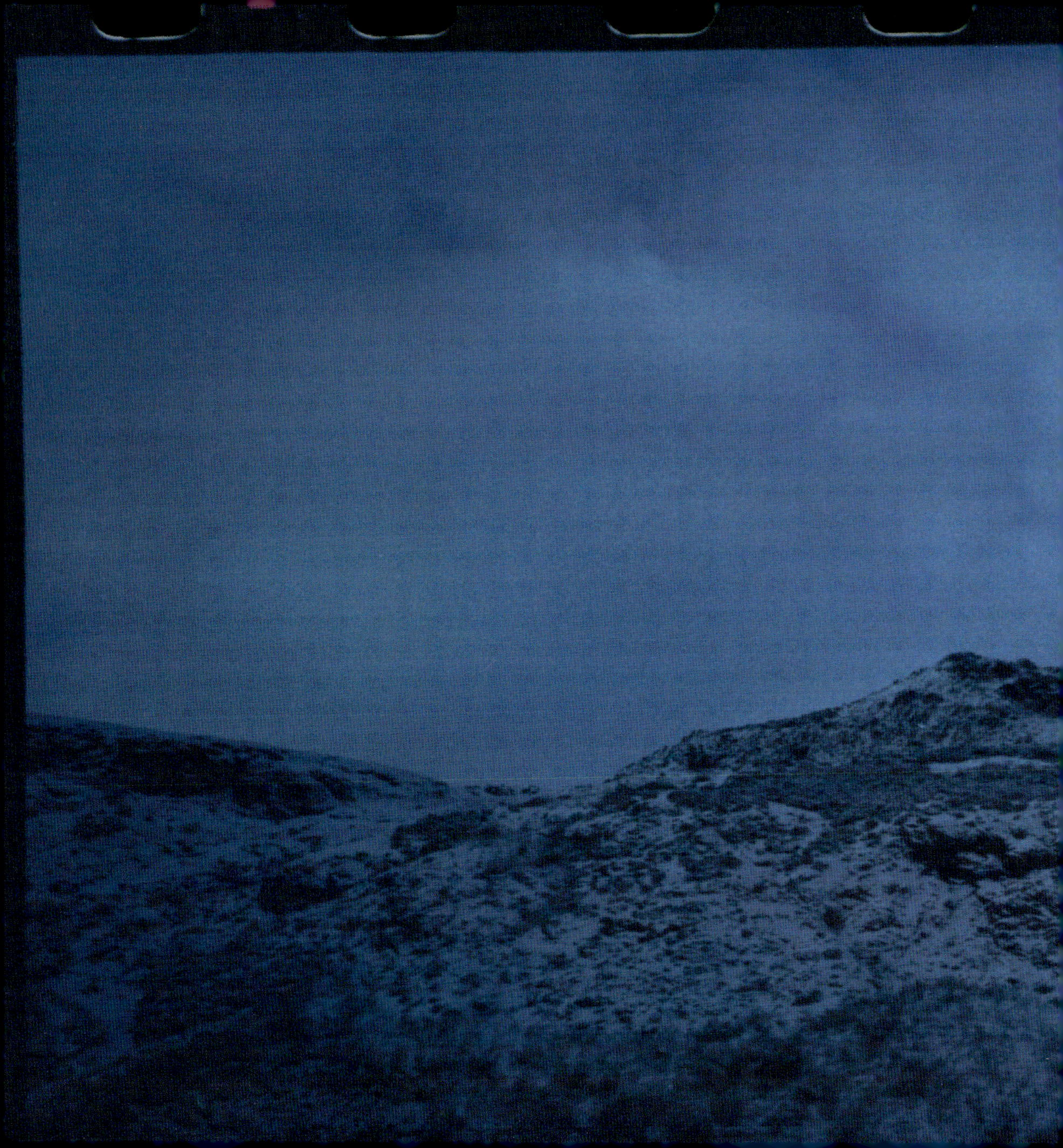

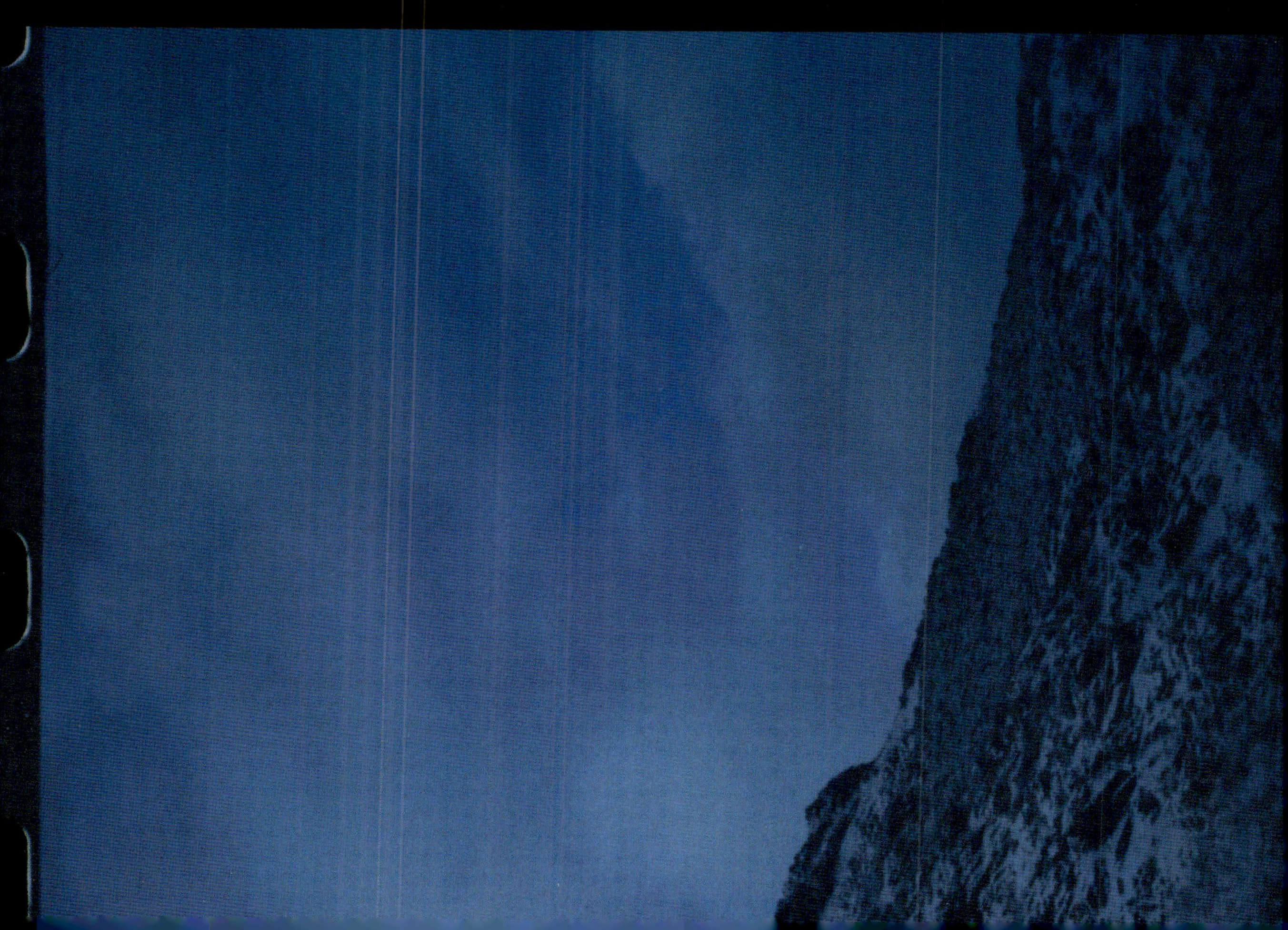

Chapter 2:
SMALL FORMAT RESURGENCE

Small format **revisited**

Digital technology has not muscled in on the film camera market—it has kicked down the door and pummeled its analog brethren into submission. To most people, 35mm SLR cameras are no longer seen as desirable, and the ridiculously low used camera prices certainly don't suggest that this is a phoenix that will one day rise from the ashes. Yet in this bleak wasteland of discarded camera bodies, manual focus lenses, and sundry filters and other accessories that are no longer required, there's still a glimmer of life: despite having had a largely fatal impact on the film camera market, digital technology has failed miserably to kill off the humble plastic camera.

To a certain extent the credit lies at the feet of one company: Lomography. Or, more specifically, it lies at the feet of the two Austrian students who (re)discovered the quirks of the LOMO LC-A in the early 1990s and convinced people that a camera from the past was the way forward. From this moment, the face of the analog photography market was set to change, and the company that was set up to distribute the original LC-A—Lomographische AG—has grown into a manufacturing and marketing behemoth that is synonymous with plastic cameras and lo-fi photography. Indeed, Lomography has become so big that it's easy to think that it is where plastic cameras both start and end.

Lomography is not the only player in the market, despite what appears to be overwhelming evidence to the contrary. Although far less prolific (and without the distribution and marketing clout of Lomography), Holga continues to make inroads into the 35mm market with alternatives to its medium format models, while Japanese company PowerShovel has been manufacturing and distributing its own unique slice of plastic camera goodness under the SuperHeadz name since the start of the millennium.

It is also incorrect to think that the small-format plastic camera market is the preserve of "full frame" 35mm cameras. In recent years there has been a trend for smaller image formats (perhaps due to cost), and this has seen a modest resurgence in cameras that provide a modern twist to the classic half-frame format that was popular in the 1960s and 1970s. These have been joined by sub-miniature models designed to shoot ever-so-elusive 110 format film, while mainstream player Fujifilm has seen its Instax Mini range gain a following among lo-fi enthusiasts. So, whether you feel the need to shoot "straight" 35mm, squeeze two, three, or even more images onto a single frame, or pick up a camera that takes a less conventional film-type, the thriving small-format plastic camera market is sure to have something to help you get your kicks.

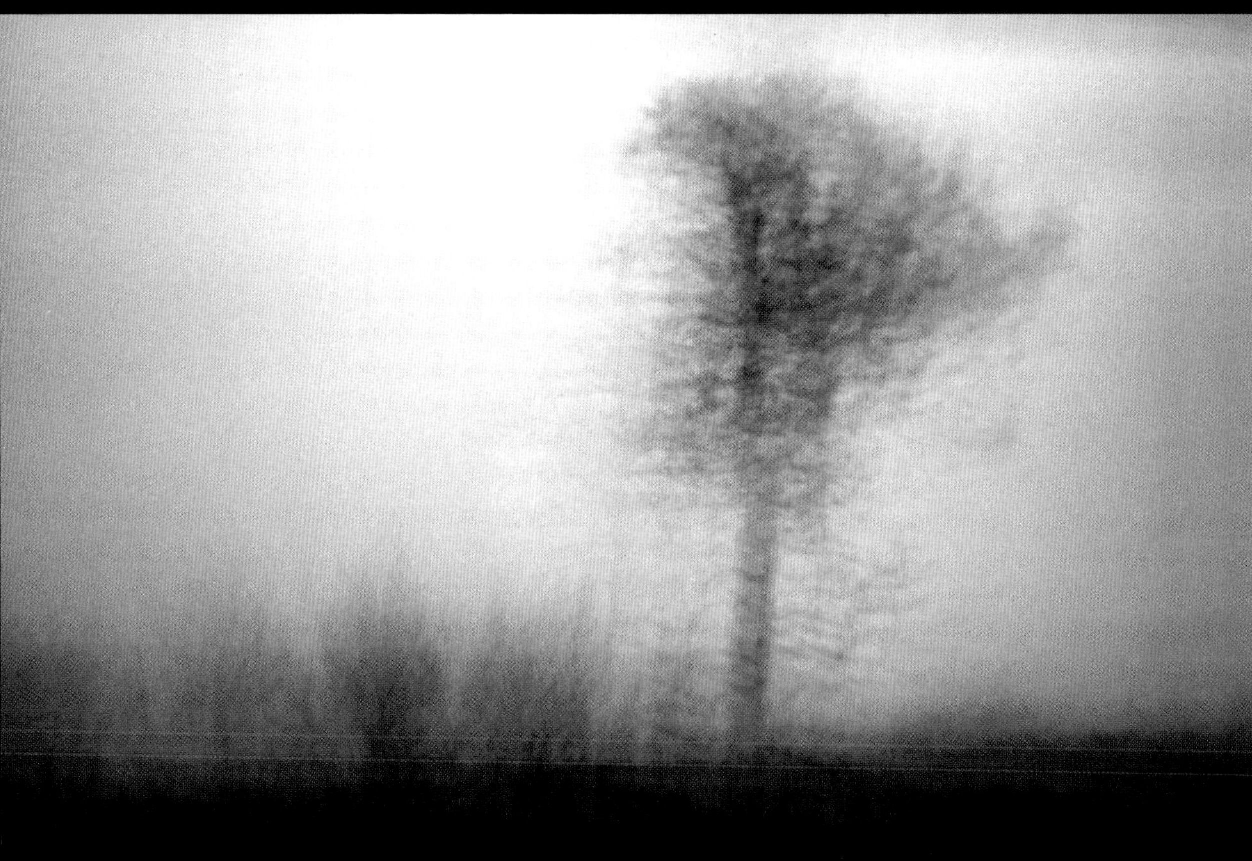

CAMERA: Holga 135
FILM: Rollei Retro 400s
EXPOSURE: Multiple exposure

Plastic cameras encourage experimentation, but this can
prove expensive with medium format models. Using 35mm
film can often be more affordable.

Small-format **film**

With many film manufacturers now just a footnote in the archives, the days when you could walk into your local drugstore and pick your favorite emulsion from a bunch of different 35mm film stocks are over. In some towns you might not have much of a choice of film even if you head to a photo store—things are that bleak.

Thankfully, the Internet doesn't suffer in quite the same way, and Ebay is awash with people selling film described as being ideal for "Lomo" photography. If you're prepared to look around you may find a specific emulsion that you thought was no longer available.

However, you don't have to rely on "extinct" film, and despite the general downturn in sales (compared to the pre-digital days) there is now a wide range of "creative" films available, in addition to the more traditional color negative, color slide, and black-and-white options. Unsurprisingly, one of the names behind this is Lomography, which has added both color and black-and-white film to its product line, as well as films designed for cross-processing (Lomography X-pro) and redscale (Lomography RedScale). The Rollei-branded "Creative Edition" films are also worth exploring if you're looking for something different: Blackbird gives black-and-white negatives with dense blacks; Crossbird is a slide film that cross-processes well in C41 (negative) chemistry; and Nightbird and Redbird are ISO 800 and ISO 400 redscale films respectively.

Even more unusual is Revolog film, which is handmade in Austria. There are nine varieties in 35mm format, including such delights as "Volvox," "Rasp," and "Kolor." Each emulsion brings its own unique effect to the 35mm party, be it an underlying texture to your images or a color effect that's entirely dependent on the processing. Yet no matter how unconventional the film, all current 35mm emulsions use the same basic processes that were used in the past: Revolog's Tesla films may add lightning style flash effects to the film, but they still use a standard C41 process. Ditto Rollei's Nightbird and Redbird films—they're still 35mm negative films, using a standard negative process, despite the red mask. So, if your local lab or drugstore can handle regular negative films it can handle these: just be sure to warn them that the result might not look "right" if you want to avoid your film ending up in their trash!

> **TIP:**
> Check how the film's been stored before committing to buying it: although film can survive for several years past its "process by" date if it's stored in a fridge or freezer, the colors will start to shift on very old color emulsions, and the sensitivity will decrease with both color and black-and-white. This will be more pronounced if the film's been kept in a warm environment. It could be that this adds to the lo-fi effect, and there's also the possibility that cross-processing the film could have an interesting (but potentially unrepeatable) effect, but as a rule, if you want to be certain of getting a reasonable result you need to make sure the film's been stored somewhere cool, and not on top of a radiator in direct sunlight.

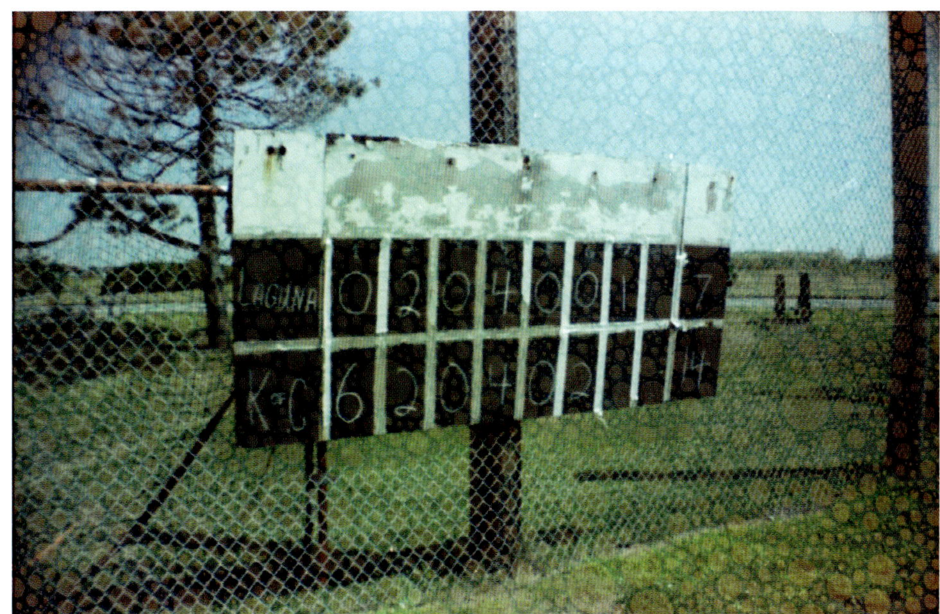

CAMERA: Lomography La Sardina
FILM: Revolog Volvox
EXPOSURE: 1/100 sec. @ f/8

Revolog is a new player in the 35mm film market, producing a unique range of handmade emulsions that are perfect for lo-fi enthusiasts.

110 film

If you fancy toying with a sub-miniature 110-format camera, then you're probably already aware that it isn't going to be easy to track down the film: Kodak may have got the 110 ball rolling in 1972, but has long since ceased production (of all film now), while Fuji stopped contributing to the 110 cause in 2009.

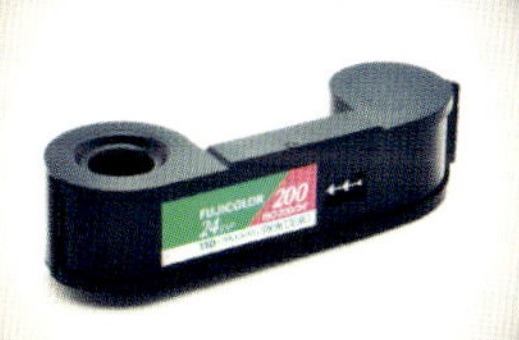

Although 110 film is not currently being produced, stores such as The Frugal Photographer still stockpile it, and eBay offers a lottery of film that may or may not be past its best (although all 110 film is now past its "process before" date).

Interesting to 110 enthusiasts is German film manufacturer, Adox's "110 film project," which aims to make its Adox Pan 400 black-and-white film (as well as a color film) available in 110 format. If this happens, not only will there be a new film on the market (a rarity in itself), but there will be a new 110 format film on the market—something that would have been unprecedented a few years ago.

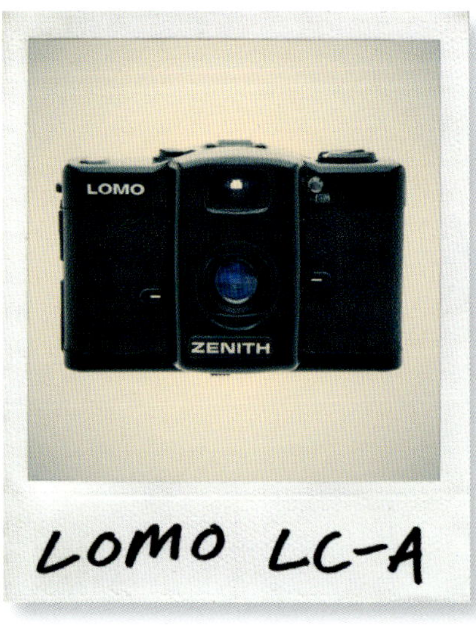

LOMO LC-A

CAMERA: LC-A
MANUFACTURER: LOMO
FILM TYPE: 35mm
IMAGE FORMAT: 36mm x 24mm
LENS: 32mm
FOCUS: Four preset distance settings (0.8m, 1.5m, 3m, Infinity)
APERTURES: f/2.8, f/4, f/5.6, f/8, f/11, f/16
SHUTTER SPEEDS: 1/500 sec.–2 min.
OTHER FEATURES: Standard hotshoe Tripod mount

No discussion of plastic (or toy) cameras and/or the lo-fi aesthetic would be complete without including the LOMO LC-A. This is the camera that inspired the birth of Lomography in the 1990s, and one that still attracts photographers to film, despite it being almost 30 years since it first appeared.

What is perhaps more surprising (not to mention somewhat ironic) given that the LC-A is now one of the most recognizable and iconic film cameras of all time, is that it was conceived as a copy of another camera: the Cosina CX-2. Yet during the translation from Japanese to Russian, something happened, and the rugged, utilitarian, homegrown compact camera that was designed for the socialist masses gained that one thing that would make it special—its Minitar 1 lens.

LOMO wasn't in a position to invest as much in the optics for the LC-A as Cosina perhaps could: this was to be a camera for the masses, not the monied few. The compromise was a simple 32mm focal length lens with a maximum aperture of f/2.8 that satisfied the need for low production costs, while retaining reasonable performance. Most notably, the multicoated lens appeared to enhance contrast (which also helps to give the appearance of "crisp" pictures) and boost color, while the obvious vignetting produces the distinct "tunnel vision" look that has come to typify lo-fi photography.

Focusing is achieved using four preset "zones," with a lever to the right of the lens (as you look at the front of the camera) offering distance options of 0.8m, 1.5m, 3m, and Infinity. On the opposite side of the lens are the aperture

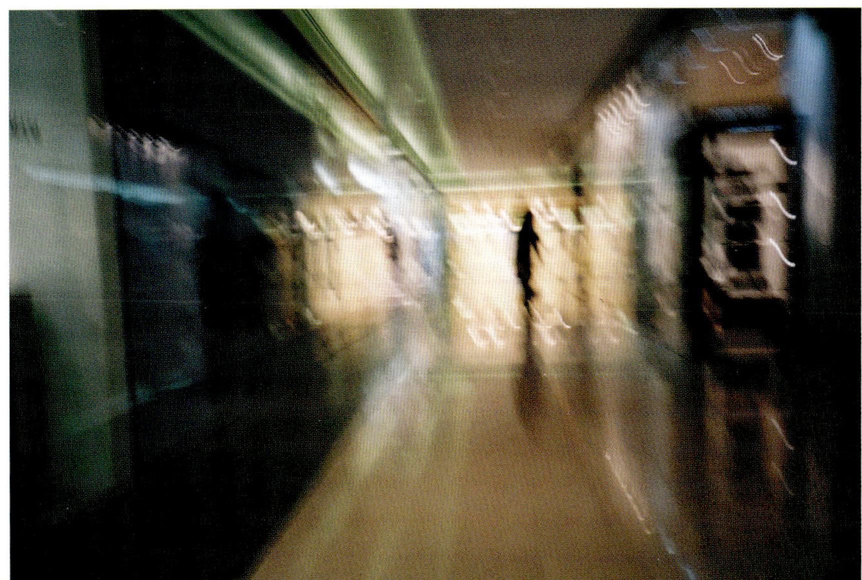

CAMERA: LOMO LC-A
FILM: Unknown
EXPOSURE: Unrecorded

The LC-A's automatic exposure system provides shutter speeds of up to 2 minutes, which is perfect for recording motion blur.

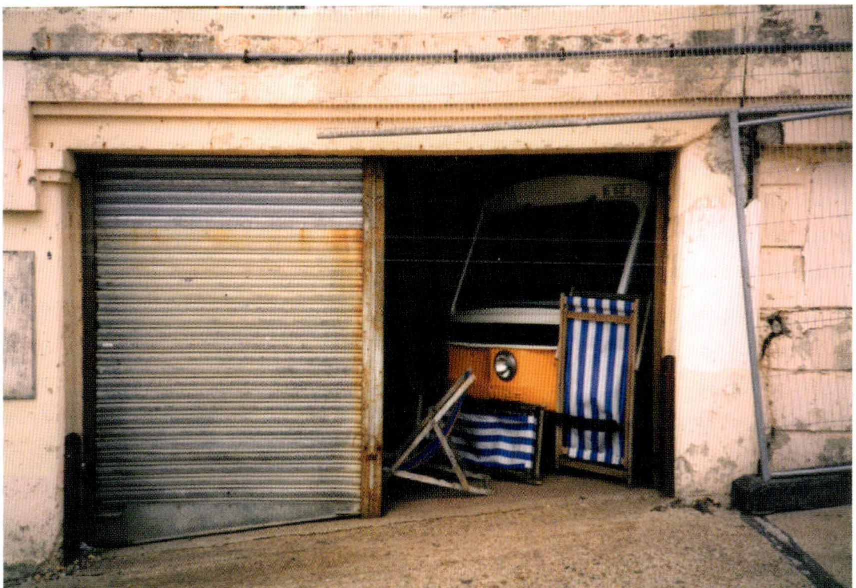

CAMERA: LOMO LC-A
FILM: Kodak Gold 200
EXPOSURE: Unrecorded

The LC-A's compact body makes it the ideal "carry anywhere" camera.

CAMERA: LOMO LC-A
FILM: Kodak Gold 200
EXPOSURE: Unrecorded

The motivation behind
this picture was to
experiment with
different angles: holding
the camera against a
wall in this case.

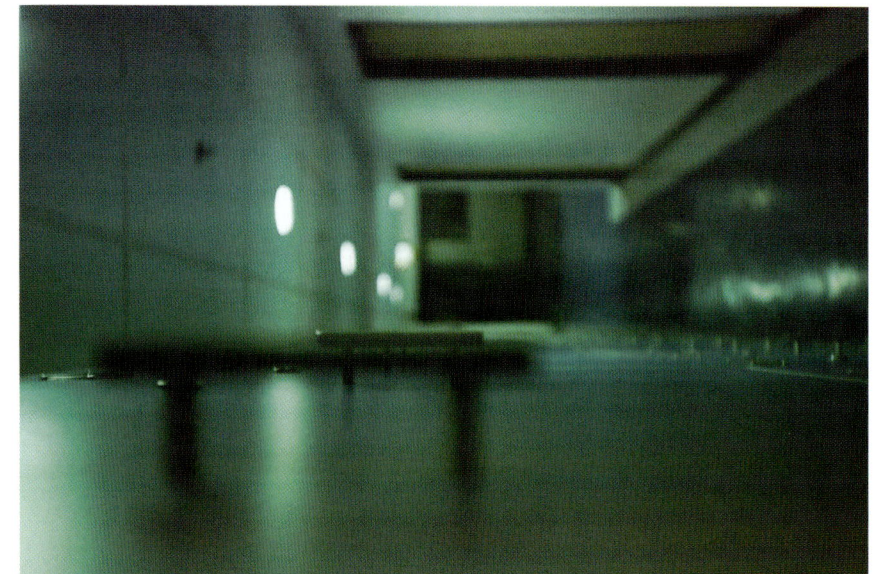

CAMERA: LOMO LC-A
FILM: Jessops 100 (cross
processed)
EXPOSURE: Unrecorded

The LC-A's 32mm
Minitar lens can add
a wideangle dynamic
when used up close to
your subject.

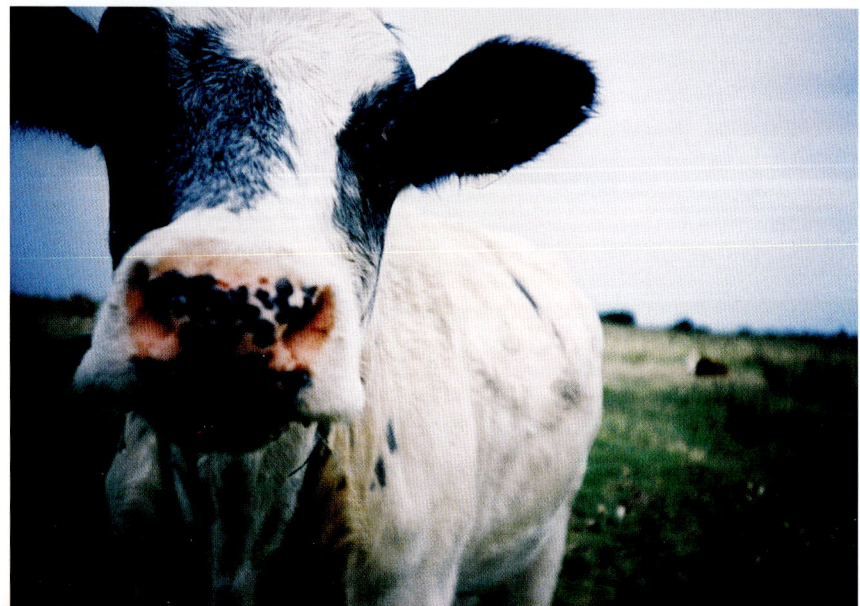

settings, although the only one that you will use regularly is "A," which activates the LC-A's comparatively sophisticated automatic exposure system. This chooses the aperture and shutter speed for you, and works well in most shooting scenarios. However, it is especially useful for low-light work, as the LC-A can deliver an automatic exposure lasting from 1/500 sec. up to 2 minutes—longer than some digital SLRs can manage. It is also possible to choose an aperture manually, although this is designed for flash use, rather than general photography, and sets the shutter speed to a fixed 1/60 sec.

However, the late 1980s heralded a time of great change for Russian camera manufacturers. As the USSR began its death throes, and capitalism lurked around the corner, LOMO's camera production became more sporadic: the last Lubitels rolled off the production line in 1988–89, followed by the Smenas in the early 1990s. The LC-A was more fortunate, as the increasing openness of the east led to a pair of adventurous Austrians heading to Prague where they encountered the little LOMO and its unique creative outlook.

Returning home they began importing and redistributing the eastern gem, encouraging a cult following to grow around it. This evolved into what we know today as Lomography, but it was only a matter of time before the LC-A went the same way as its LOMO stablemates. In 1994 LOMO closed down its entire camera production facility.

New skin

If your LC-A's looking tired, there are plenty of people willing to sell you a replacement "skin." Most of these are self-adhesive, so it's a case of removing the old covering carefully (often the hardest part of the job) and then sticking on the new one. With this LC-A the entire process took less than an hour from start to finish, and it has transformed the camera from its original black to a vibrant red to match its communist roots.

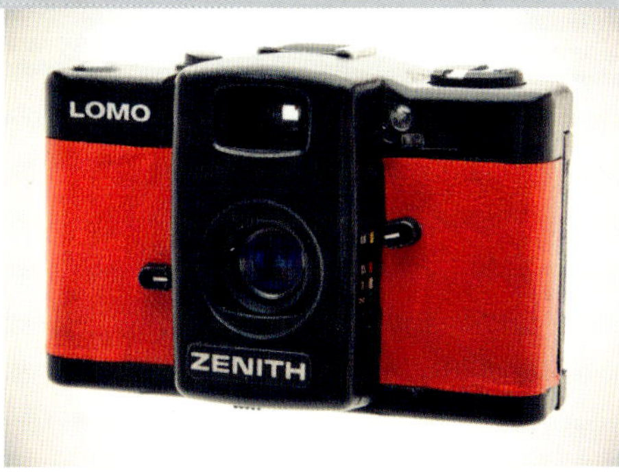

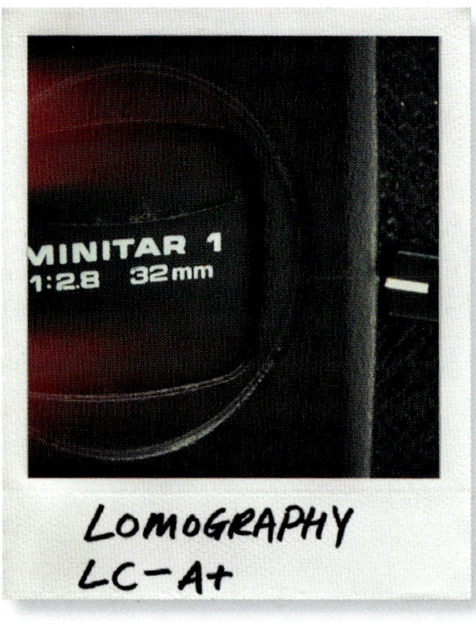

LOMOGRAPHY
LC-A+

CAMERA: LC-A+
MANUFACTURER: Lomography
FILM TYPE: 35mm
IMAGE FORMAT: 36mm x 24mm
LENS: 32mm
FOCUS: Four preset distance settings
(0.8m, 1.5m, 3m, Infinity)
APERTURES: f/2.8, f/4, f/5.6, f/8, f/11, f/16 (Automatic)
SHUTTER SPEEDS: 1/500 sec.–unlimited
OTHER FEATURES: Multiple exposure switch
Lens accessory mount
Standard hotshoe
Cable release socket
Tripod mount

Although LOMO ceased camera production in 1994, this proved to be a mere "blip" in the grand scheme of things, and just a year later Lomography was once again receiving shipments of shiny new LC-As. The Lomography/LOMO alliance continued to fuel Western demand for another decade, but in 2005 Russian production halted once more.

This time there was no miraculous resurrection, so Lomography turned to China instead, partnering with Colibri Manufacturers to release the all-new LC-A+ toward the end of 2006. Production continues today, with limited edition models encouraging enthusiastic Lomographers to part with their cash.

Key differences

Lomography's LC-A+ is very similar to the LC-A in both its appearance and the images that it produces, but notable differences exist:
• Grooves on the front of the LC-A+ allow a number of optional optical accessories to be attached
• Aperture selection is fully automatic, with no manual settings for flash photography
• ISO range increased to ISO 1600 to allow metering with faster films
• Threaded shutter-release button allows a

CAMERA: LOMO LC-A
FILM: Kodak ColorPlus 200
EXPOSURE: Unrecorded

Lomography's LC-A+ uses the same lens specification as the original LC-A, but with the exception of LC-A+ RL variant, production of the Minitar 1 is now in China.

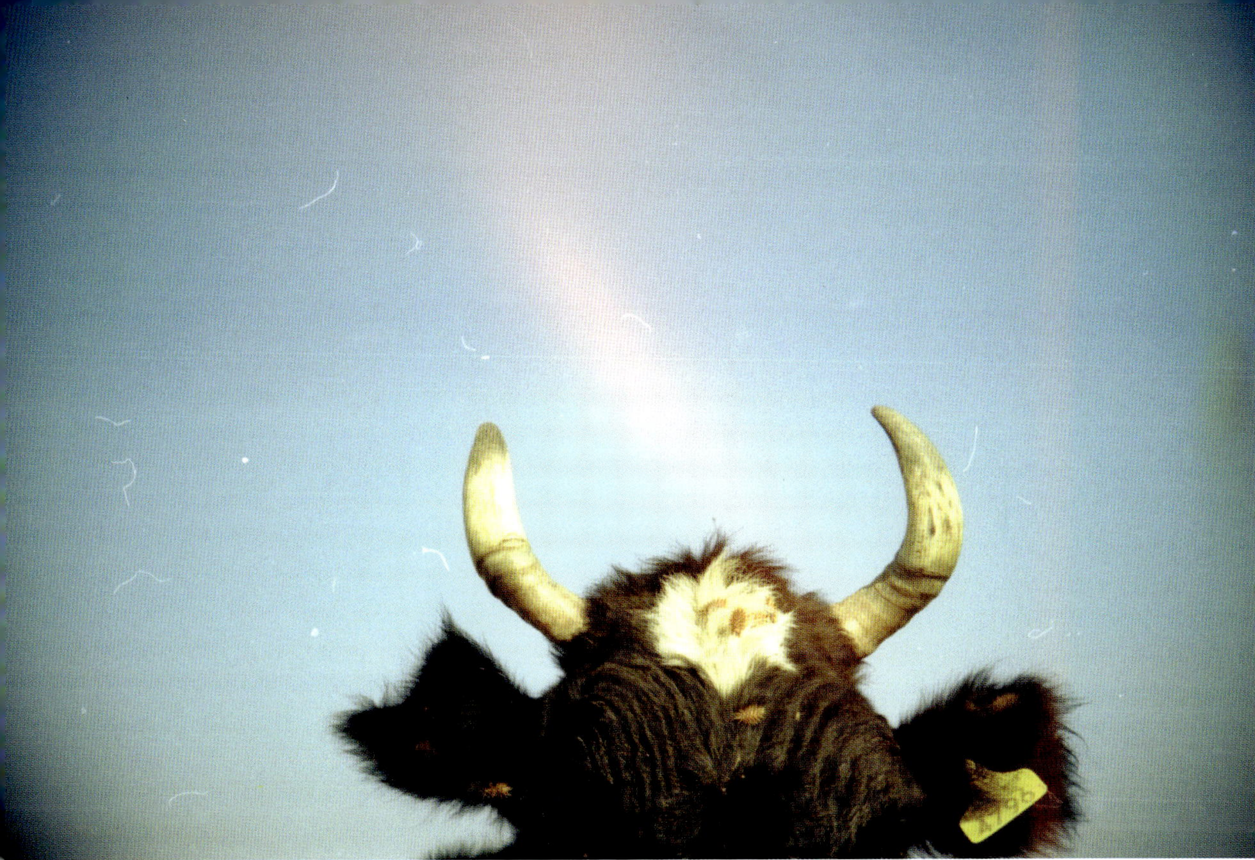

Lomo LC-Wide

Lomography's LC-Wide is a new addition to the company's line-up, but one that is beyond the scope of this book—at £329 (over $500), it's definitely a more serious proposition than the plastic cameras featured here. However, for the sake of completeness, this wide-boy's highlights include:

- A fixed 17mm f/4.5 Minigon 1 Ultra-Wide Angle lens
- Three image formats: 36mm x 24mm, 24mm x 24mm, and 17mm x 24mm (half frame)
- Two preset focus distances (0.4–0.9m, 0.9m–Infinity)
- Fully automatic shooting (as with the LC-A+), with 1/500 sec.–''unlimited'' exposure times
- Multiple exposure facility

cable release to be used for long exposures
• Multiple exposure (MX) feature for those who want to stack multiple images.
• LC-A+ camera body and Minitar 1 lens are both made in China to original specifications. LC-A+ RL variant combines a Chinese camera. body with a Russian Minitar 1 lens produced in the LOMO factory.

Accessories

Owning an LC-A+ doesn't necessarily end with buying the camera, as Lomography produces a host of accessories. Some of these, such as the Krab underwater housing, are based on accessories that were available for the original LC-A, while others are more recent additions, such as the Colorsplash flash, the Lomo ringflash, and an instant film back that allows you to load up with Fuji's Instax Mini film. However, at the top of the new developments list are supplementary lenses that you can employ to expand your creative repertoire:

Fisheye adaptor: Converts the LC-A+'s Minitar 1 into a 170-degree fisheye lens.

Wide-angle lens: Widens the angle of view of the LC-A+, changing the focal length from 32mm to 20mm. A hotshoe-mounted viewfinder helps you see what you'll be shooting.

Tunnelvision lens: Adds softly focused, dark vignettes to your images to really focus attention at the center of the frame. Doubles as a close-up lens, and also works on 35mm Holga cameras.

Splitzer: Allows you to selectively conceal and reveal parts of the scene. Use in conjunction with the LC-A+'s multiple exposure facility to create in-camera montages.

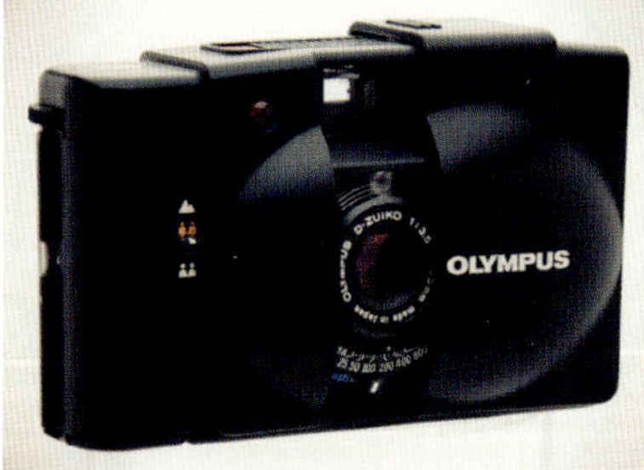

The Olympus XA2 is a n alternative to the cult cameras such as the LC-A+, and bargains abound.

LC-A+ Alternatives

The closest alternative to an LC-A+ is the LOMO LC-A (obviously!), followed by the Cosina CX-1 or CX-2 that they're based on, but all of these cult cameras come at a price, especially the Japanese "originals." A more cost-effective, and popular, option is the Olympus XA2. With its CdS exposure meter, programmed exposure, "zone focus," and four-element 35mm f/3.5 lens it's functionality is similar to an LC-A+, and the used market is awash with bargains. The colors from the Zuiko lens are less vivid than those form the LC-A+, and the contrast is not quite so high, but you can expect slight vignetting, and a strong chance of light leaks if the back seals are worn: that ultra-cheap, "well-worn" example could be a lo-fi hero!

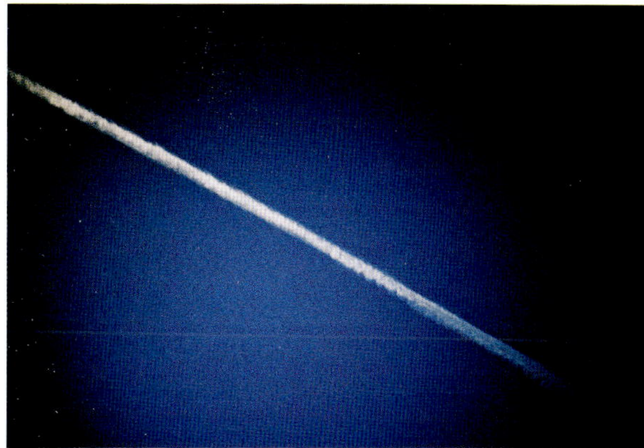

A simple "grab shot" of an aircraft contrail creates a stunning abstract image.

Cross-processing has meant that the blue of the water contrasts with the warm brown edge of a swimming pool.

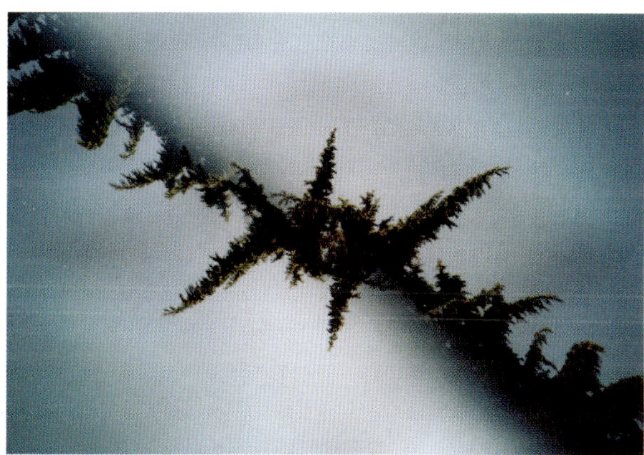

Lomography's "Splitzer" lets you selectively expose different parts of the film by covering up sections of the lens.

When you get your photos printed at a lab they crop the image to fit the paper, but check the negatives and you'll be amazed what else is hiding at the edges of the LC-A+'s frame.

Technique: Multiple exposures

In the previous chapter you saw how easy it can be to create multiple exposures with a medium format camera. If the shutter and winding mechanisms are not coupled, the same sentiment applies to small format cameras as well. So if you're shooting with a Holga 135, for example, you can simply fire the shutter as many times as you like before you wind the film on.

However, in 35mm and 110 cameras it is far more common for the film advance and shutter cocking mechanisms to be coupled, so that when you wind on, the shutter is made ready for the next exposure. This is undoubtedly convenient for everyday shooting, and certainly helps prevent you accidentally exposing the same frame twice, but what if double or triple exposures are precisely what you are after?

In some instances, the camera manufacturers have preempted this desire, and fitted their camera with a multiple exposure switch that enables you to reset the shutter without winding the film: the Lomography LC-A+, Holga TIM, and Fisheye 2 are just a few of the cameras in this chapter that will allow you to do this. Not all small format cameras offer this facility though, in which case you have to "trick" the camera into thinking you have advanced the film so it will allow you to fire it again. This technique will work with any 35mm camera with manual rewind:

1. Take a shot as normal, but DO NOT wind on the film.
2. Turn the rewind crank to tension the film.
3. Press the rewind button as if you were about to rewind your film.
4. Wind on the film while holding the rewind crank to prevent it from turning.
5. Make your second exposure and repeat the process to add a third exposure, or wind on as normal.

What you are doing here is activating the camera's rewind mechanism, which releases the wind-on spool. So, when you "wind on" after taking your first shot, the film isn't actually transported through the camera, but the shutter is readied to shoot again. This is unlikely to create perfect multiple exposures, as the film always shifts slightly, but it will enable you to combine several images on the same (approximate) frame.

CAMERA: Lomography LC-A+
FILM: Fuji Superia 100
EXPOSURE: Unrecorded

Multiple exposures aren't always easy on 35mm film, but an increasing number of cameras now have MX switches to make it as straightforward as possible.

"

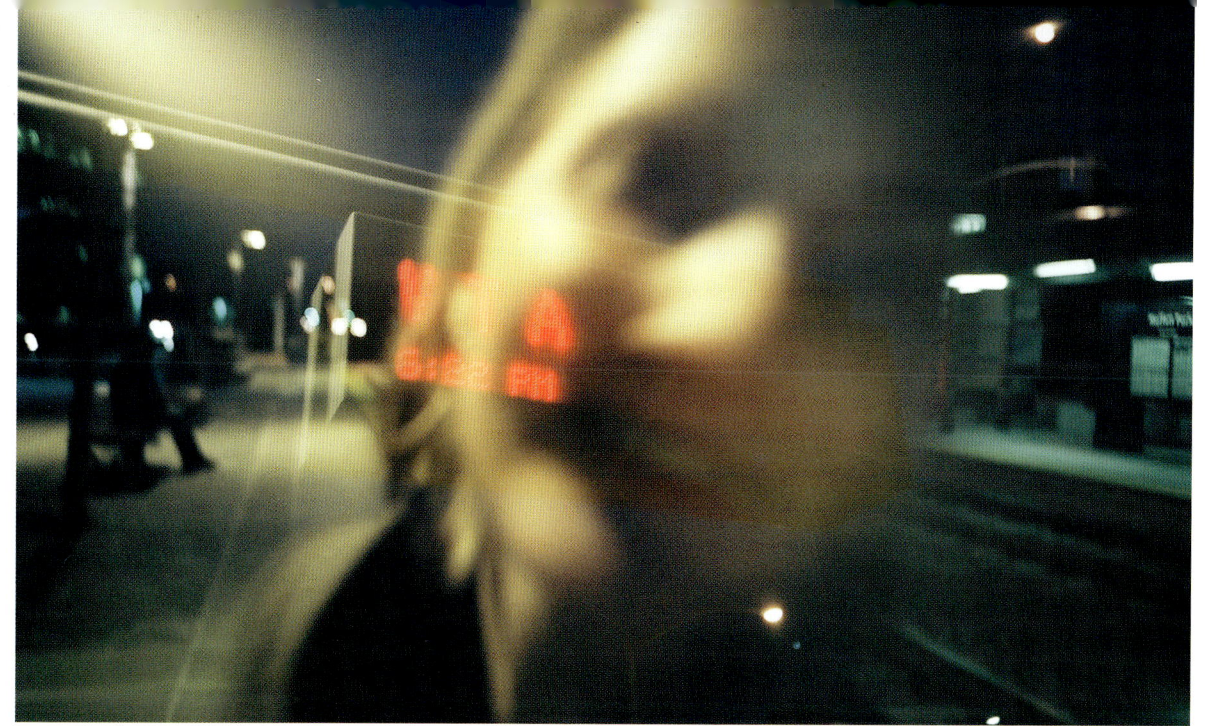

Multiple reloads

Double exposing a single frame (or even consecutive frames) is great, but if you're shooting them over a fairly short timescale you might be limited in terms of location. You can overcome this by exposing an entire roll of film and then reloading it into your camera and shooting it again—at a different time and in an entirely different place.

Start by drawing a mark on your film (and camera) so you can realign the film the next time you load it. Shoot as normal, and once you've shot your film the first time round, rewind it, leaving the end of the film (the "leader") out of the cassette. You can normally tell when the film is released from the spool inside the camera because there will be a discernible "click" and the rewind crank will become looser—at this point the exposed film will be in the cassette, but the leader will be out.

Now you can reload it, aligning the marks you made initially, and shoot again. If you want to get really creative, you could even load it into a different camera!

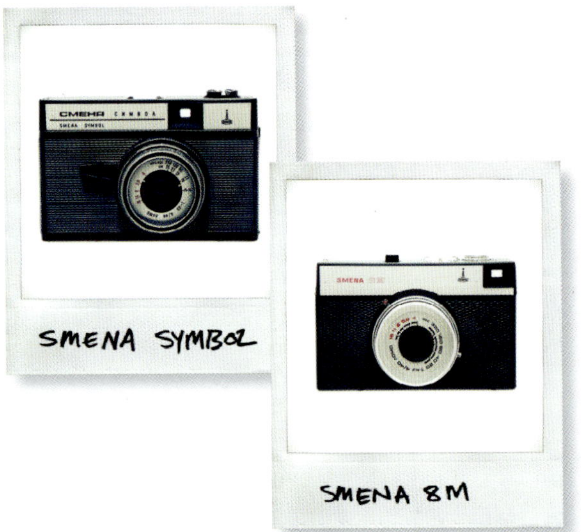

CAMERA:	Smena Symbol
MANUFACTURER:	LOMO
FILM TYPE:	35mm
IMAGE FORMAT:	36mm x 24mm
LENS:	40mm
FOCUS:	1m–Infinity
APERTURES:	f/4, f/5.6, f/8, f/11, f/16
SHUTTER SPEEDS:	1/250 sec.–1/15 sec., B (Bulb)
OTHER FEATURES:	Standard hotshoe Tripod mount

CAMERA:	Smena 8M
MANUFACTURER:	LOMO
FILM TYPE:	35mm
IMAGE FORMAT:	36mm x 24mm
LENS:	40mm
FOCUS:	1m–Infinity
APERTURES:	f/4, f/5.6, f/8, f/11, f/16
SHUTTER SPEEDS:	1/250 sec.–1/15 sec., B (Bulb)
OTHER FEATURES:	PC flash sync socket Tripod mount

Although it's the LC-A that largely draws the crowds to LOMO, a Smena is definitely worth thinking about if you fancy something a little more utilitarian. The first Smena camera appeared in the early 1950s, but it's the slightly later Smena Symbol and Smena 8M that are the ones to go for. Both were launched in the early 1970s, with production continuing for over 20 years, so this duo offers a great combination of availability, affordability, and good old-fashioned usability.

As you might expect from a camera designed and made in the Soviet Union during the 1970s, there are few frills on either model, and at a fundamental level these plastic troopers are hard to separate. The 40mm, f/4 (coated) triplet lens is common to both, and although not the most refined design, it can deliver surprisingly sharp results if you focus accurately. This is not guaranteed, though, as focusing relies solely on the distance scale marked on the lens (which may or may not be entirely accurate).

The 8M and Symbol also share a reliance on manual exposure, with a modest range of apertures and shutter speeds providing both cameras with a genuinely useful level of control. The B setting is great for making long exposures with the 8M, but less helpful on the Symbol, which doesn't have a cable release thread. As a result, you have to physically hold the lens-mounted shutter-release lever down. This guarantees a blurred result, even if you have your camera mounted on a tripod.

Where they differ most is in the winding mechanism and in their flash compatibility. The

8M has separate winding and shutter cocking mechanisms, whereas the Symbol has a coupled film advance that readies the shutter and winds the film at the same time. In real terms this means that it is much easier to use the Symbol, as you don't have to worry about accidental double exposures: if you haven't wound the film on, the shutter will not fire again. The flip side to this is that deliberate multiple exposures are much harder to make using the Symbol. They're not impossible to produce, but the Smena 8M makes the process easier.

Regarding flash compatibility, the 8M utilizes a PC flash sync socket on the lens, while the Symbol synchronizes with a flash via a hotshoe. As a result, it's easier to get a flash off-camera with the 8M (or plug in a studio flash), but this can also be achieved using an adapter in the Symbol's hotshoe.

Ultimately, which Smena you opt for is largely a personal choice: the Symbol is the more user-friendly of the two when it comes to general purpose shooting, but the 8M offers greater creativity for multiple and long exposures. Perhaps the answer is to buy one of each of these examples of affordable Soviet plastic?

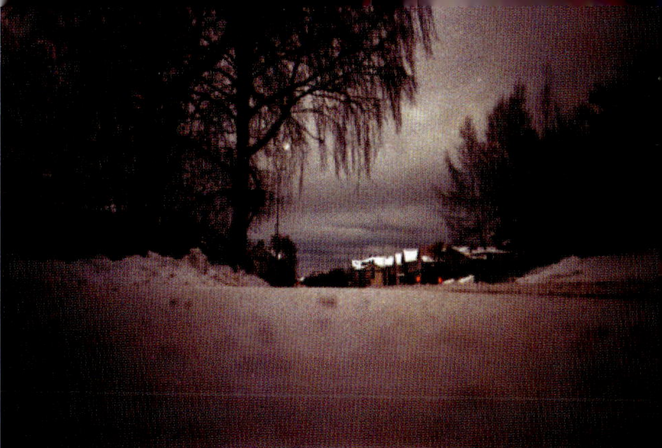

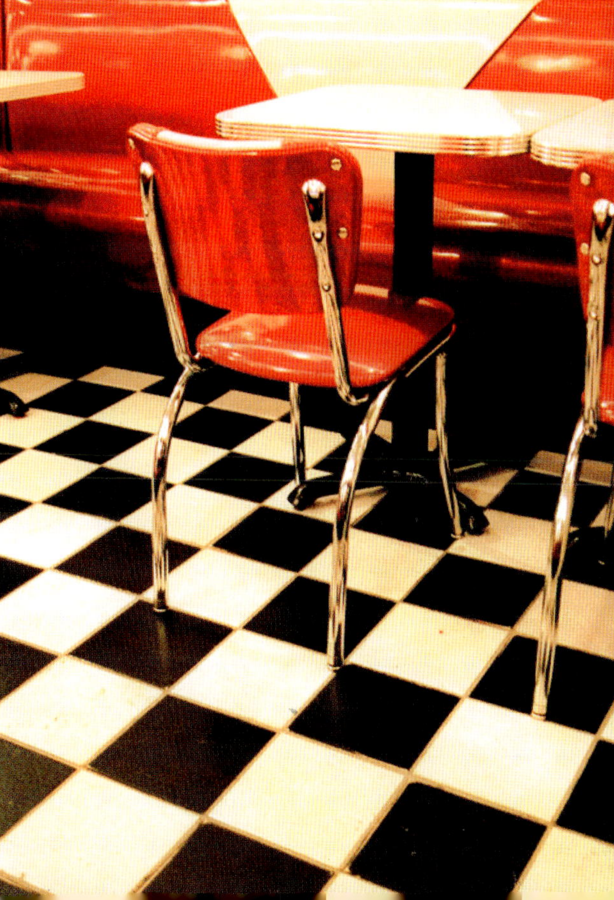

Top right:
CAMERA: LOMO Smena 8M
FILM: Unknown
EXPOSURE: Unrecorded

Using the Smena's weather symbols will give you an idea of the exposure required, or at least provide a starting point!

Right:
CAMERA: LOMO Smena 8M
FILM: Unknown
EXPOSURE: Unrecorded

A wide range of aperture and shutter speed settings make the Smena Symbol and 8M very versatile.

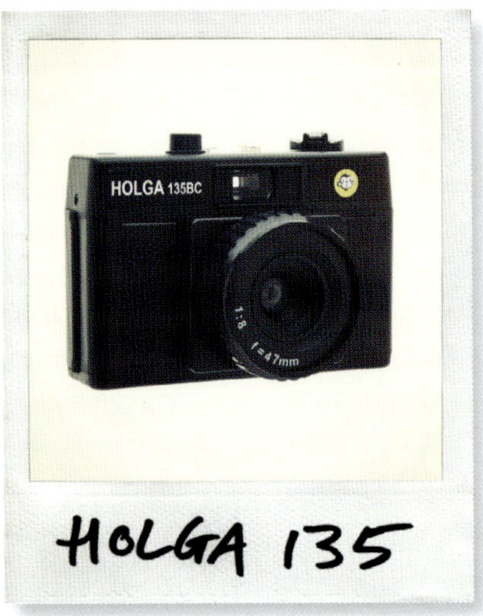

HOLGA 135

CAMERA:	Holga 135/135BC
MANUFACTURER:	Holga
FILM TYPE:	35mm
IMAGE FORMAT:	36mm x 24mm
LENS:	47mm
FOCUS:	4 marked distances (1m, 2m, 6m, Infinity)
APERTURES:	Cloudy (f/8), Sunny (f/11)
SHUTTER SPEED:	N (1/100 sec.), B (Bulb)
OTHER FEATURES:	Tripod mount Cable release socket Standard hotshoe

CAMERA:	Holga 135PC
MANUFACTURER:	Holga
FILM TYPE:	35mm
IMAGE FORMAT:	36mm x 24mm
LENS:	Pinhole
FOCUS:	N/A
APERTURE:	f/175 (approx.)
SHUTTER SPEEDS:	B (Bulb)
OTHER FEATURES:	Tripod mount Cable release socket

Ever since Mr Lee launched his first medium-format camera for the masses, the Holga name has been synonymous with lo-fi photography. As you saw in the previous chapter, the Holga 120 range has grown significantly in the intervening years, and it has also been joined by a burgeoning number of cameras designed for 35mm film. This makes a lot of sense, because while medium format roll film was common in China when the first Holga was released in the early 1980s, 35mm film is now more prevalent, no matter where you are in the world.

Initially, the company released two 35mm Holgas in 2005. Only a limited number were made, but their sell-out success was enough to convince Holga that a 35mm plastic camera was viable, even in the rapidly expanding digital realm. As a result, three 35mm Holgas were launched, this time on an unlimited production line, aiming to deliver the distinct medium format Holga look on a rectangular 35mm frame.

The "basic" 35mm model is the Holga 135, which takes its lead from the equally basic Holga 120N. This means you get N and B shutter speeds (1/100 sec. and Bulb, respectively), the familiar aperture duo of Cloudy (f/8) and Sunny (f/11), and focusing ranging from 1m–Infinity in four discrete steps. Other notable features include a standard hotshoe, a frame-counter, and a threaded shutter-release button (for a cable release): all sensible stuff.

Like its medium format counterpart the Holga 135 doesn't have a linked shutter/winding mechanism, which is both a blessing and a curse. On the one hand, multiple exposures simply require you to press the shutter-release button more than once, so you can produce multilayered images with ease. On the other hand, there's nothing to stop you from accidentally making a double exposure if you forget to wind on or the shutter-release button gets pressed by accident.

With so many similarities to its medium format stablemate, it would follow that focus fall-off, vignetting, and light leaks are the order of the day with the Holga 135. Yet while the results lean in that direction, the Holga 135 doesn't deliver the intensity of a 6cm x 6cm shot taken with a medium format Holga—it's more of a "diluted Holga" look than the true medium format experience.

However, photographers who are seeking the "concentrated Holga" look shouldn't be despondent, as this is where the Holga 135BC (Black Corners/Bent Corners) steps in. This is essentially the same camera as the standard 135, but with one crucial difference: it has a thin plastic "mask" behind the lens. This simple

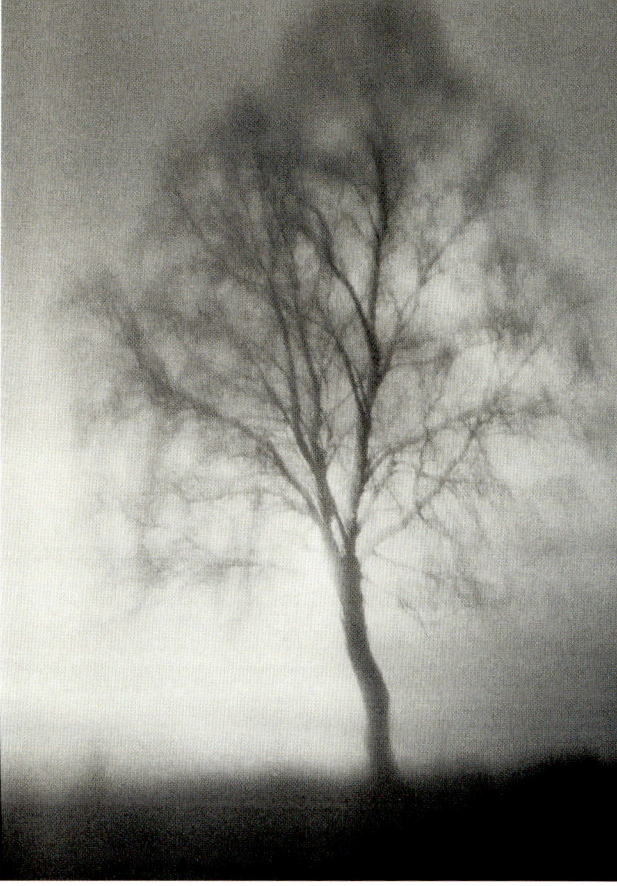

CAMERA: Holga 135
FILM: Fomapan 400
EXPOSURE: f/8 (Bulb)

Holding the Holga 135's shutter open in "B" mode can create ethereal, dreamlike images.

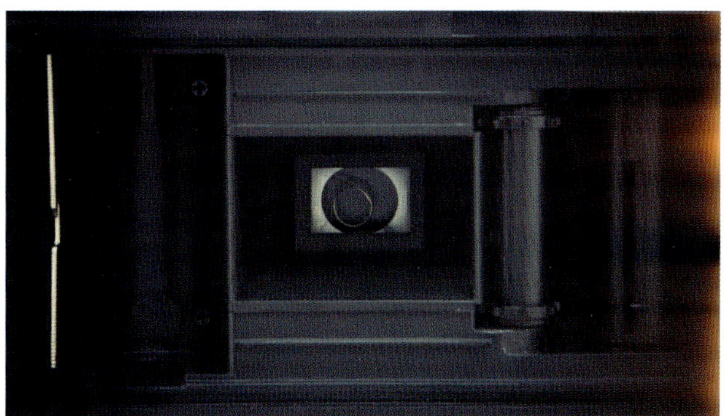

The 135BC's darkened corners are created by a plastic mask that sits behind the lens.

addition enhances vignetting, increases corner softness, and is the reason why the 135BC is the 35mm Holga that most people go for.

The third of the original Holga 135s—the 135PC—is something of an oddity as it eschews the plastic lens ethos that typifies a Holga and replaces it with a pinhole lens. Superficially, the 135PC is the same size and shape as a regular 135, but here the similarities end. Gone is the hotshoe, the focusing, the variable aperture settings, and the 1/100 sec. shutter speed, leaving you with a fixed aperture of approximately f/175 and exposure durations that are controlled manually using the B (Bulb) setting. This is to be expected with a pinhole camera, but it does raise one fundamental question once again: without the iconic optical qualities from a plastic (or glass) Holga lens, can the 135PC be described as a "true" Holga?

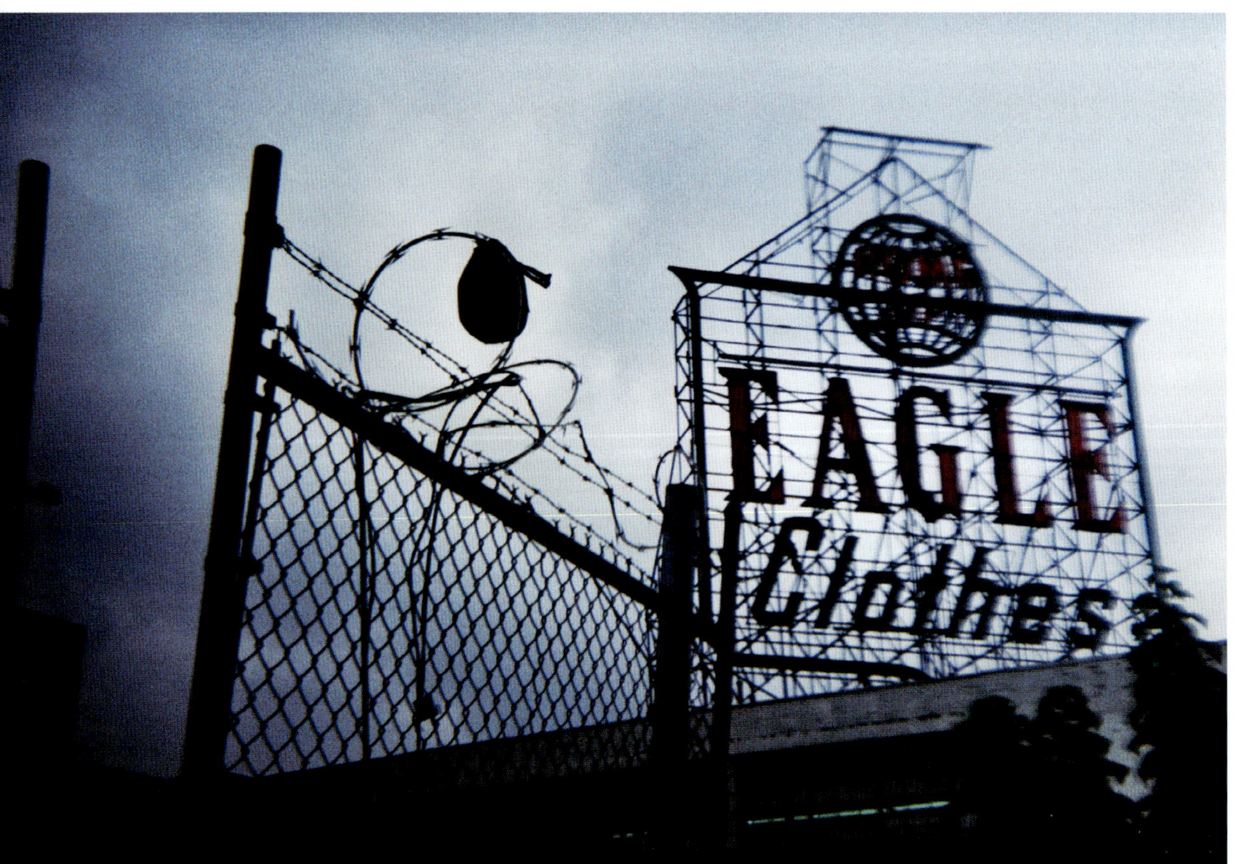

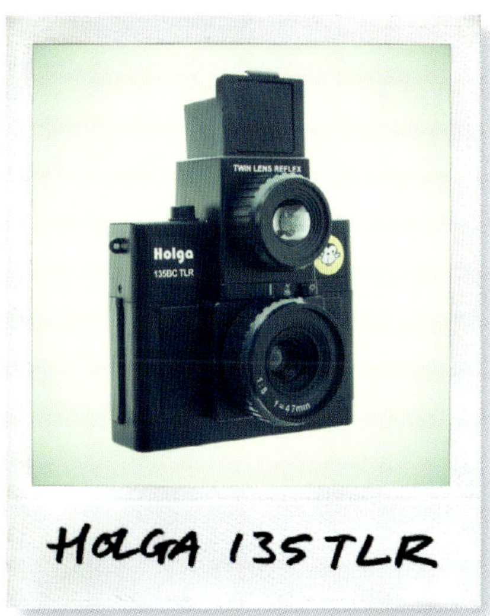

CAMERA:	Holga 135TLR/135TLR BC
MANUFACTURER:	Holga
FILM TYPE:	35mm
IMAGE FORMAT:	36mm x 24mm
LENS:	47mm
FOCUS:	4 preset distance settings (1m, 2m, 6m, Infinity)
APERTURES:	Cloudy (f/8), Sunny (f/11)
SHUTTER SPEEDS:	N (1/100 sec.), B (Bulb)
OTHER FEATURES:	Tripod mount Cable release socket Standard hotshoe

Holga's 35mm TLR cameras may be latecomers to Holga's 135 party, but the BC and non-BC models open up some new options. The only difference between the TLRs and their standard counterparts (either BC or non-BC) is, rather obviously, the twin lens reflex viewing system—in all other respects they are identical. This means there will be little difference between an image from a TLR Holga and one taken with a standard 35mm Holga, beyond the naturally inherent variations of individual cameras. So deciding whether to go for a standard camera or a TLR comes down to one simple question: which one best suits your shooting style?

The TLR option is great if you like to seek out unusual camera angles. It's much easier to peer down the viewing "chimney" and compose shots with the camera at ground level, for example, and you can also hold the camera upside down, above your head, for high-angle pictures.

However, if you often find yourself fitting a flash, the 135TLRs aren't quite so great. Sure, the cameras have got a hotshoe, the same as the regular 135s, but its proximity to the raised viewfinder severely limits your choice of flash—Holga's tall and narrow H-160 flash is the "built for purpose" solution, although it may be too weak for some people.

CAMERA: Holga 135
FILM: Unknown (expired and cross-processed)
EXPOSURE: Unrecorded

Cross-processing expired film can create some fantastic color and contrast shifts.

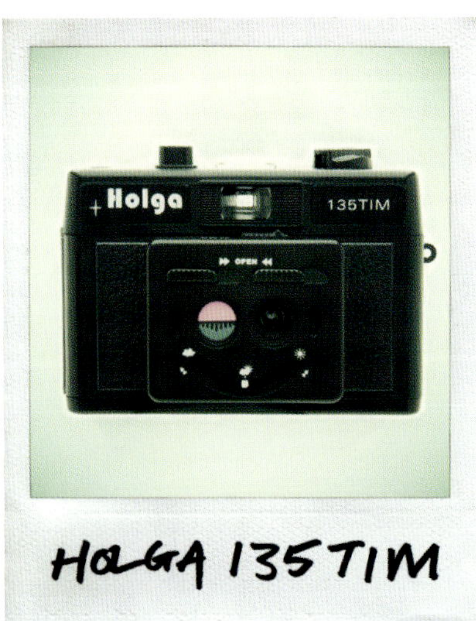

HOLGA 135 TIM

CAMERA:	Holga 135TIM
MANUFACTURER:	Holga
FILM TYPE:	35mm
IMAGE FORMAT:	24mm x 18mm
LENS:	29mm
FOCUS:	Fixed
APERTURES:	Cloudy (f/8), Partial cloud (f/11), Sunny (f/22)
SHUTTER SPEED:	1/100 sec.
OTHER FEATURES:	Tripod mount Cable release socket Standard hotshoe Shoots single half frame images or stereo pairs

Meet the Holga 135TIM, aka Twin Image Maker, aka "Tim." He's a curious addition to Holga's 35mm range, and one that is probably for the "got-to-catch-them-all" Holga collector, rather than someone looking for a quirky plastic camera. That's not to say that Tim isn't quirky—he's the very epitome of "peculiar."

What makes Tim unique is the smiling lens unit that's been attached to the front of a regular Holga 135 camera body. The unit houses a pair of lenses that serve one of two purposes: to shoot half-frame images or, with close-up subject, stereo pairs.

The problem for me is that Tim does neither one of these things in a straightforward fashion, which makes using him a frustrating experience. It's not long before his grin switches from being endearing, to vaguely smug, and then downright conceited—give it time and you will believe this camera is laughing at you, make no mistake!

So what's the problem? Well, first off, let's look at the stereo side of things. To achieve a successful 3D effect, a pair of images needs to be taken using lenses that are spaced roughly the same distance apart as our own eyes. Tim's eyes are clearly much closer together, which means his 3D capabilities are limited to only very close subjects (at which point focus can be an issue).

CAMERA: Holga TIM
FILM: Kodak Gold 400
EXPOSURE: 1/100 sec. @ f/11

Holga's TIM might be awkward to use, but it can still deliver interesting lo-fi results.

At least the process of shooting a stereo pair is straightforward: you start by opening both of Tim's "eyes" (lenses), and then, when he's giving you a sunken-eyed, skeletal stare, you set his "smile" (the aperture) and press the shutter-release button. Both lenses fire simultaneously, recording a pair of images on a single frame.

"Straightforward" isn't a word I'd use to describe Tim's half-frame prowess. To successfully shoot half-frame images, you need to:
• Open one of Tim's eyes so he's winking at you
• Shoot
• Slide the MX (multiple exposure) switch on the top of the lens unit to reset the shutter
• Close the open eye
• Open the other eye
• Take your second shot
• Wind on using the winding wheel on the back of the camera.

This might not sound like an overly convoluted process, but it only works if you shoot continuously, or have a good memory—the slightest distraction and you'll wonder which lens you used last, and whether you've wound on or not. The result is that you either have to wind on and risk wasting a frame, or shoot and hope for the best: you might create a double exposure, but you might not. The more frequently you get distracted between shots, the more often this will happen.

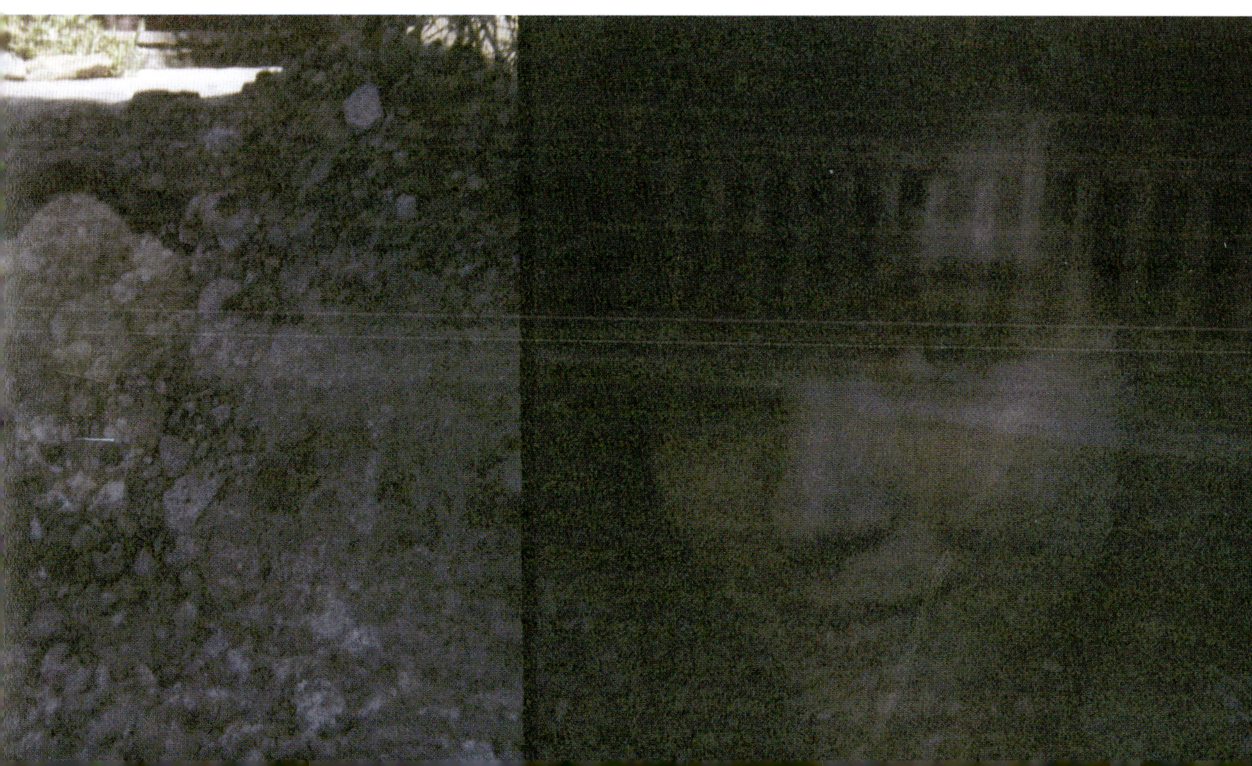

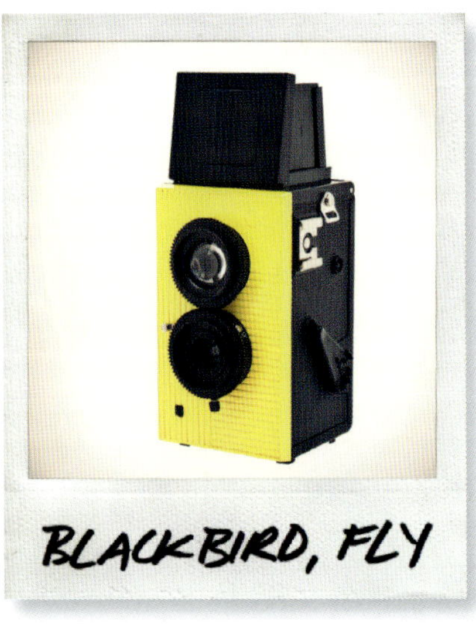

CAMERA:	Blackbird, Fly
MANUFACTURER:	SuperHeadz
FILM TYPE:	35mm
IMAGE FORMATS:	Regular format (36mm x 24mm)
	Square format (24mm x 24mm)
	Full format (36mm x 36mm)
LENS:	33mm
FOCUS:	0.8m–Infinity
APERTURES:	Cloudy (f/7), Fine (f/11)
SHUTTER SPEED:	1/125 sec., B (Bulb)
NOTES:	Tripod mount
	Standard hotshoe

One of the advantages of using plastic to make a camera, rather than metal, is that it can be colored easily, which means the same camera can be produced in a variety of finishes. It doesn't necessarily make any difference to the shots it takes, or how it works (unless the manufacturers makes that happen intentionally), but it does allow you to pick a camera based on its style as well as its functionality.

Style is something that the Blackbird, Fly from SuperHeadz has plenty of—as well as six "flat" color options (black, white, yellow, orange, red, and blue), the company produces limited edition models that will guarantee you stand out from the crowd. Of course, standing out from the crowd is something that happens naturally when you're using a Blackbird, Fly, thanks to its classic, now rarely seen, twin-lens design.

However, unlike the vast majority of twin-lens reflex (TLR) cameras, the Blackbird, Fly uses standard 35mm film, rather than medium format roll film. Not only that, but it offers a choice of three image formats: 24mm x 24mm square, standard 36mm x 24mm, and a large 36mm x 36mm square that exposes right the way across the film, including the sprocket area. To achieve the smaller two formats a plastic mask is fitted into the back of the camera, while shooting without a mask gives you the larger "sprocket shot" option. In all cases you have to choose

CAMERA: Blackbird, Fly
FILM: Ilford HP5+
EXPOSURE: Unrecorded

With the 35mm mask removed, the Blackbird, Fly can shoot over your film's sprocket holes.

your format before you load your film, and there's a strong argument for simply shooting at the maximum size—you can always crop your images to a smaller rectangle or square if you want to.

As with all TLR cameras, you compose your images by looking down through the waist-level viewfinder, and the Blackbird, Fly (or BBF as it will be known from here on) has frame guides to indicate the various image formats. What it does not do, though, is give you any indication of focus—it is purely for framing. Instead, you have to rely on the distances marked above the top (viewing) lens to set the focus on the lower (taking) lens.

Setting the exposure is also a little rough 'n' ready, because you don't have a great deal of choice. The shutter speed (1/125 sec. or B) is set using a small switch on the lower left side of the camera front (as you look at it), while a metal lever next to the lower lens determines the aperture: the choice is f/7 (cloudy) or f/11 (sunny). Given the small maximum aperture, and relatively fast shutter speed, this means you will need to load up with fast film (ISO 400 or above) unless you are shooting on a bright day. Alternatively, if the light levels dip, you can fit a flash into the BBF's side-mounted hotshoe, but this is an ungainly solution and a flash isn't something you'd want attached all the time.

It is well worth accepting the BBF's slightly unrefined approach though, as the results delivered by the 33mm wide-angle plastic lens can be pure lo-fi magic, with soft edges and a chance of light leaks due to the plastic body shell. The separate wind-on and shutter mechanisms make it incredibly straightforward to create a multiple exposures as well, both intentionally and accidentally. Couple this with the novel TLR design and various color options, and you end up with a great all-rounder, albeit one that's at the slightly more expensive end of the plastic camera scale.

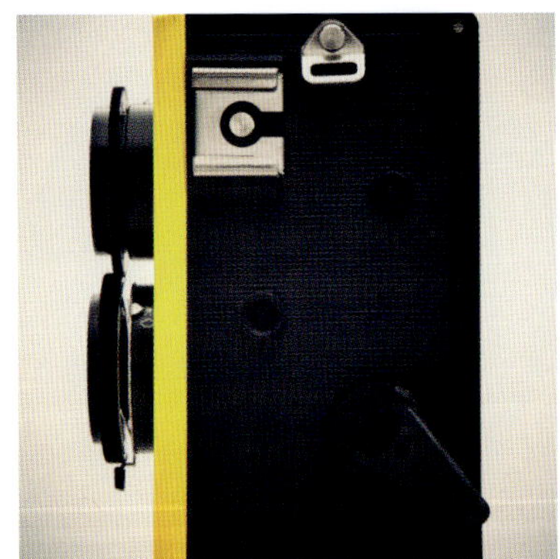

A "live" hotshoe enables you to use flash if you want to, but the side-mounted position is somewhat inconvenient for continual use.

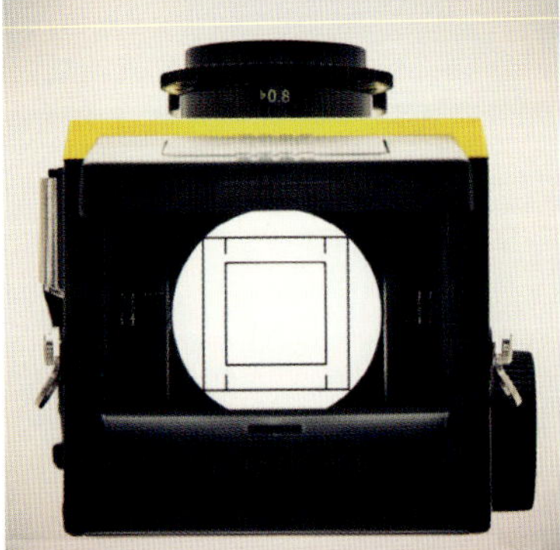

The Blackbird, Fly features multiple frame lines on the waist-level viewing screen, to help you accurately frame your shots no matter what format you choose.

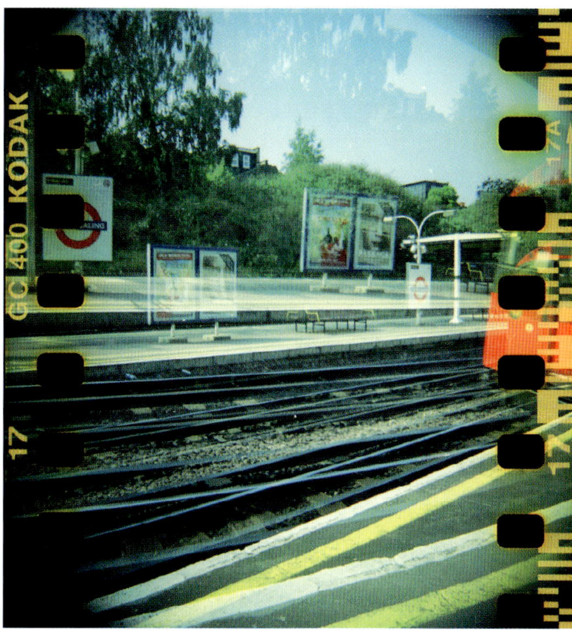

CAMERA: Blackbird, Fly
FILM: Kodak Gold 400
EXPOSURE: Unrecorded

The Blackbird, Fly lets you
pretty much do anything you
want with multiple exposures
and part winding. This was
a frame from a whole roll of
multiple exposures.

TIP:
Although the BBF offers multiple image formats, there's
little to be gained by shooting the smaller 24mm x 24mm
square because it's effectively just a cropped "full frame"
shot. Also, the camera winds the film on by the exact
same amount as it does for the larger, rectangular format,
so you'll still only get 36 exposures from a 36-exposure
film—they will just have a bigger gap between them.

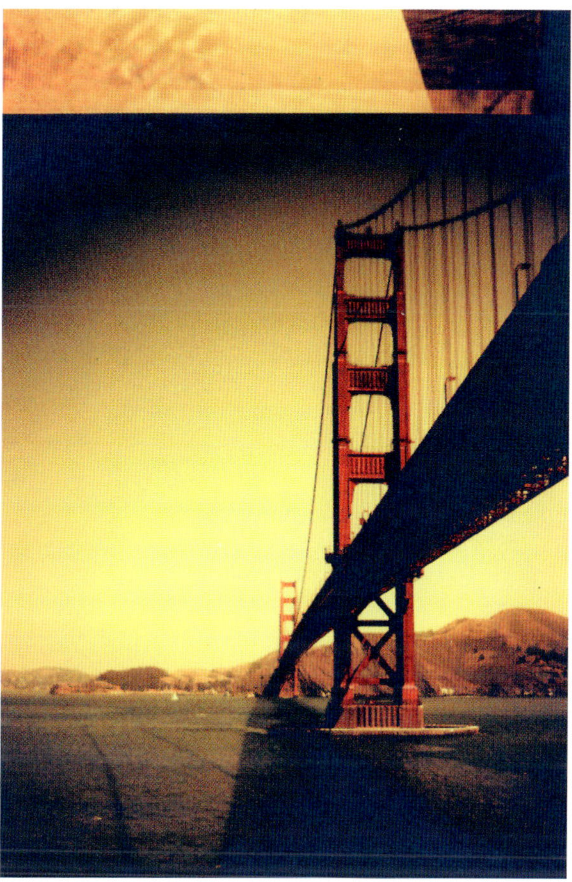

CAMERA: Blackbird, Fly
FILM: Lomography Redscale
EXPOSURE: Unrecorded

Redscale film seemed an
appropriate treatment for
the rusty red primer hue of
the landmark Golden Gate
bridge in San Francisco, USA.

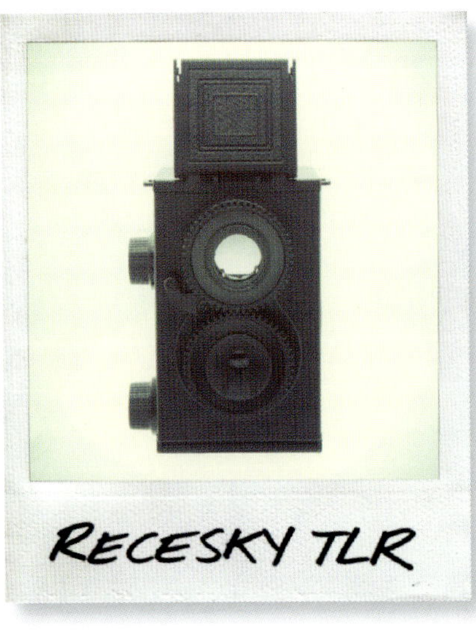

CAMERA: Recesky TLR
MANUFACTURER: Recesky
FILM TYPE: 35mm
IMAGE FORMAT: 36mm x 24mm
LENS: 33mm
FOCUS: Approx.   0.5m–Infinity
APERTURE: f/11
SHUTTER SPEED: Approx. 1/125 sec.
NOTES: Tripod mount

Like the Blackbird, Fly, the Recesky TLR is a 35mm twin lens reflex camera, but this one has a serious twist: you have to put it together yourself. The packing and instructions suggest it will take one hour to transform the polystyrene tray of parts into a fully-functional TLR, but I have to confess it took me twice as long as that—and I'm usually pretty good with this type of thing.

As many people have found, the main stumbling block is the assembly of the shutter mechanism, which is slightly surprising considering it consists of just three pieces of plastic and three springs. However, at this point the instructions aren't particularly clear, so you might find yourself scratching your head for a few minutes and trying different assembly permutations before you hit the right one. Alternatively, there is a host of material online that can help you out—both web sites and "how to" videos—so it's definitely just a minor setback.

But why bother going to this effort when you could buy a readymade Blackbird, Fly instead? Well, first off there's no escaping the thrill of actually making something for yourself and then setting out to see if it works. Providing you've followed the instructions reasonably carefully there's no reason why it shouldn't, and the results you get may well be like no other camera you own.

The main reason for this is the 33mm lens: a simple single-element meniscus lens that does nothing to control edge softness, fringing, flare, vignetting, and distortion. Throw in light leaks that are almost mandatory thanks to the "hand-crafted" nature of the camera, and the Recesky TLR typifies everything that should be celebrated with plastic cameras and the lo-fi aesthetic.

Of course, you have to accept some limitations: there's a single aperture and shutter speed; winding your film on is very imprecise and can easily result in overlapping frames; focusing can be inaccurate, depending on how precisely you fit the viewing and taking lenses; and there's no flash capability. However, at least the Recesky allows you to use the viewing lens and screen to focus—the same cannot be said for the significantly more expensive Blackbird, Fly!

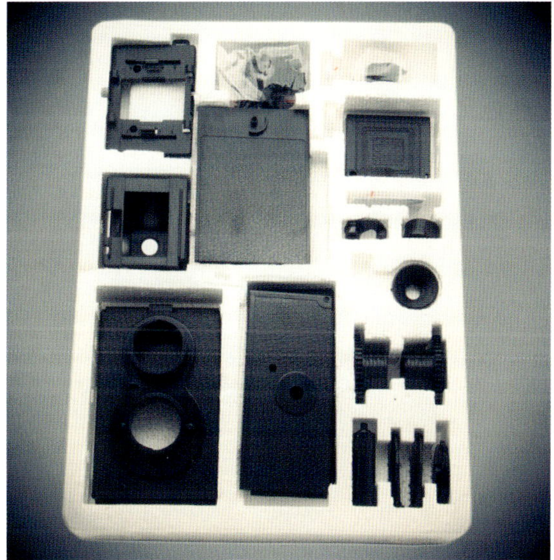

A tray of plastic camera parts, ready to be trasnformed into a Recesky TLR. All you need is a screwdriver and a little patience.

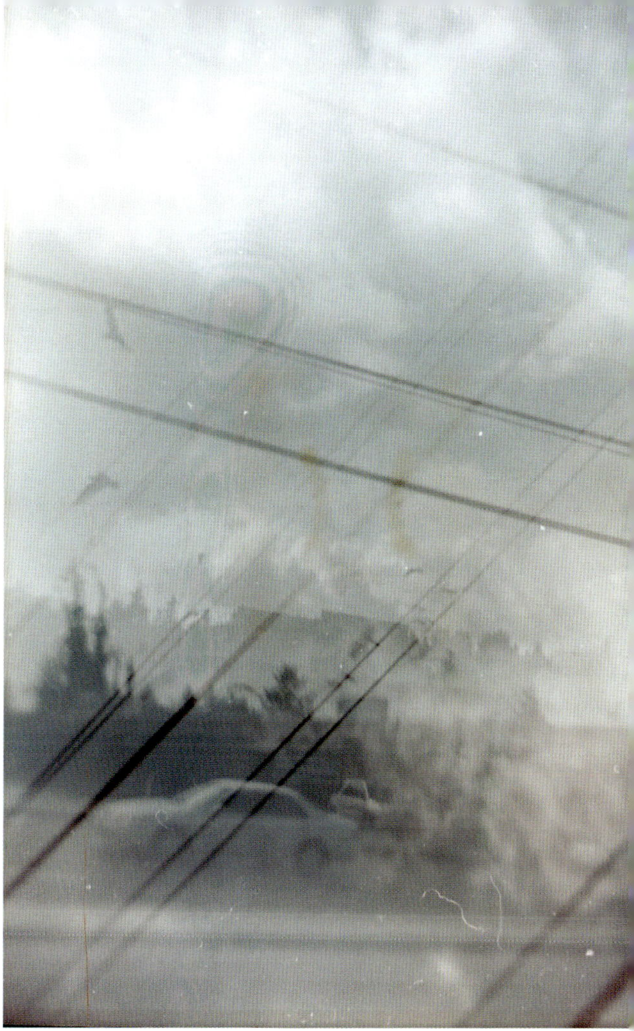

CAMERA: Recesky TLR
FILM: Fuji Superia 400
EXPOSURE: Unrecorded

The Recesky TLR is a clone of the "Gakkenflex," a build-it-yourself camera given away with issue 25 of *Otona no kagaku* magazine, published in Japan by Gakken.

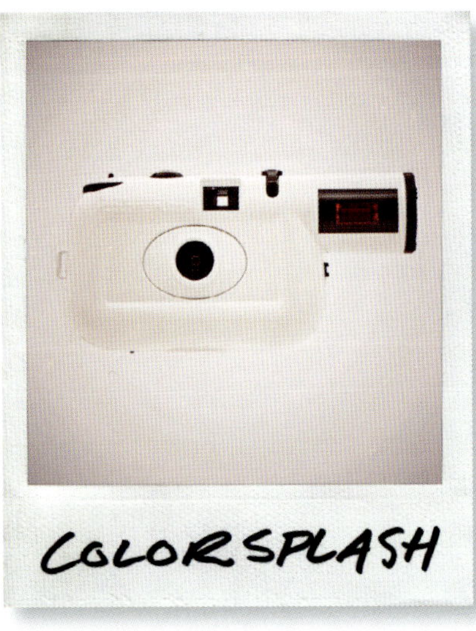

CAMERA: Colorsplash
MANUFACTURER: Lomography
FILM TYPE: 35mm
IMAGE FORMATS: 36mm x 24mm
LENS: Focal length not given
FOCUS: Fixed (approx. 0.2m–Infinity)
APERTURE: Aperture not given
SHUTTER SPEEDS: 1/125 sec., Bulb
NOTES: Built-in color flash
Multiple limited edition models and color options are also available, but ultra-glossy white remains the standard model.

In its standard, iconic, gloss-white-with-black-detailing finish, Lomography's Colorsplash camera looks as though it was designed specifically as the plaything for George Lucas' Stormtroopers, perhaps so they could snap a distant moon as they took a little R&R away from the Death Star? Certainly the results that can be achieved with this camera can be "out of this world."

This is because the Colorsplash's built-in color flash allows you to "dial" a colored gel in front it—just like the color flash in certain Holga models. Like the Holgas, the default colors are red, yellow, blue, and "white" (unfiltered), but here the similarity ends, since the Colorsplash allows two of these filters to be replaced. Nine additional gels are supplied with the camera, but you could, with a little care, make your own filters as well, so the color options are near endless. A word of caution though: the filter door isn't particularly robust, even by plastic camera standards, and as it needs to be prised off with a screwdriver (or similar) a little care is needed. Thankfully, this isn't an integral part of the camera, so it's not the end of the world if (when?) the worst happens.

The flash can be used with either of the Colorsplash's shutter speeds: "Sun" (1/125 sec.) or "Moon" (B). In B mode, the flash fires at the end of the exposure (known as second curtain flash), which is great for moving subjects as any blurred movement will appear to trail behind them (like a "speed blur") rather than in front of them. In low-light conditions you can also use the B option to create heavily blurred backgrounds by deliberately moving the camera during the exposure: the flash will kick in at the end to add a sharp subject to the shot.

Of course, you don't have to use flash, but that rather misses the point of the camera; without the flash it becomes a 35mm point-and-shoot camera with a slightly wide-angle lens, and there are plenty of those around that don't cost as much. However, I guarantee that none of them will look quite so unique!

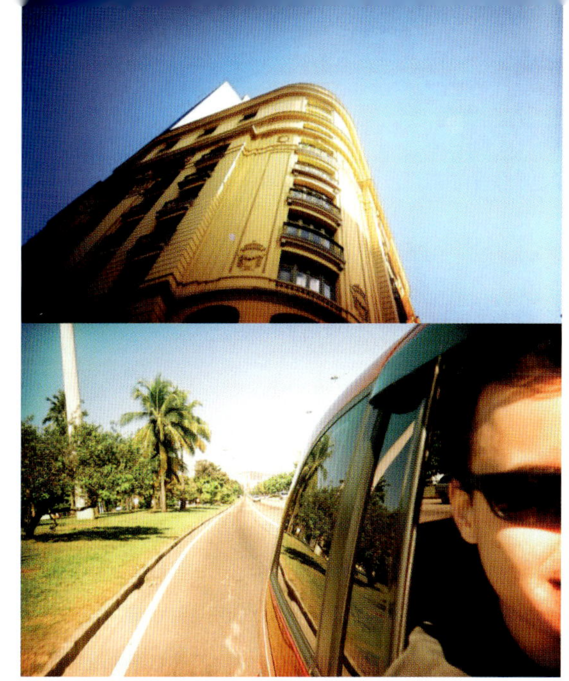

Both images, right
CAMERA: Lomography Colorsplash
FILM: Unknown
EXPOSURE: 1/125 sec.

Without the flash, the Colorsplash becomes a useful wideangle plastic camera, although the precise focal length remains a mystery.

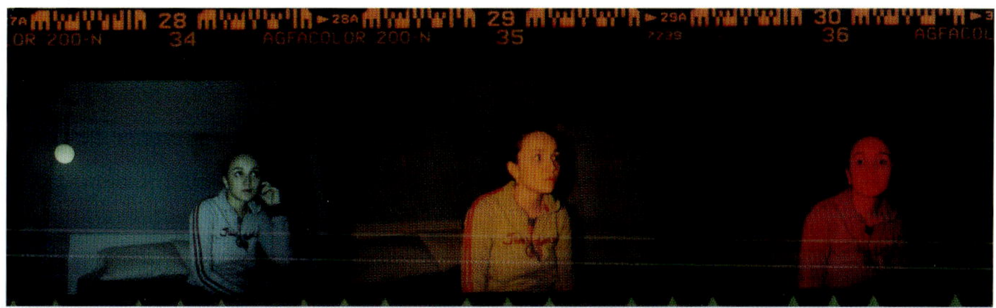

CAMERA: Lomography Colorsplash
FILM: Agfacolor 200
EXPOSURE: 1/125 sec.

The Colorsplash's built-in flash enables you to get a variety of "looks" with very little effort.

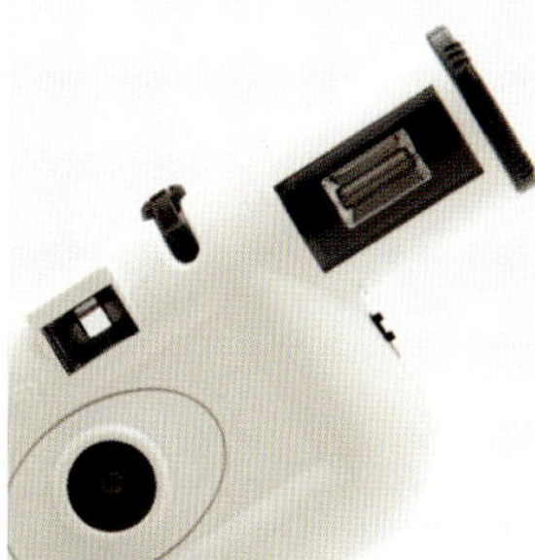
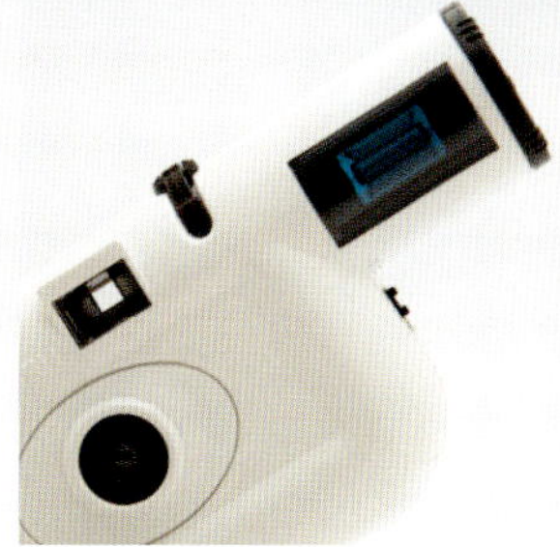
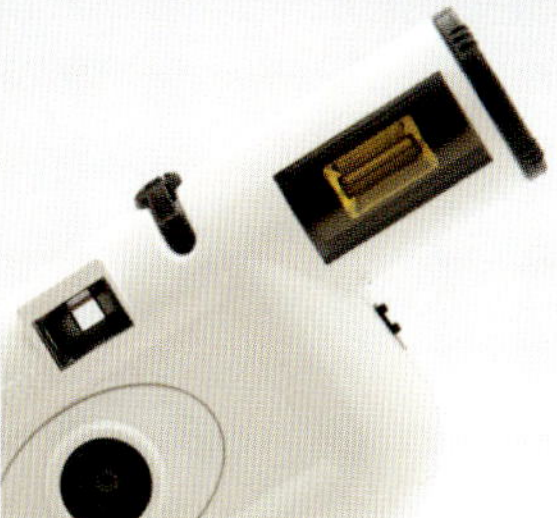
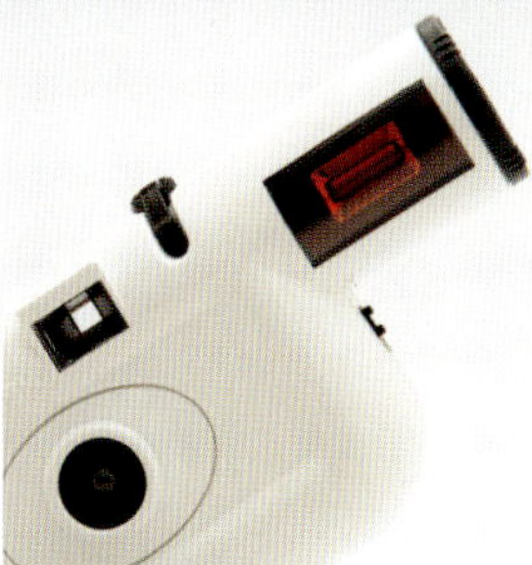

Technique: Cross-processing

If you spend just a few minutes looking at plastic camera photographs online, you're guaranteed to see a whole load of cross-processed shots. Some will be good, some bad, and some can be downright ugly, but that's not the point: plastic cameras and cross-processing were made for each other! But what exactly is it?

Cross-processing is simply taking one type of color film (negative or slide) and processing it in the other one's chemistry—so slide film goes through the C41 process usually used for negative film, and negative film is run through the E6 slide film process. Slide film through negative chemistry (or "E6 through C41" if you want to sound like a pro at the lab) is the most popular choice, and generally speaking it's the one that will produce the best results. Certainly, if you're looking at a shot with skewed colors and "popped" contrast, you're looking at E6 through C41. Doing it the other way (C41 neg film through E6 slide chemistry) tends to give dark, flat results unless you start playing around with your exposures and processing times.

However, no film is designed to be abused in this way, which is why the colors shift in protest, the contrast changes, and grain is often amplified. But that's why you're cross-processing to start with—you want something less conventional. Less boringly predictable. And unpredictability really is the name of the game here. With the exception of the films featured in the box, top right, there's no real way of determining precisely what the results will be with any given film. Some films can be cross-processed more successfully than others, but slight changes in exposure, or the temperature and "freshness" of the chemistry, can have a significant impact on the end result.

The key is to experiment. Grab some film and try it. Try over- and underexposing shots to see what difference that makes, and even consider having your film "pushed" or "pulled" at the processing stage (see box, bottom right). Either way, keep meticulous notes so you can find a starting point for your future rolls, but remember that when it comes to cross-processing, nothing is guaranteed!

TIP:
When cross-processing E6 (slide) film, downrating it (rating an ISO 200 film at ISO 100, for example) and then pull-processing it by 1 stop can help reduce high contrast.

Reinventing a classic

Cross-processing is not a new technique, so much of experimentation has already been done for you: Agfa's RSX 200 slide film was great cross-processed through C41 chemistry, for example. Although Agfa is no longer active in the traditional photographic market, its legacy lives on with Rollei's Creative Edition Crossbird film and Lomography's X-Pro 200. Both films are based on Agfa RSX 200, making them ideal for cross-processing, as well as for producing conventional slides.

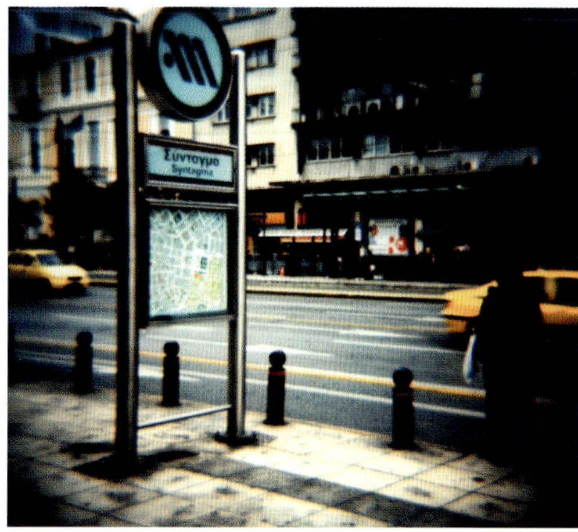

CAMERA: Holga 120N
FILM: Kodak Ektachrome E100VS (cross-processed)
EXPOSURE: 1/100 sec. @ f/8

Shot on slide film then cross-processed for a dreamy, saturated look. No other filters or effects were applied.

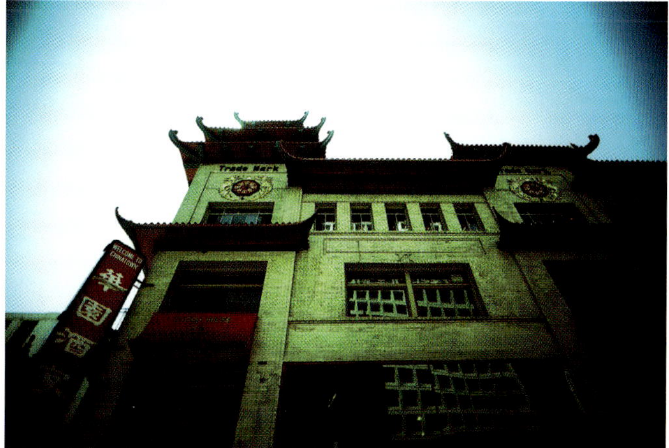

CAMERA: Vivitar Ultra Wide & Slim
FILM: Fuji Provia 100F (cross-processed)
EXPOSURE: 1/125 sec. @ f/11

Increased contrast and color shifts are typical of cross-processing E6 slide film in the C41 chemistry designed for color negative film.

Push/pull processing

"Pushing" and "pulling" are terms used in film processing to indicate deliberate over- or underdevelopment. In conventional film photography push-processing is the more common of the two, and would be used to "uprate" the ISO of a film—you could shoot an ISO 100 film as if it was ISO 200 (or ISO 400), and then have it push-processed by 1 stop (or 2 stops) to compensate. The contrast and grain will increase, but the exposures will be OK.

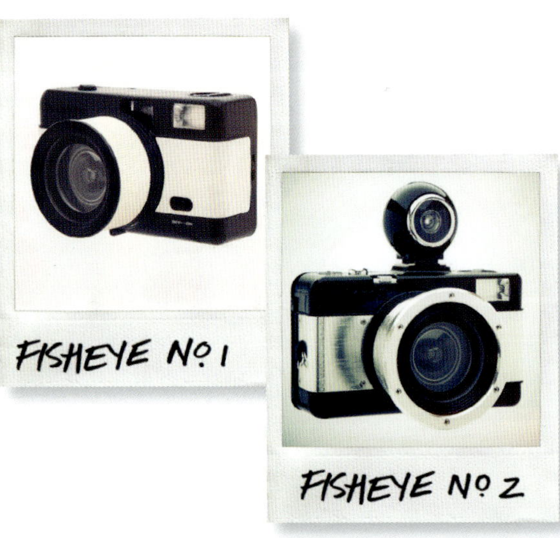

CAMERA:	Fisheye No.1
MANUFACTURER:	Lomography
FILM TYPE:	35mm
IMAGE FORMAT:	36mm x 24mm
LENS:	10mm
FOCUS:	Fixed
APERTURE:	f/8
SHUTTER SPEED:	1/100 sec.
OTHER FEATURES:	Built-in flash

CAMERA:	Fisheye No.2
NOTES:	As Fisheye No.1, but gains a fisheye viewfinder, multiple exposure switch, Bulb mode, and standard hotshoe

It would be unthinkable to attach a fisheye lens permanently to an SLR or other interchangeable lens camera, but with its Fisheye cameras Lomography has created a pair of fixed-lens, super-wide plastic snappers that make shooting circular images through a 10mm lens all the time, somehow seem "right."

The duo offers the same fundamental attributes in terms of lens, aperture, shutter speeds, and built-in flash, but Fisheye No. 2 is slightly more sophisticated thanks to the fisheye viewfinder, Bulb mode, multiple exposure button, and standard hotshoe that it brings to the extreme-angle party. It also features a tougher-looking outer shell that uses brushed aluminum and exposed screw heads to give it a quasi-industrial feel. Fisheye No. 1 may be slightly less expensive, but Fisheye No. 2 is worth the additional cost if you're certain that you want your photography to be less square.

CAMERA: Lomography Fisheye No.2
FILM: Kodak Portra 800
EXPOSURE: 1/100 sec. @ f/9

An underwater shot taken using the optional underwater housing that is available for the Fisheye camera.

TIP:

With a 170-degree viewing angle, and a lens that produces "true" fisheye, circular images, these cameras won't suit everyone, and it's easy to become disheartened with early results. However, the reason for most disappointment is often quite simple: you need to be as close as possible if you want to stand any chance of filling the super-wide frame. If you move just slightly further back, everything can (and will) becomes a tiny speck in the goldfish bowl of life that the fisheye lens sees.

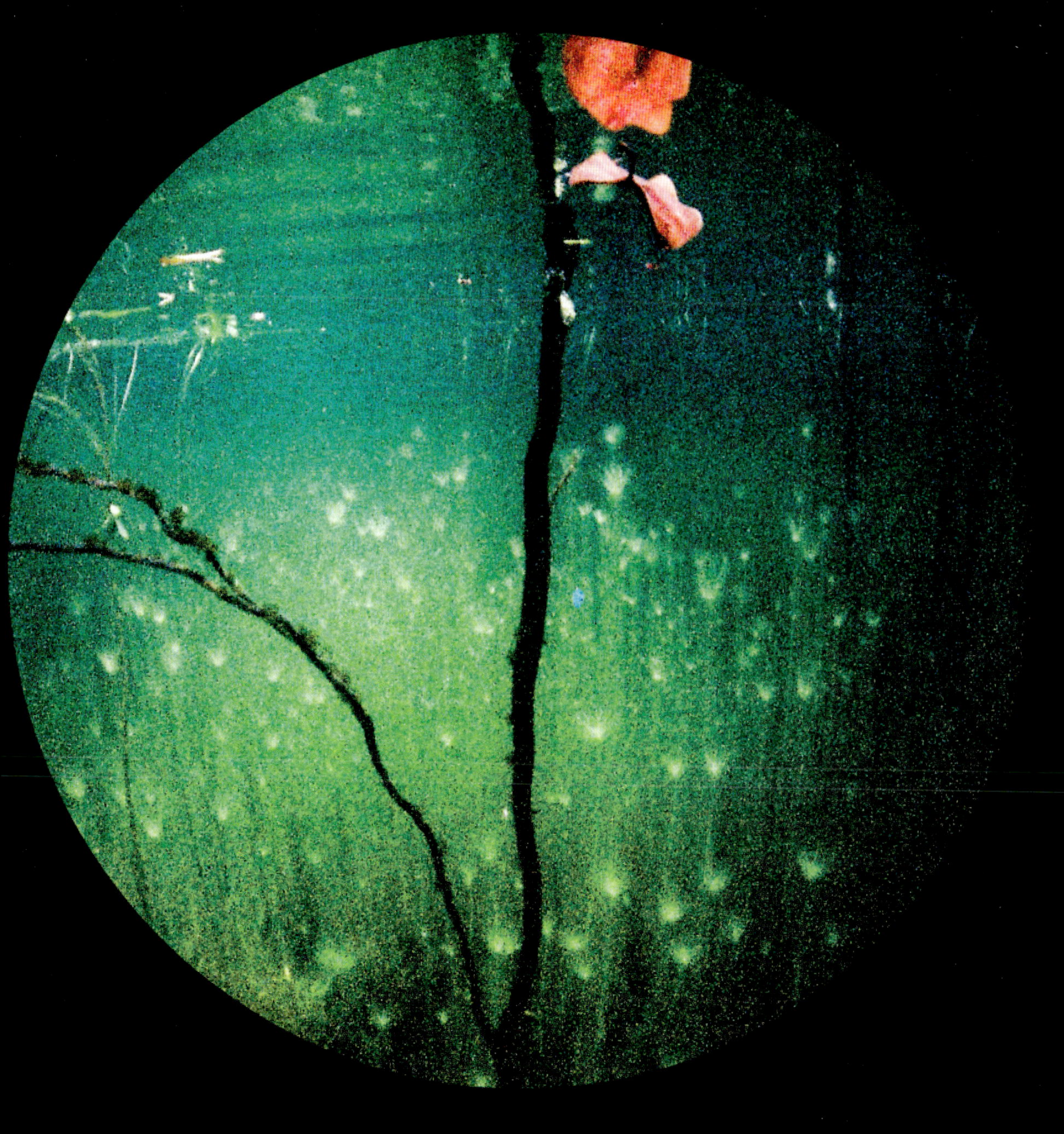

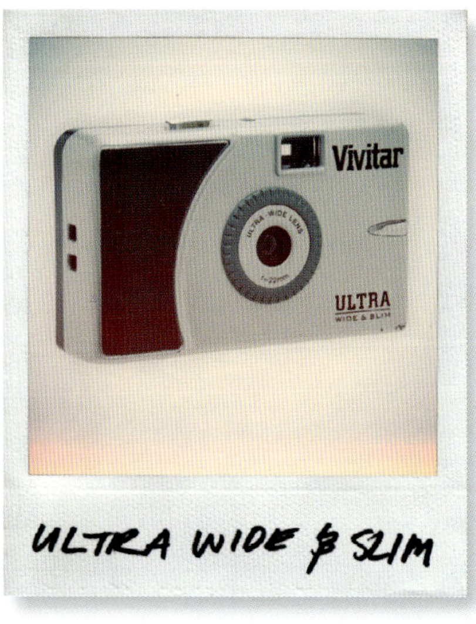

ULTRA WIDE & SLIM

CAMERA:	Ultra Wide & Slim
MANUFACTURER:	Vivitar
FILM TYPE:	35mm
IMAGE FORMAT:	36mm x 24mm
LENS:	22mm
FOCUS:	Fixed (approx. 1m–Infinity)
APERTURE:	f/11
SHUTTER SPEED:	1/125 sec.

Vivitar's Ultra Wide & Slim (UWS) is about as basic a point-and-shoot camera as you can get: the focal length is fixed; the focus is fixed; the aperture is fixed; and the shutter speed is—you guessed it—fixed. There's no hotshoe, no cable release thread, no Bulb mode, and no tripod socket either. In fact, all you can do is point the camera, press the shutter-release button, wind-on, and then rewind your film when you've finished the roll.

Yet despite fundamentally doing—and offering—so little, numerous "clones" of this camera have appeared since Vivitar ceased production, including the Eximus Wide and Slim, Jelly Lens UWS, Rainbow V, and the SuperHeadz range that is made up of at least 10 colored models including Black Slim Devil, White Angel, Pink Dress, and Blue Ribbon.

The reason for this resurgence in its popularity is simple: it's because of the lens. With a focal length of just 22mm, the UWS' ultra wide-angle optic was, for a number of years, in a lo-fi class of its own, combining heavy vignetting with extreme flare, and the possibility of light leaks from the camera body. Being so wide, you can forgive the fixed focus and small aperture—depth of field will ensure that almost everything is in focus from foreground to background. This really is a camera where the photographer's eye far exceeds the technology being used!

The only downside is that the original Vivitar model was discontinued years ago, so as the camera has become popular again, demand (and therefore the price) has risen: you may find yourself drawn into an expensive bidding "war" if you look for the camera on eBay.

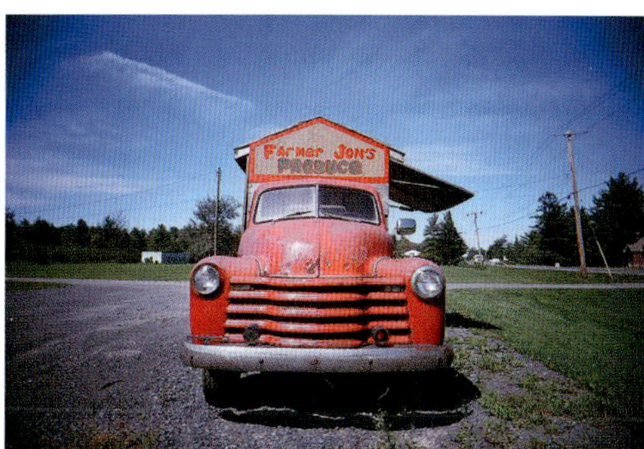

CAMERA: Vivitar Ultra Wide & Slim
FILM: Agfacolor 200
EXPOSURE: 1/125 sec. @ f/11

Significant corner shading typifies the UWS' 22mm, wideangle lens.

TIPS:

The UWS' wide viewing angle and narrow camera body mean that it is all too easy for your fingers to encroach into the corners of your shots. To help prevent this, hold the camera with just your thumb and forefinger, resting your digits on the top and bottom of its shell, rather than gripping the sides and front of the body.

With its relatively fast shutter speed (1/125 sec.) and small aperture (f/11), the UWS doesn't allow much light to hit your film for very long, so you need to choose your film to match the conditions. Loading up with ISO 400 film (or faster) is generally recommended, especially on overcast days, although you might get away with ISO 200 film on a bright, sunny day.

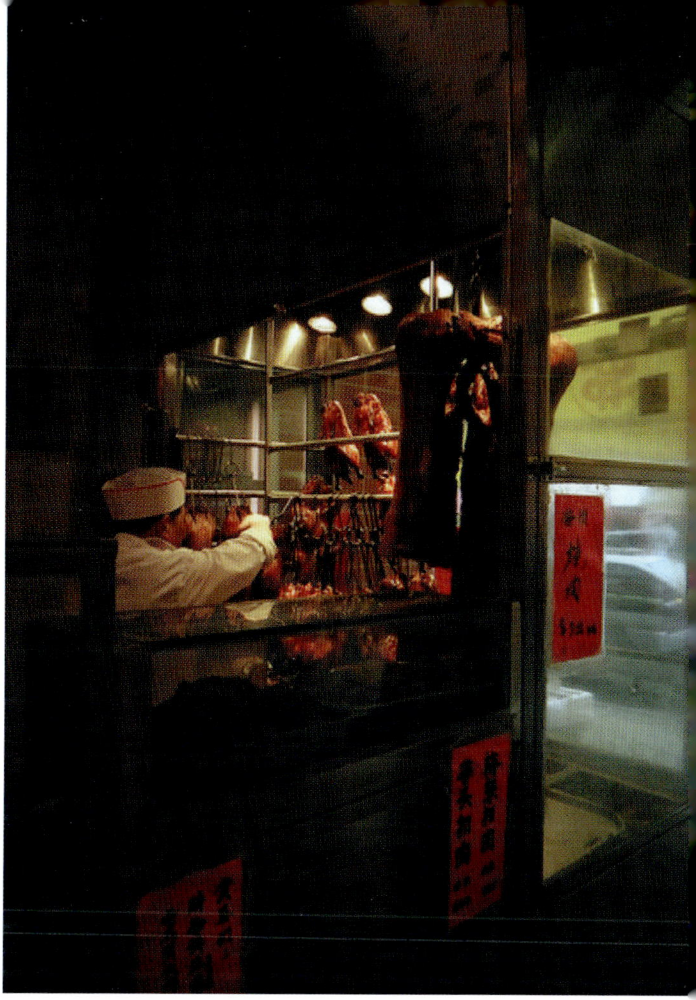

CAMERA: Vivitar Ultra Wide & Slim
FILM: Unknown
EXPOSURE: 1/125 sec. @ f/11

The UWS' fast shutter speed and small aperture aren't conducive to low-light photography, but with a fast film it can be possible.

In loving memory of Mrs Teresa Y.H. Wong (1937–2012)

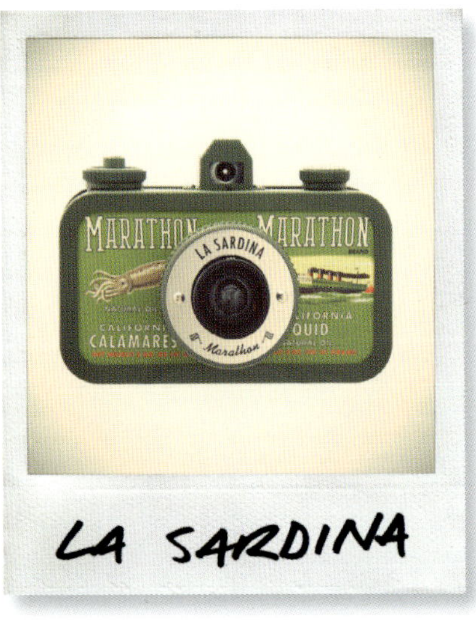

LA SARDINA

CAMERA:	La Sardina
MANUFACTURER:	Lomography
FILM TYPE:	35mm
IMAGE FORMAT:	36mm x 24mm
LENS:	22mm
FOCUS:	2 settings (0.6m–1m, 1m–Infinity)
APERTURE:	f/8
SHUTTER SPEED:	N (1/100 sec.), B (Bulb)
OTHER FEATURES:	Collapsible lens
	Multiple exposure button
	Optional flash
	Cable release socket
	Two standard tripod mounts

Whether you opt for one of the wallet-friendly plastic La Sardina models, or go for a more expensive metal-shelled option, the internal workings of these 35mm cameras are the same. Each one is centered on an ultra-wide 22mm lens that needs to be rotated out from the body before you can shoot: rotated back in it effectively locks the shutter and makes the camera more compact.

The focal length matches that of the Ultra Wide & Slim (see page 102), which is a rarity in 35mm camera terms, but while the angle of view is similar, the performance is not: La Sardina delivers softer results than the UWS. These can be described either as "dreamier" or "worse," depending on the quality that is most important to you. What can't be disputed is that Lomography's offering is more versatile than the UWS. There are two focus settings, allowing you to focus down to 2 feet, and while La Sardina's aperture and shutter speed are fixed (at f/8 and 1/125 sec.), this combination is more than 1 stop "faster" than the UWS, meaning you can shoot with slower film, or in lower light. Additional low-light functionality comes from a B setting, and you can hook up a flash, although the unique connection limits your options to a couple of Lomography flashes, and nearly doubles the price of the basic camera.

In its standard guise a multiple exposure facility, partial rewind (to create "endless" panoramas), and a pair of tripod mounts for landscape and portrait format shooting add to the camera's versatility and round off a great-looking package that should appeal to shooters unafraid to take a walk on the wide side.

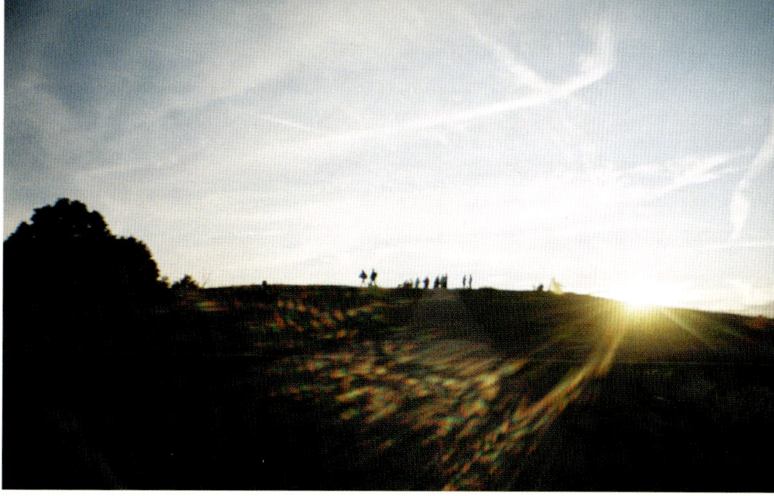

Top left:
CAMERA: La Sardina
FILM: Kodak BW400CN
EXPOSURE: 1/100 sec. @ f/8

La Sardina's 22mm lens is great for creating a dramatic wideangle perspective.

Left:
CAMERA: La Sardina
FILM: Unknown
EXPOSURE: 1/100 sec. @ f/8

Images from La Sardina are softer than those from the UWS, although some people prefer this.

CAMERA: La Sardina
FILM: Unknown
EXPOSURE: 1/100 sec. @ f/8

Aimed toward the sun you can expect extreme flare from La Sardina's wideangle lens.

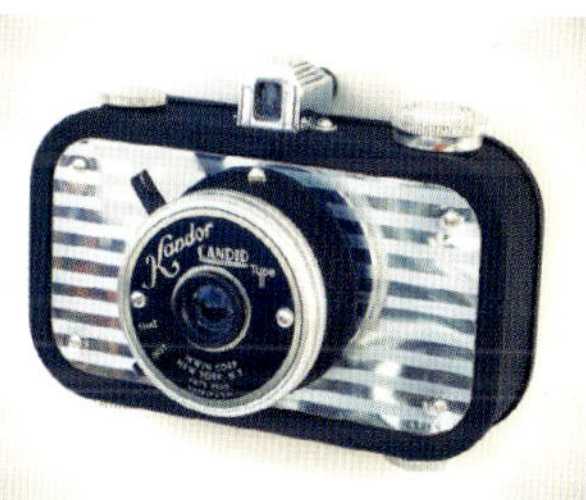

In the can

Lomography's La Sardina is an homage to the "sardine can" cameras of the 1930s, especially the Kandor Candid from New York's Irwin Corporation (pictured). These cameras got their name because their flat, metal bodies with rounded corners made them look like... well, sardine cans. In fact, it is rumored that early Kandor models used actual sardine cans for the camera body. However, the curvaceous body is where the similarities end: the Candid takes 127-format film and produces 3cm x 4cm images using a fairly pedestrian 50mm. La Sardina does not.

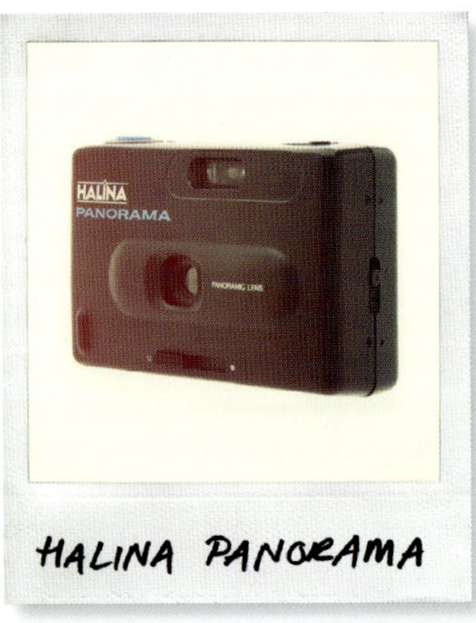

HALINA PANORAMA

CAMERA:	Halina Panorama
MANUFACTURER:	Haking
FILM TYPE:	35mm
IMAGE FORMAT:	36mm x 13mm
LENS:	28mm
FOCUS:	Fixed (approx. 1m–Infinity)
APERTURE:	f/11
SHUTTER SPEED:	1/125 sec.
OTHER FEATURES:	Halina Panorama-F has built-in flash

The Halina Panorama is a camera with many names: before Chinese manufacturer Haking took over the Ansco name, it was known as the Ansco Pix Panorama, and it also appeared as the Revue Panorama for European retailer Foto-Quelle.

Regardless of the name on the front, the cameras are all the same, with each one delivering panoramic images measuring 36mm x 13mm onto standard 35mm film. This 1:2.7 image ratio is achieved in a laughably simplistic way: a plastic mask in the back of the camera physically crops the area of the film that is exposed to light, while the front of the camera body is designed with a "widescreen" viewfinder window to match. You could achieve the exact same effect using any full-frame 35mm camera and cropping your shots.

However, while the way in which the panoramic image is formed is rudimentary, it's also incredibly effective, as every stage of the process—from looking through the viewfinder to printing your shots—stays strictly panoramic. There are also none of the hassles associated with cropping your prints, as everything the Panorama produces will be printed with movie-style black bars top and bottom unless you have your prints made on panoramic paper or scan your shots. Even better, these cameras (and others like them) regularly turn up in yard sales, thrift stores, and Ebay auctions at insanely low prices, so if you're looking to create panoramas with point-and-shoot simplicity, perhaps your search is over?

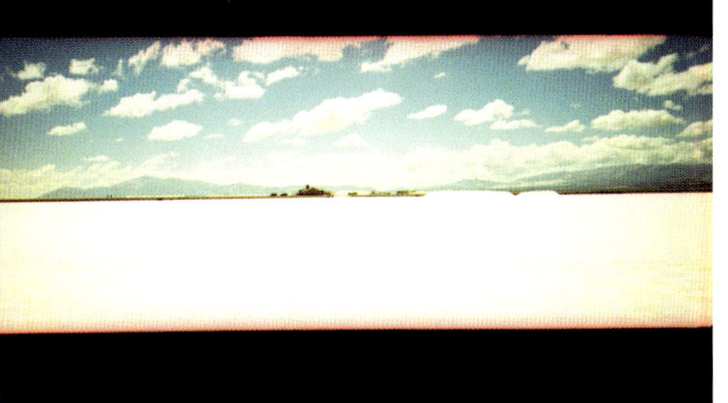

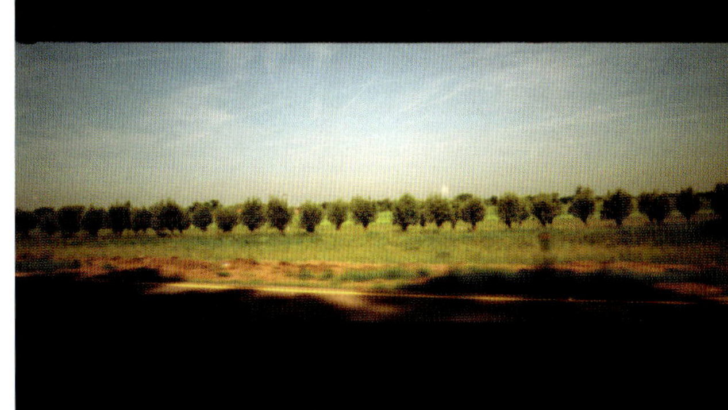

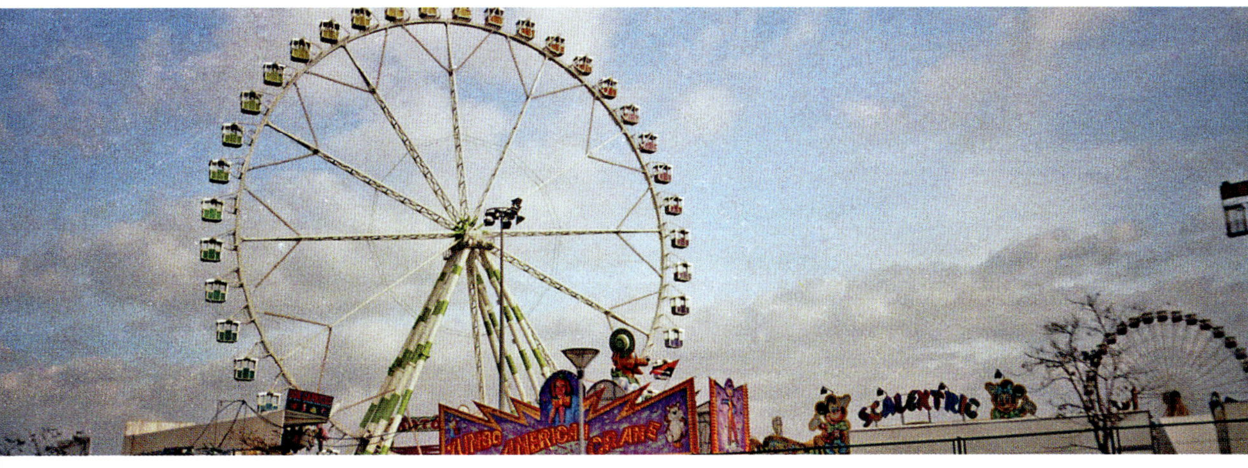

Top left:
CAMERA: Halina Panorama
FILM: Argenti Godochrome
EXPOSURE: 1/125 sec. @ f/11

Cross-processed transparency film produces a dramatic, high contrast result from the Halina Panorama.

Above:
CAMERA: Halina Panorama
FILM: Kodak Gold 400
EXPOSURE: 1/125 sec. @ f/11

Vignetting and soft focus creeps into the edges of shots taken with the Panorama, but this camera isn't a bad performer.

Top right:
CAMERA: Halina Panorama
FILM: Unknown
EXPOSURE: 1/125 sec. @ f/11

The Halina's panoramic format is great for landscapes, and it really enhances horizontal lines.

Halina Panorama-F

To improve the Panorama's low-light performance Haking added a built-in flash and created the Halina Panorama-F. As it has a manual on/off switch the flash can also be used as a fill-light on brighter days, making the "F" variant the slightly more versatile option.

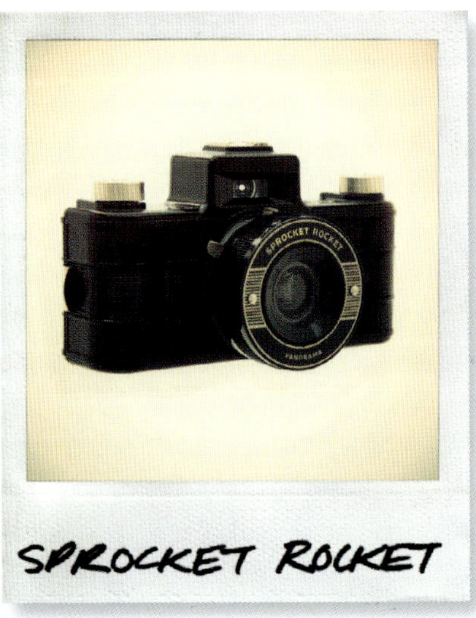

CAMERA: Sprocket Rocket
MANUFACTURER: Lomography
FILM TYPE: 35mm
IMAGE FORMAT: 72mm x 33mm (without mask)
72mm x 24mm (with mask)
LENS: 30mm
FOCUS: Two preset distance settings
(0.6m–1m, 1m–Infinity)
APERTURES: Cloudy (f/10.8), Sunny (f/16)
SHUTTER SPEEDS: N (1/100 sec.), B (Bulb)
OTHER FEATURES: Tripod mount
Cable release socket
Standard hotshoe

If you like panoramic images, extreme wide-angle views, sprocket shots, overlapping frames, multiple exposures, or any combination of these, Sprocket Rocket will get your pulse racing because it offers all this and more. Looking like a vintage, art deco, Bakelite camera (but constructed from modern plastics), the Sprocket Rocket is a panoramic shooter that delivers 72mm wide images onto standard 35mm film, either with or without sprocket holes.

The viewfinder gives an indication of what the 30mm lens can see, but be prepared for a seriously wide-angle view: this is a 30mm focal length on what is essentially a cropped medium-format frame. The lens gives a super-wide, 106-degree viewing angle. A token level of control over your exposures is provided by two aperture settings (f/10.8 and f/16), although the fixed 1/100 sec. shutter speed means you'll need a fast film to get good exposures—ISO 400 stock is best, but you may need to go faster still if the light levels dip and you don't want to switch the shutter speed to B or fit a flash.

Since Sprocket Rocket essentially delivers a cropped 6cm x 7cm medium format frame (on 35mm film), you don't need to enlarge your shots as much as you would with a "standard" full-frame 35mm camera, so the grain won't be enlarged as much either. The flip side is the larger frame size reduces the number of shots you'll get per roll (half the indicated number; 18 panoramas on a 36 exposure film), so Sprocket Rocket isn't the most economical 35mm camera. That's a small price to pay though: few plastic cameras can achieve the same result, and even fewer look so darned sexy doing it!

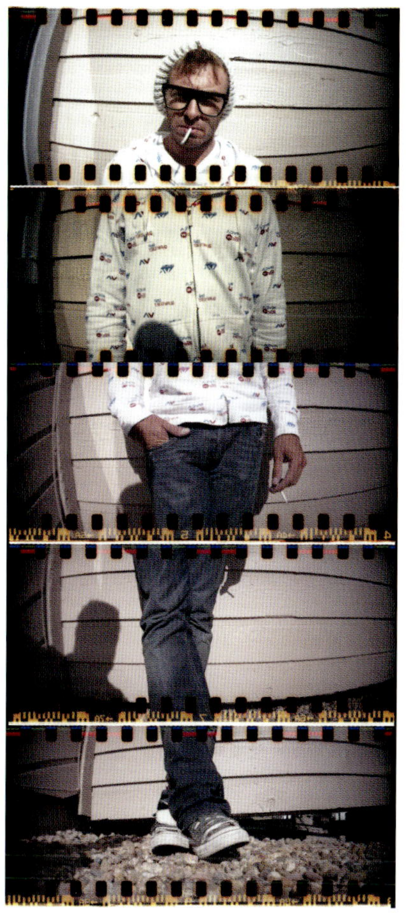

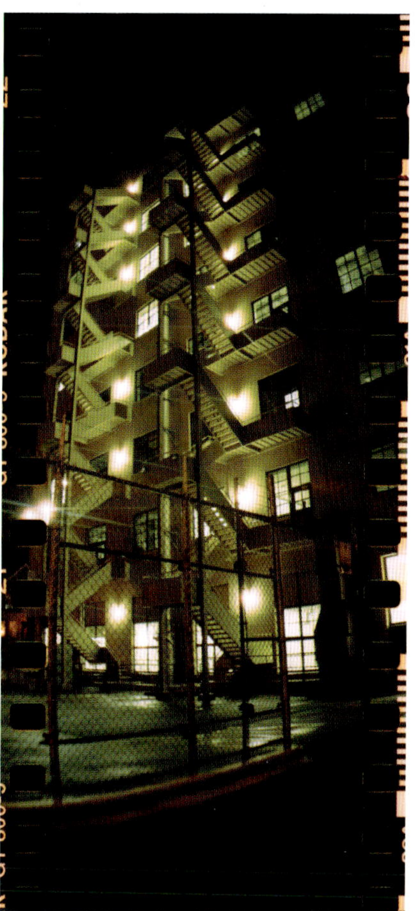

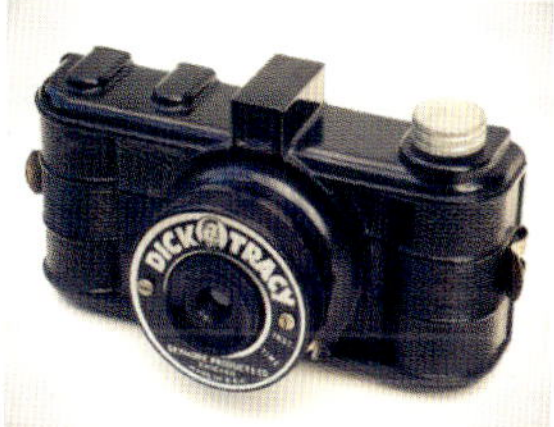

Roots

Although Lomography doesn't reference it directly, Sprocket Rocket bears an uncanny resemblance to a range of cameras based on a 1938 design patent by Jack Galter. As camera collector and historian John Kratz notes: "That same camera design was used for cameras with at least 20 different names, made by at least half as many 'companies' (the reality is that most of the manufacturers that made those cameras were one and the same). I usually refer to it, however, as the 'Dick Tracy' camera, because the Dick Tracy was only made with that body style, and was quite possibly the most popular camera of that design."

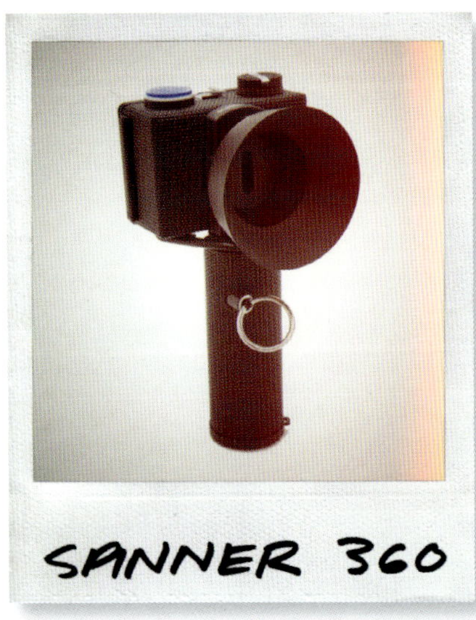

CAMERA:	Spinner 360
MANUFACTURER:	Lomography
FILM TYPE:	35mm
IMAGE FORMAT:	Up to 8 panoramas on a 36-exposure film (full 360-degree shots)
LENS:	25mm
FOCUS:	Fixed (1m–Infinity)
APERTURES:	Cloudy (f/8), Sunny (f/16)
SHUTTER SPEEDS:	Between 1/250 sec. and 1/125 sec.
OTHER FEATURES:	Built-in spirit level Pull-cord shutter release Tripod mount

Lomography's Spinner 360 takes panoramic photography to its natural conclusion by allowing you to shoot full 360-degree shots of your surroundings. It achieves this by "spinning" the camera (the clue's in the name!) on top of the vertical handgrip. As the camera spins, the film inside is pulled past a slit behind the lens, and this slit delivers a continuous exposure.

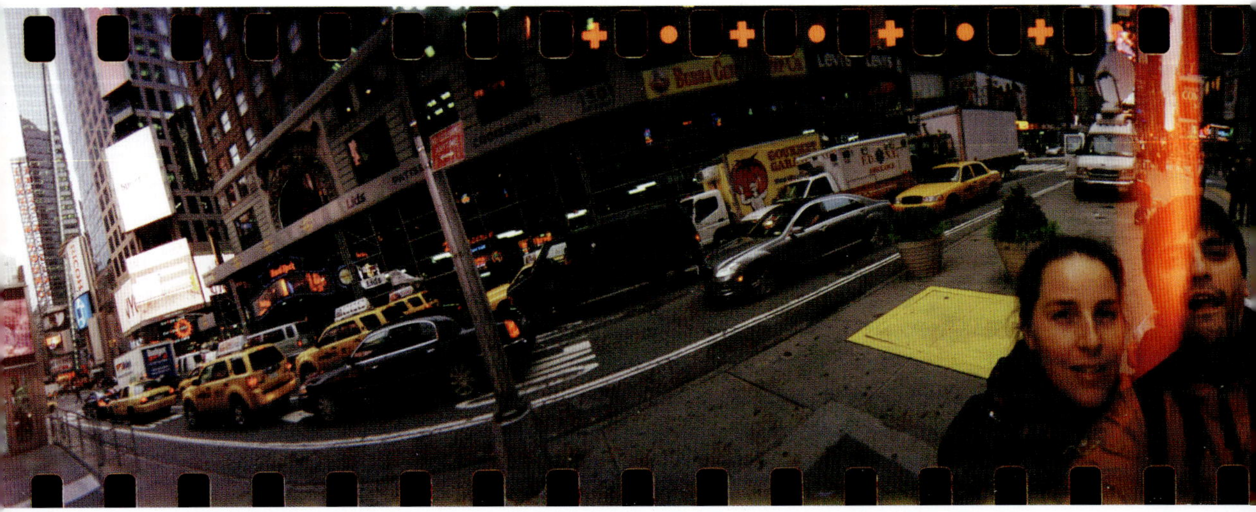

To get the camera spinning you use the pull-cord in the handgrip, rather than a traditional shutter-release button, and this cord also determines the angle covered by the exposure. If you pull the cord out fully (a little over 3 inches/8cm) you'll be rewarded with a full 360-degree shot, but pulling it out to a lesser extent reduces the camera's spin. It's not an exact science though, and most times it's easiest to go for the full rotation. If you do, you'll get 8 shots before a 36 exposure film is finished so it pays to pick your shots carefully.

If you're handholding the Spinner you'll find it gives a slight "kick" as it starts to spin, because the camera needs to get up to speed instantly to avoid uneven exposures. You'll also find that you appear in every shot if you're holding the camera in front of you, which is great for some shots, but there might be times when a self-portrait isn't necessary. If that's the case, holding the camera above your head will keep you out of the shot, but this isn't conducive to level shots so you may consider using a tripod, even if this goes against the plastic camera ethos of shooting spontaneously.

For a more refined experience, Lomography has produced the "Motorizer," which replaces the handgrip and pull-cord with an electric motor to spin the camera, and a remote release to trigger it. It's not low-cost option, but transforms the Spinner into a serious panoramic proposition.

CAMERA: Lomography Spinner 360
FILM: Unknown
EXPOSURE: 360-degree spin @ f/8

Unless you hold the Spinner 360 above your head, you're guaranteed to be in shot—but that's great for those "look where I've been" moments.

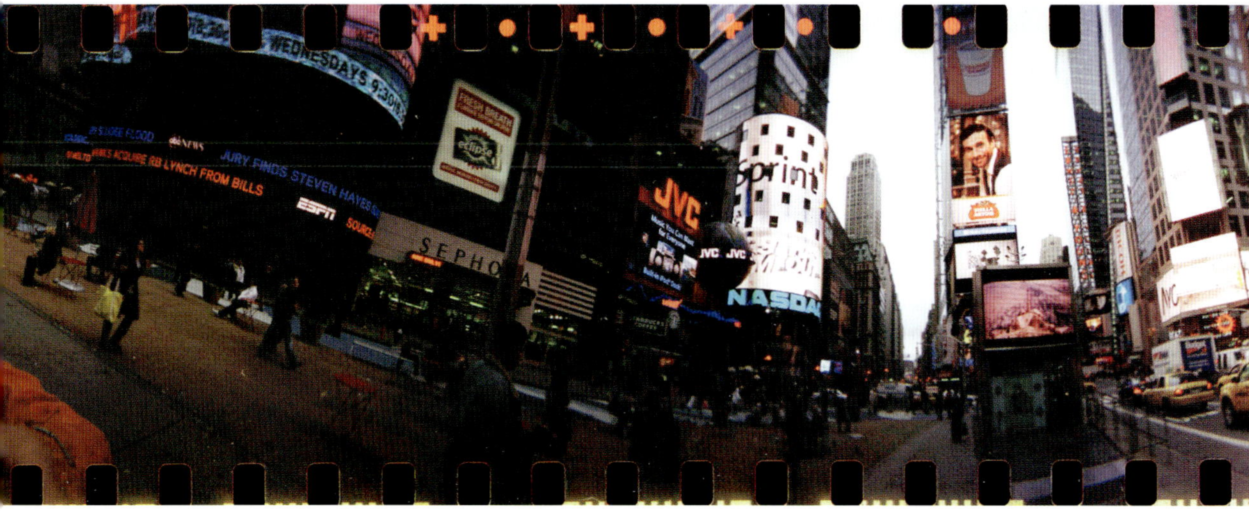

Technique: Redscale

Redscale photography demands you shoot film, as the emulsion itself is the very essence of this lo-fi technique. This is because redscale images are produced by photographing through the back of a color film, so the light passes through the emulsion's red-sensitive layer first: this is what creates the distinctive "red" look (although the results can actually vary from magenta/blue through to strong reds/yellows).

What this means is that your film needs to be loaded back-to-front in your camera, so the emulsion is facing away from the lens. There are two ways you can achieve this, but the easiest is to use a commercial redscale film such as Lomography's Redscale (available in both 35mm and 120 formats) or Rollei's Redbird or Nightbird (35mm only). If you are using any of these films you simply load your camera as you would with a "normal" film and start shooting. The alternative to buying redscale film is to "roll your own," which requires access to a darkroom, delivers unpredictable results, and demands experimentation to determine the right exposure settings. It's a hassle, but the flip side is you can use a much wider range of emulsions (providing different redscale "looks") and it's also going to be cheaper.

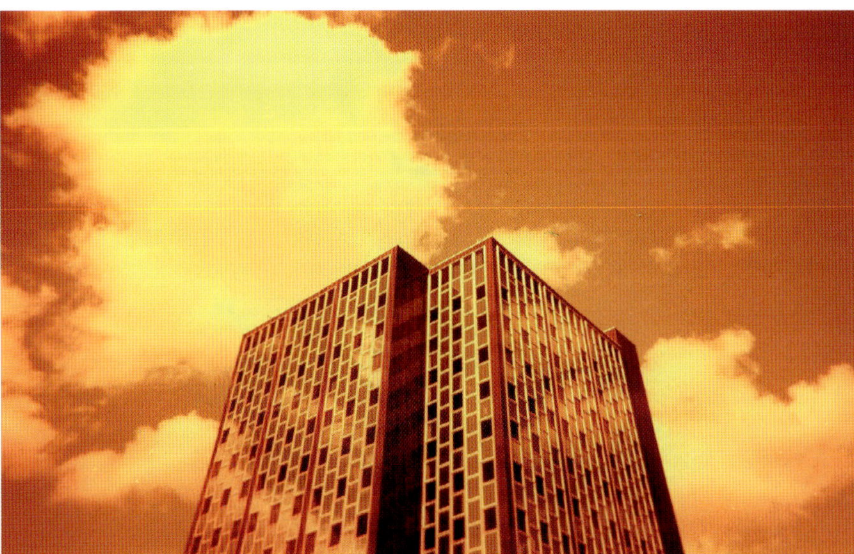

CAMERA: Snap Snap
FILM: Lomography Redscale 100
EXPOSURE: Unrecorded

Lomography's ready-rolled Redscale film can transform your subject into rich shades of red, orange, and yellow.

Roll your own 35mm redscale film

You will need:

1 x unexposed 35mm color film (ISO 400 negative film is ideal for most fixed-exposure plastic cameras)
1 x 35mm "scrap" film (the cheaper the better)
Scissors
Adhesive tape
Darkroom (or changing bag)

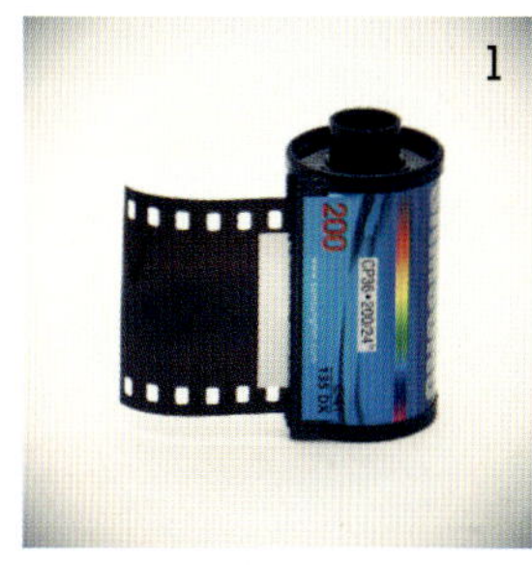

1. Take your scrap roll of film and pull all of the film out of the cassette, (although not so hard that you rip it off the spool inside). Cut the film, leaving an inch or two sticking out of the cassette.

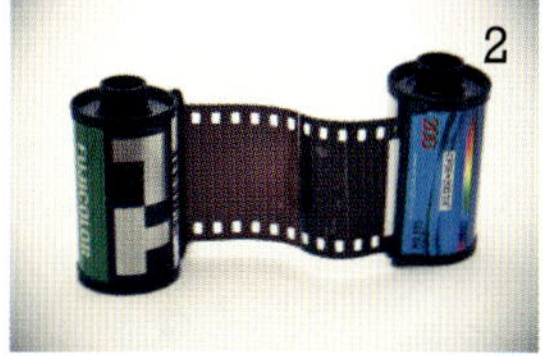

2. Trim the end of your unexposed color film to remove the "leader" and use adhesive tape to attach it to the stub sticking out of the scrap cassette. Make sure that the emulsion of the film is facing in the opposite direction to the emulsion of the stub.

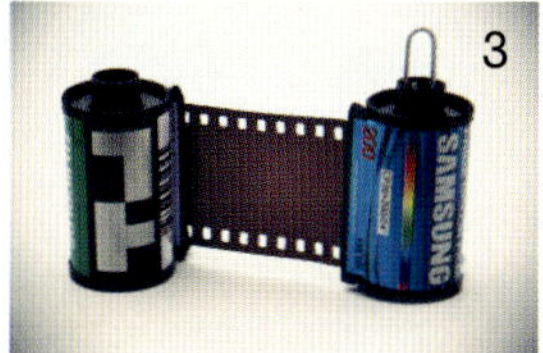

3. IN TOTAL DARKNESS (a darkroom or changing bag), wind the unexposed film into your scrap cassette—a paperclip can be used as a crude "winder" to make the process easier. When the film is fully wound onto the new spool, cut it, leaving a small piece outside the cassette. You have now rolled your redscale film.

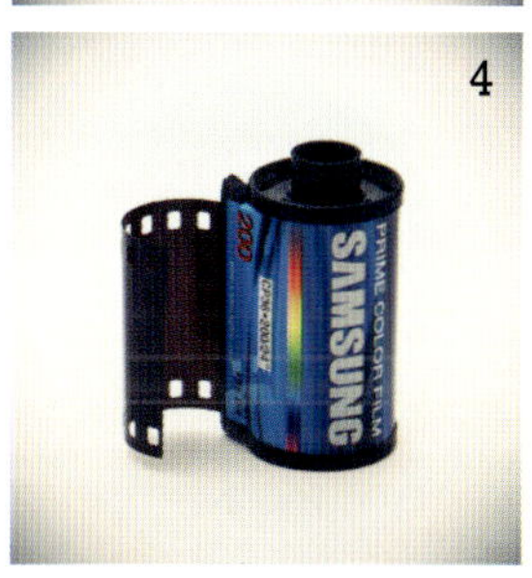

4. Back in the light, trim the end of your redscale film so it is roughly the same shape as a standard film leader and load it into your chosen camera.

You can shoot as normal, but it is a good idea to bracket your shots if your camera allows it, as the exposure can affect the color of your redscale images. This isn't essential. Once the roll's finished, you can process it as normal, but be sure to explain to the lab why your film's back to front, and perhaps mention that your shots might look a bit red...

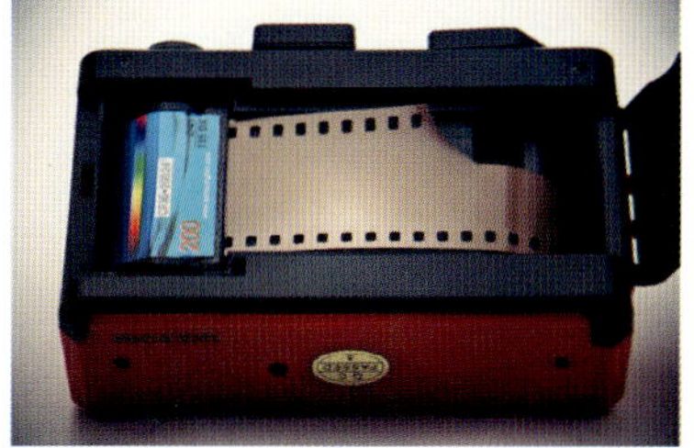

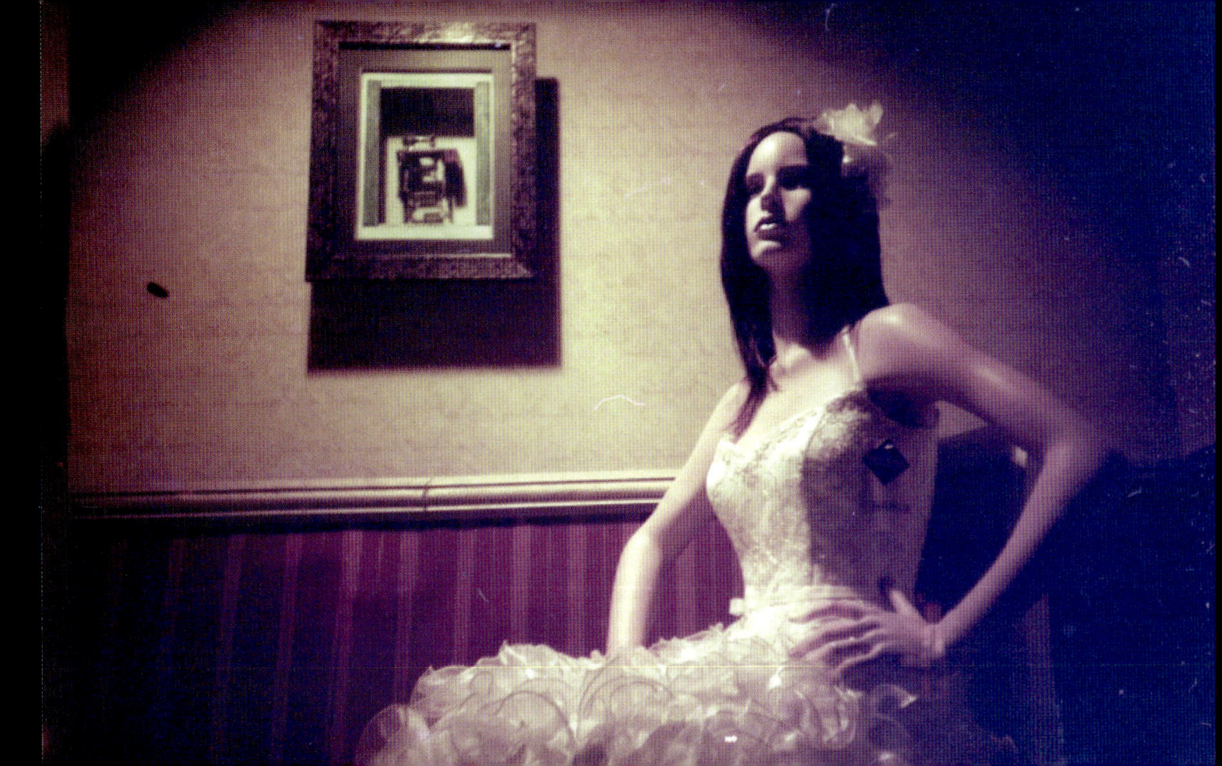

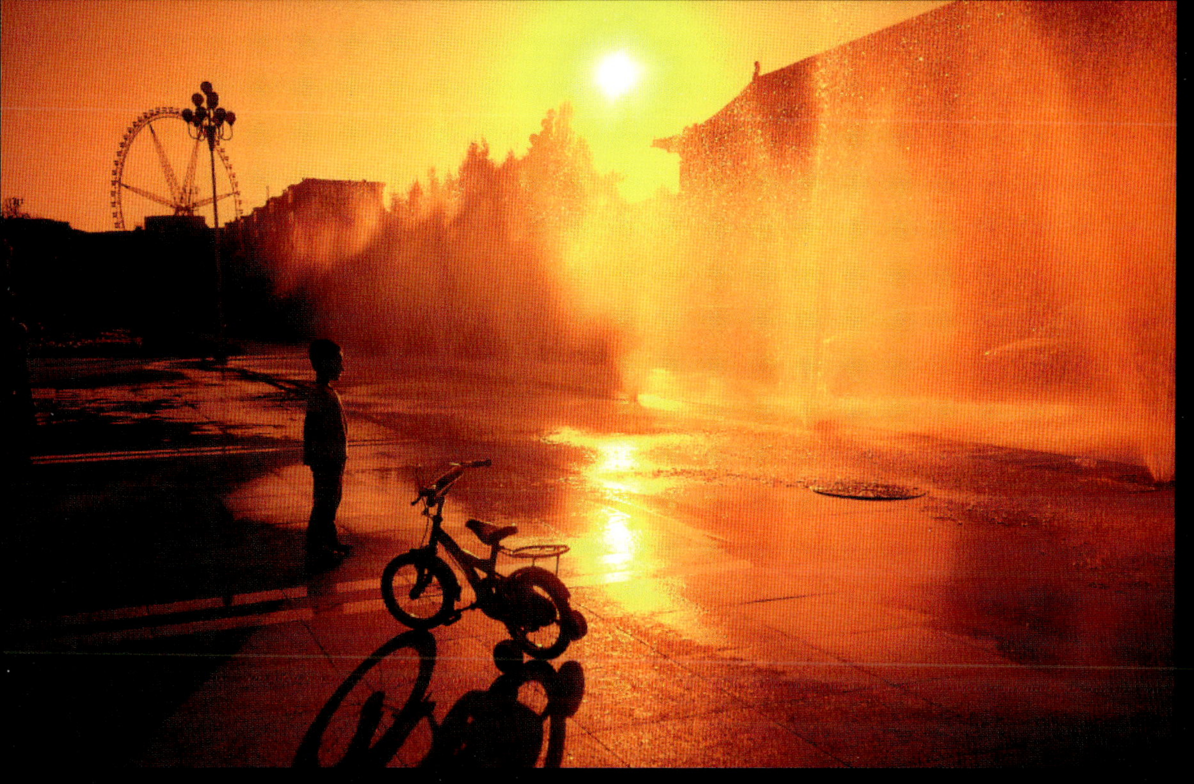

CAMERA: LOMO LC-A
FILM: Lomography Redscale XR 50-200
EXPOSURE: Unrecorded

Silhouettes and bold graphic shapes make great redscale
subjects. As with black and white photography tone,
rather than color, becomes an important factor.

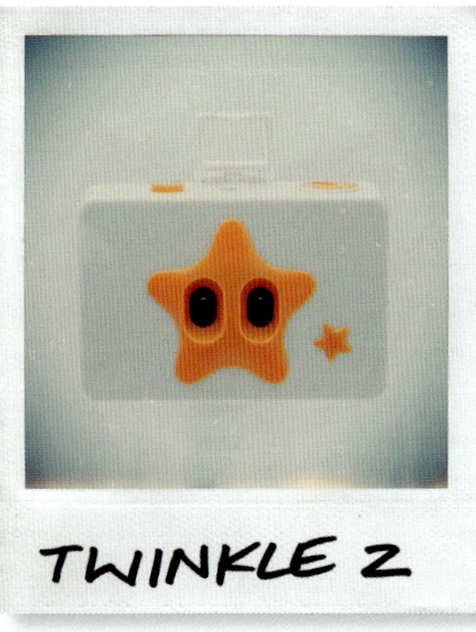

CAMERA:	Twinkle 2
MANUFACTURER:	Unknown
FILM TYPE:	35mm
IMAGE FORMAT:	2 images on 36mm x 24mm frame
LENS:	28mm (x2)
FOCUS:	Fixed (1m–Infinity)
APERTURE:	f/8
SHUTTER SPEED:	1/100 sec.

Along with the Robot 3 and Action 4 that appear later in this chapter, the Twinkle 2 forms part of a trio of cameras that are commonly referred to as "Disderi" cameras. This is more a reference to French photographer André-Adolphe-Eugène Disdéri who pioneered multilens photography in the 1850s than it is to any specific manufacturer—certainly the camera (and it's packaging) doesn't bear a maker's name. As with the other Disderi cameras, the Twinkle 2 is available in either a black or white plastic body, with the "cutesy" star motif on the front (and other details) picked out in a contrasting green, yellow, orange, pink, or blue. You can even have it with a waterproof housing if you want to exploit its capabilities underwater.

So what exactly does the Twinkle 2 do? Well, ostensibly, it's a twin-lens "action" camera that sticks two half-frame images side-by-side on a single 35mm frame. However, unlike the Holga TIM it does this with a single press of the shutter-release button, at which point a rotating shutter behind the 28mm lenses records two moments in time separated by a fraction of a second.

As this suggests, the Twinkle 2 is at its most effective when its dual lenses are turned on moving subjects. To keep things simple there is nothing to detract you from recording a "perfect" moment (or should that be "perfect moments"), as the shutter speed, aperture, and focus are all fixed. Even framing your images isn't going to be a concern as the single viewfinder frame on the top of the camera is of no practical use at all—the only option is to point, shoot, and hope your image works out!

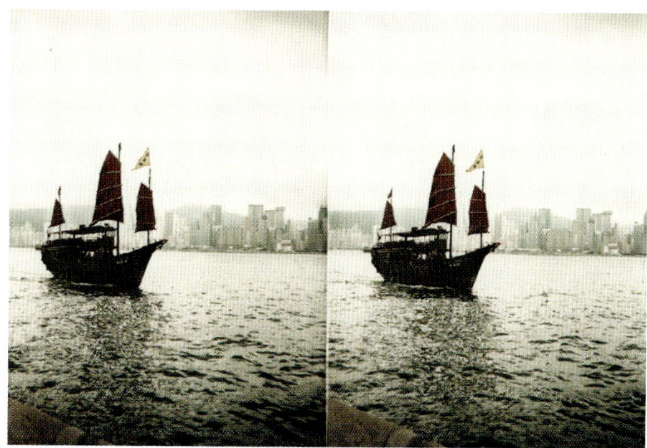

CAMERA: Twinkle 2
FILM: Unknown
EXPOSURE: 1/100sec @ f/8

The Twinkle 2 is essentially a half-frame "action camera," placing two images side-by-side in the same frame.

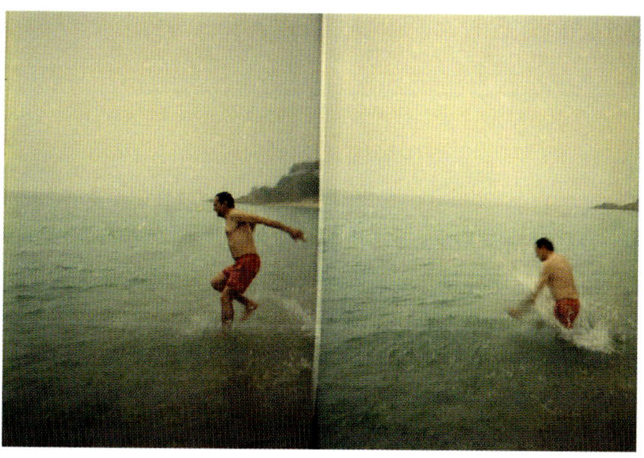

CAMERA: Twinkle 2
FILM: Unknown
EXPOSURE: 1/100sec @ f/8

The Twinkle 2 records two moments in time, separated by a split-second.

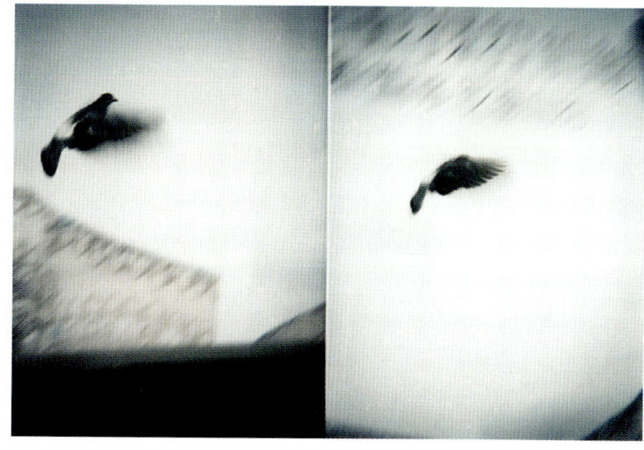

CAMERA: Twinkle 2
FILM: Unknown (expired)
EXPOSURE: 1/100sec @ f/8

The expired film loaded in the Twinkle 2 gives this shot a distinctly "old" look.

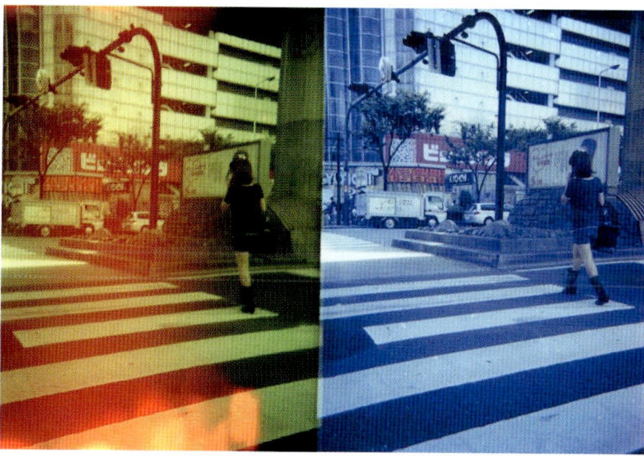

CAMERA: Twinkle 2
FILM: Unknown
EXPOSURE: 1/100sec @ f/8

Placing a piece of colored acetate over one of the lenses can create an effective color contrast.

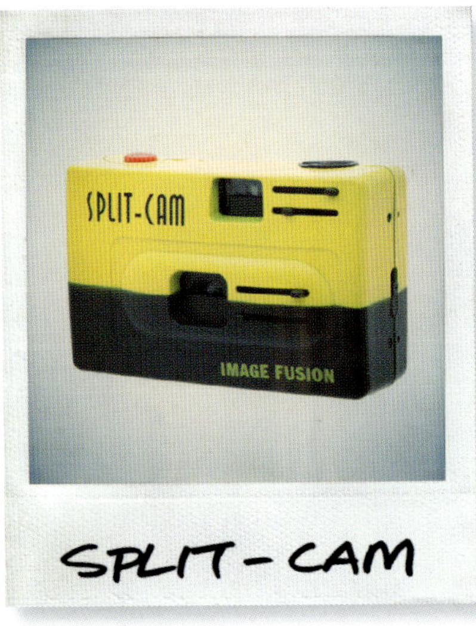

CAMERA:	Split-Cam
MANUFACTURER:	Accoutrements
FILM TYPE:	35mm
IMAGE FORMATS:	One or two images on 36mm x 24mm frame
LENS:	Focal length not given
FOCUS:	Fixed (range not given)
APERTURE:	Fixed (f-stop not given)
SHUTTER SPEED:	Fixed (duration not given)

The Split-Cam comes from the US company Accoutrements, creators of the Yodelling Pickle and Bacon Bandages amongst other gift ideas. Out of its packaging, it's immediately clear that this is a camera that also trades on novelty value rather than quality: the chunky 35mm compact camera is cheap looking, and even cheaper feeling, but don't let that put you off.

The basic premise of the Split-Cam is that you mask off half of the image (top or bottom) using sliders over the lens and viewfinder. You then shoot the "revealed" area, switch the sliders round, and shoot the other half. The result is two images on the same 35mm film frame—so you could, for example, have one person's legs attached to another person's torso. At least that's the theory. In practice, it's a frustratingly difficult process and trying to create any sort of "realistic" join is going to be a futile exercise: the masking and framing just isn't precise enough.

Again, don't let this deter you though, as the Split-Cam's shutter reset (multiple exposure) button can be used to facilitate striking full-frame multiple exposures, and with a bit of consideration it's possible to use the top and bottom masks to produce fantastic images as shown here.

You just have to accept that the process isn't "point and shoot" and you'll need to think carefully about what effect you hope to achieve. This makes the Split-Cam a challenging camera, for sure, but with a little perseverance it can be made to deliver some very unique visions.

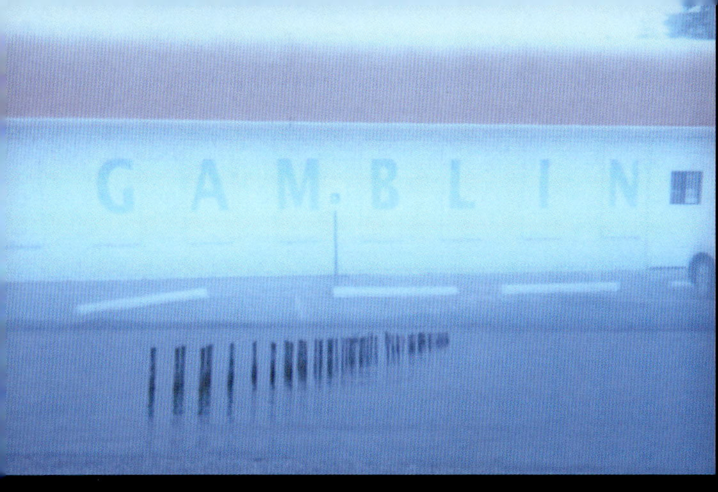

CAMERA: Split-Cam
FILM: Kodak Gold 400
EXPOSURE: Unknown

Split-Cam is a hard camera to master, but capable of creating unique images in skilled hands.

CAMERA: Split-Cam
FILM: Unknown
EXPOSURE: Unknown

Getting the best from your Split-Cam requires a small amount of planning and a whole heap of patience.

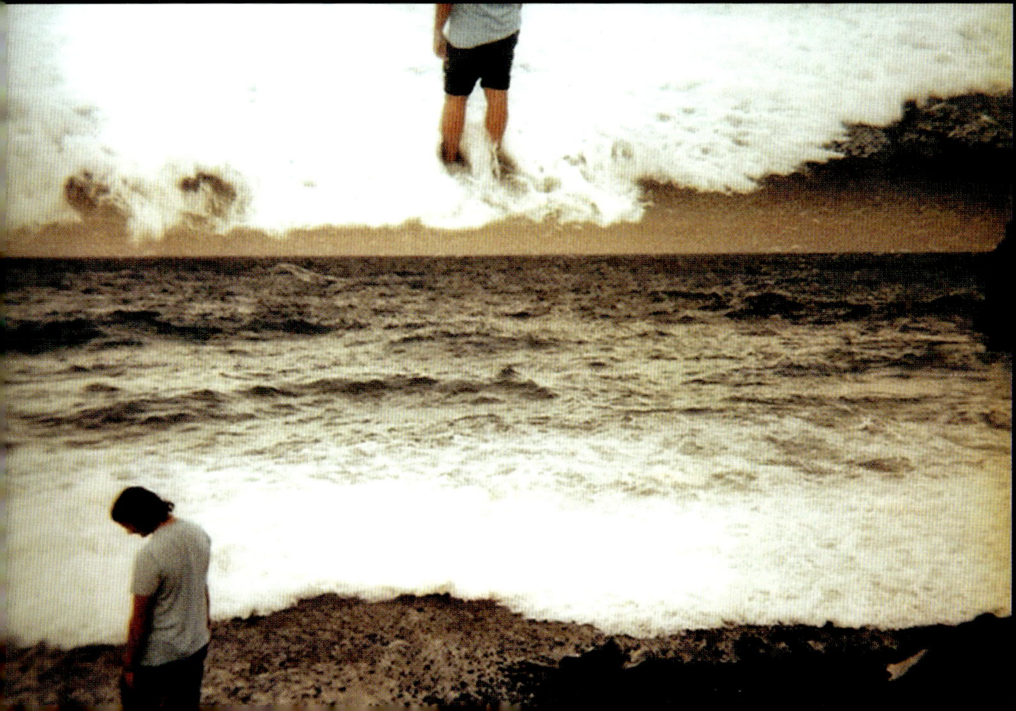

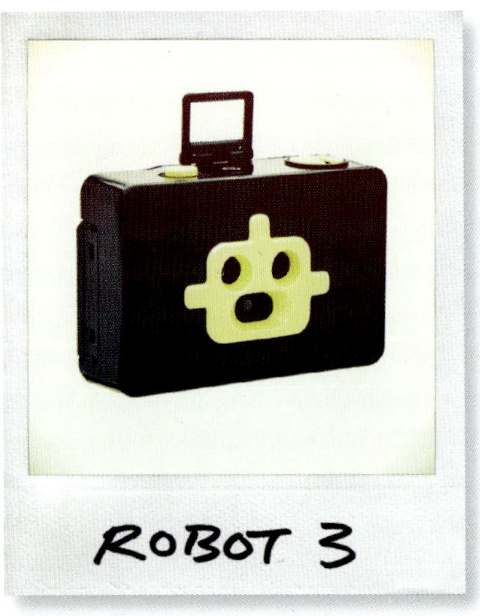

CAMERA: Robot 3
MANUFACTURER: Unknown
FILM TYPE: 35mm
IMAGE FORMAT: 3 images on 36mm x 24mm frame
LENS: 28mm (x3)
FOCUS: Fixed (1m–Infinity)
APERTURE: f/8
SHUTTER SPEED: 1/100 sec.

As with Twinkle 2, Robot 3 is a pure plastic point-and-shooter, available in a range of colors (with or without a waterproof housing) and at a bargain-basement price. There's no control over the exposure beyond choosing film speed, although with a fixed aperture of f/8 and shutter speed of 1/100 sec. even this is determined for you: ISO 400 is often the best choice unless you're shooting outdoors under bright sun.

However, while Twinkle 2 delivers two regular rectangular images per 35mm frame, Robot 3 creates a trio of exposures in the same space. These are not neat rectangles, as Robot 3 produces one elongated panoramic image with its lower lens, and two smaller, curve-topped images below. A rotating shutter reveals each of the camera's 28mm lenses in turn: the lower lens (the robot's "mouth") fires first, and then the two upper lenses (the "eyes"). This creates a look described as "the pages of an open book" and is the single most compelling reason why you should definitely add a Robot 3 to your collection.

Which lens?

Rather than expose all three lenses at once, try covering the "mouth" and shooting your film with just the Robot 3's "eyes." When you get to the end of the roll, reload the film, cover the eyes, open the mouth, and shoot the roll again. Assuming you have started shooting your film from roughly the same place second time round (marking the film and the camera can help) the result will be two distinctly different scenes occupying the same frame. This also works with other multilens cameras.

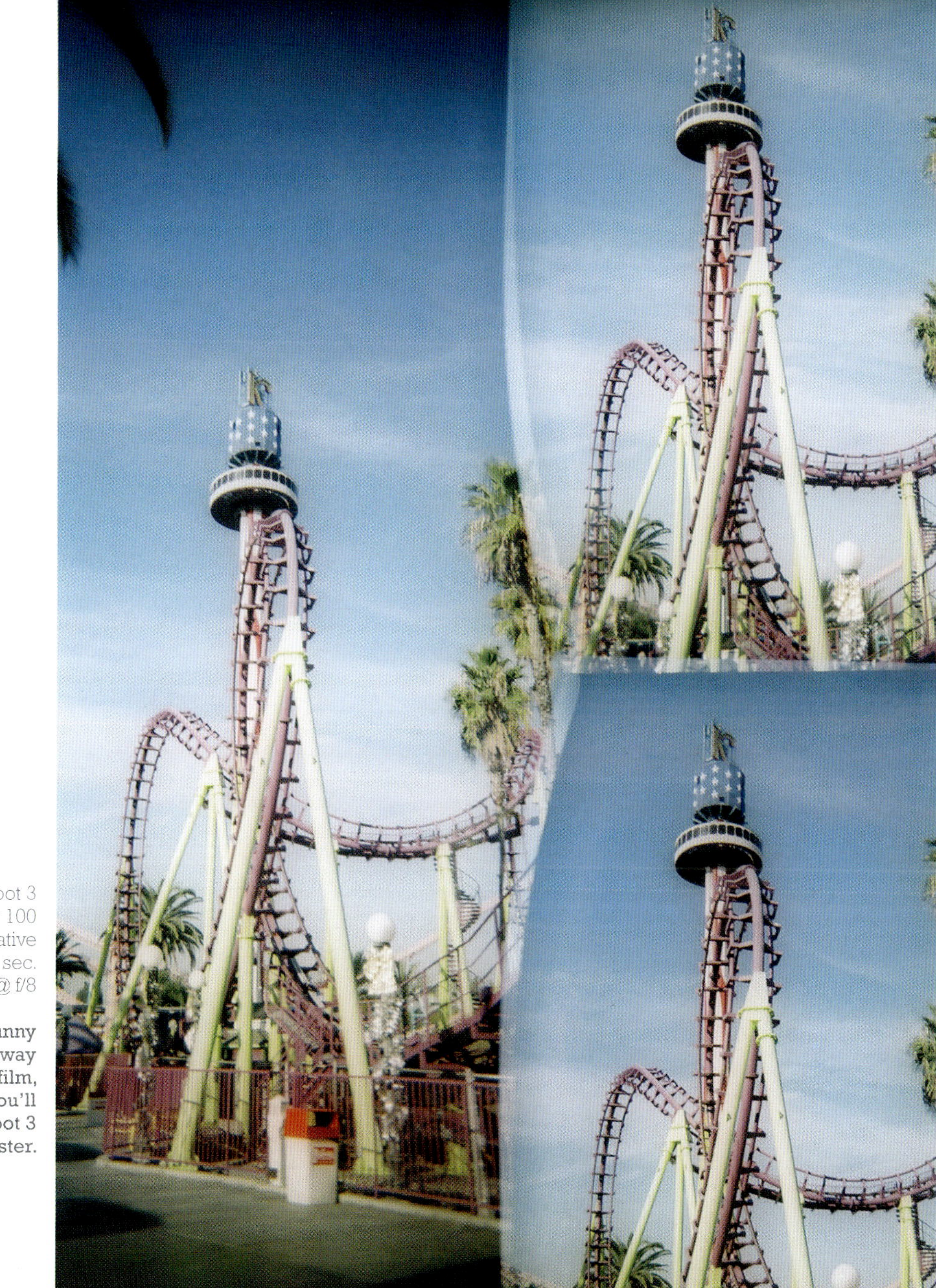

CAMERA: Robot 3
FILM: Lomography 100
color negative
EXPOSURE: 1/100 sec.
@ f/8

On a bright and sunny day you can get away with using ISO 100 film, but most times you'll need to load a Robot 3 with something faster.

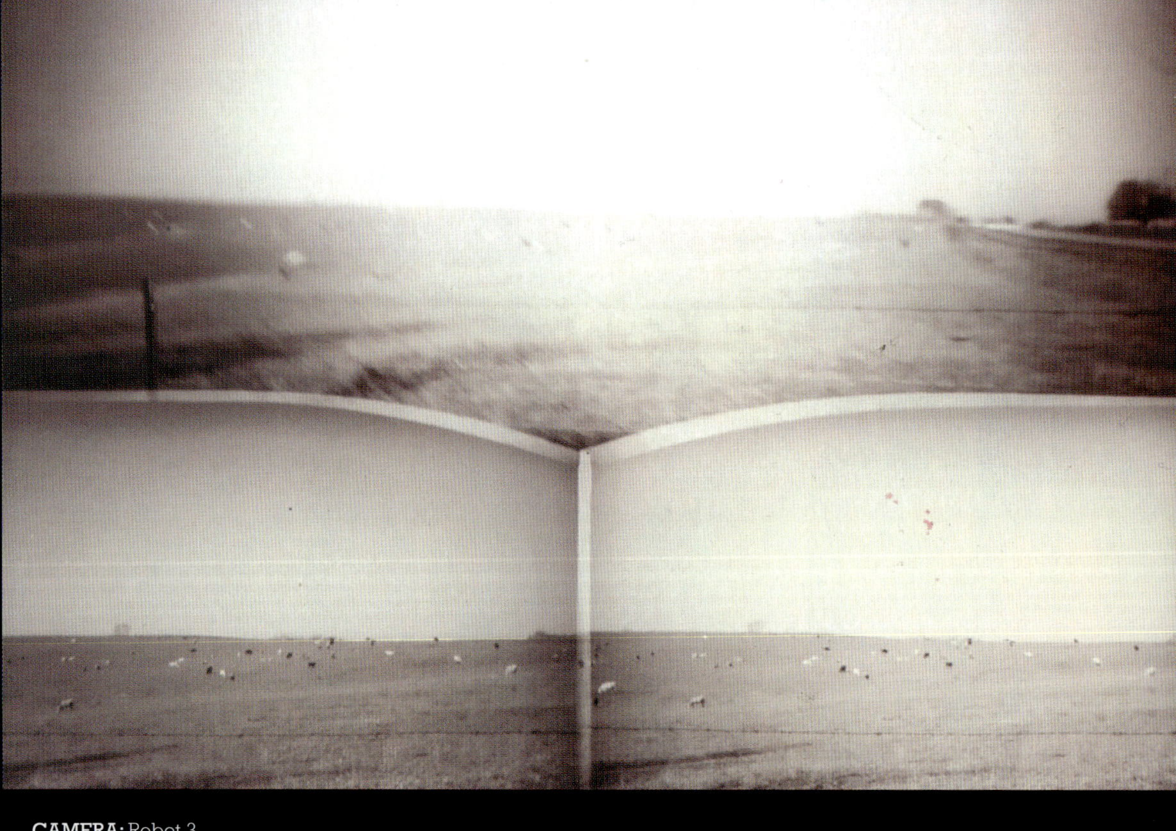

CAMERA: Robot 3
FILM: Kodak BW400CN

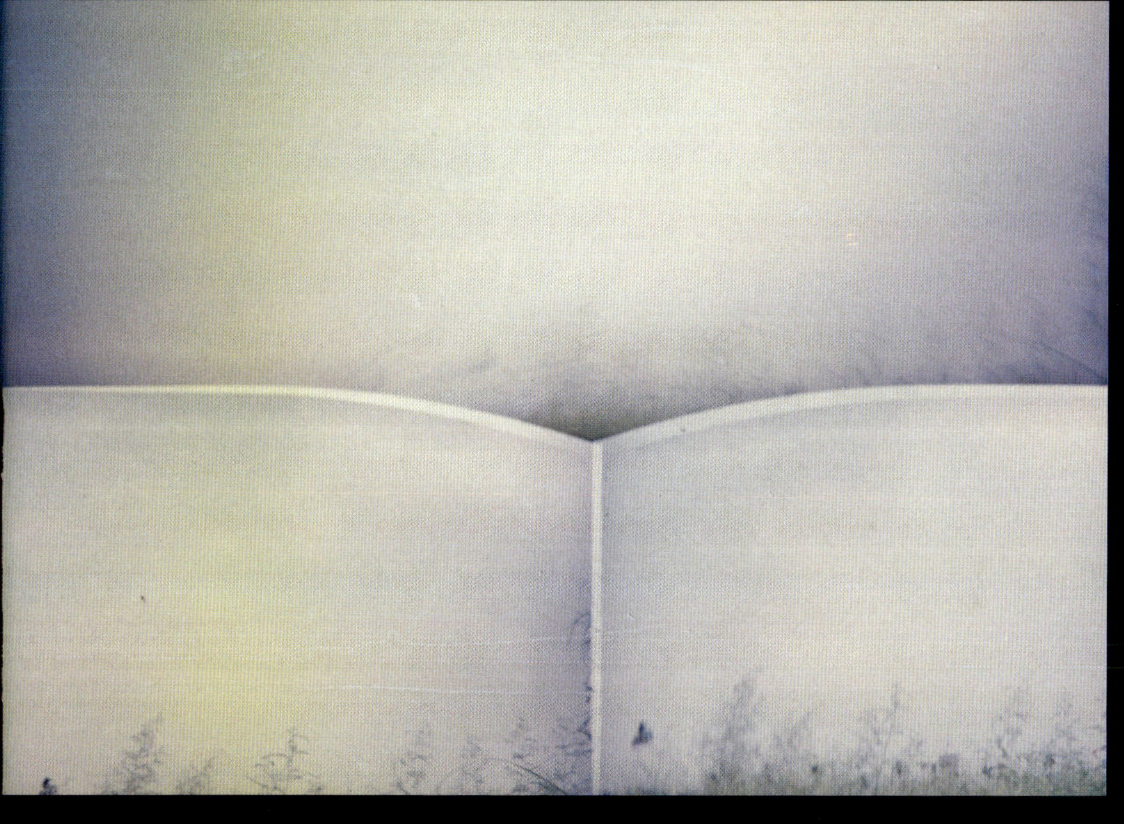

CAMERA: Robot 3
FILM: Unknown
EXPOSURE: 1/100 sec. @ f/8

Blur, vignetting, and low contrast: defects to some
people, but they can also result in sublime images.

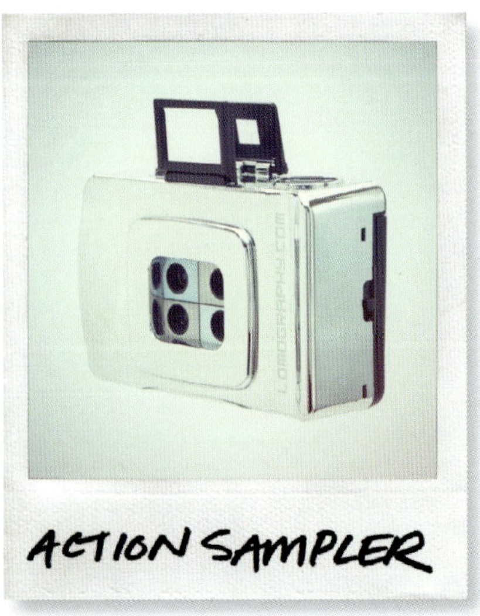

ACTION SAMPLER

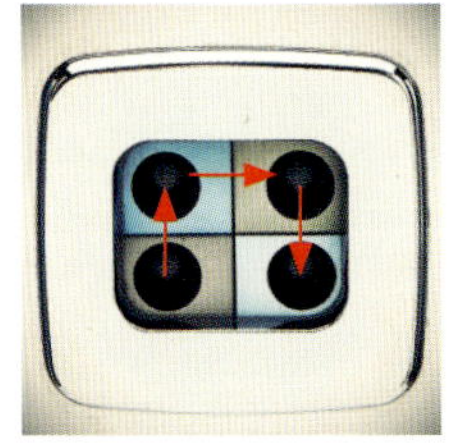

The Actionsampler's lenses fire sequentially in a clockwise direction, starting with the bottom left lens as you look at the front of the camera.

CAMERA:	Actionsampler
MANUFACTURER:	Lomography
FILM TYPE:	35mm
IMAGE FORMAT:	Four images on 36mm x 24mm frame
LENS:	26mm
FOCUS:	Fixed (1.2m–Infinity)
APERTURE:	Fixed (f-stop not given)
SHUTTER SPEED:	4 photos in 1/2 sec. (approx. 1/100 sec. per photo)

When it appeared in 1998, Actionsampler was the first product to bear the Lomography name, but it would be a fallacy to describe it as a "new" camera. Similar four-lens cameras had been around since the early 1990s, with models including the Sirius Action Tracker and the Sports 35. However, as the Sports 35 often bore corporate logos, rather than a maker's name, it was seen mainly as a promotional item, rather than a commercial prospect.

This all changed when Lomography began to distribute Actionsampler. It was transformed from a promotional tool into a desirable object, gaining a transparent outer shell and boldly colored internals so its inner machinations (but not the film!) could be seen in all their plastic glory. This was later joined by the chrome-skinned version shown here, and it is testimony to the camera's appeal that both incarnations still appear in the company's multilens lineup.

As the earlier Sports 35 model suggests, the camera was designed to capture action shots, recording four images on a single 35mm film frame. When the shutter-release button is pressed, a circular shutter spins behind the quad lenses, allowing light through each for a motion-freezing 1/100 sec. to create four sequential exposures covering 1/2 sec. of action.

In keeping with Lomography's "shoot from the hip" philosophy, Actionsampler offers zero control. While the flip-up viewing frame will give you a rough idea of what you might capture, it won't give you pin-point accuracy. Instead, just point the camera at the action and press the button—photography doesn't get much

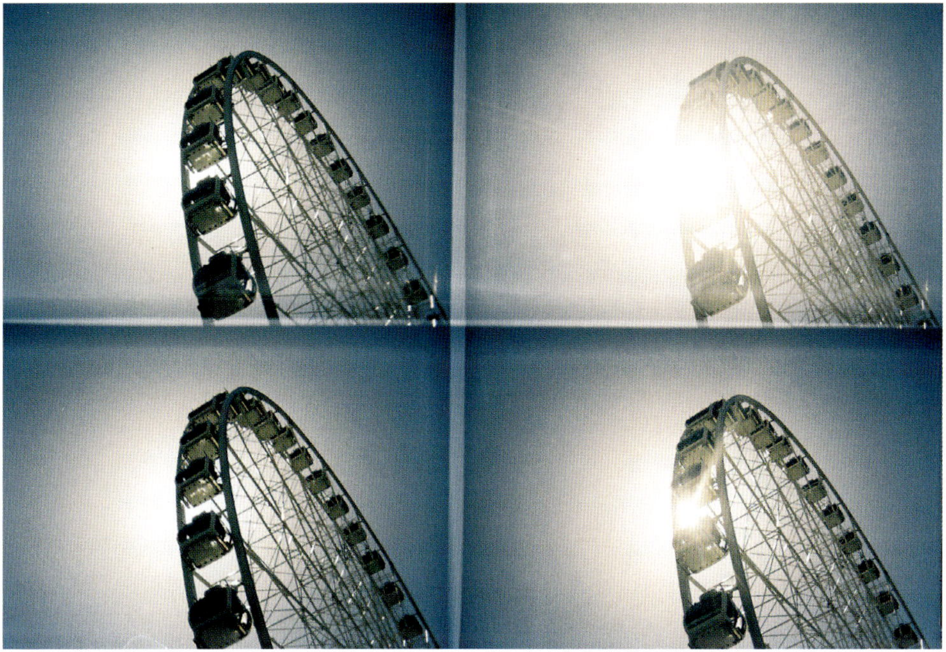

Getting flash

A third model in the Actionsampler lineup is the Actionsampler Flash, featuring a flip-up panel housing four small flashes—one synchronized to each lens. Aside from the flash, the camera is different to the regular Actionsampler in a number of other respects as well; for a start, the camera body is significantly larger and the flip-up viewing frame is replaced by a more traditional (and more useful) optical viewfinder. The most noteworthy difference, however, is the shutter speed, which makes the four sequential exposures in a more leisurely 1 sec. (rather than 1/2 sec.). In turn, each individual exposure is longer, meaning the camera is less suited for motion-freezing action shots unless you use the flash.

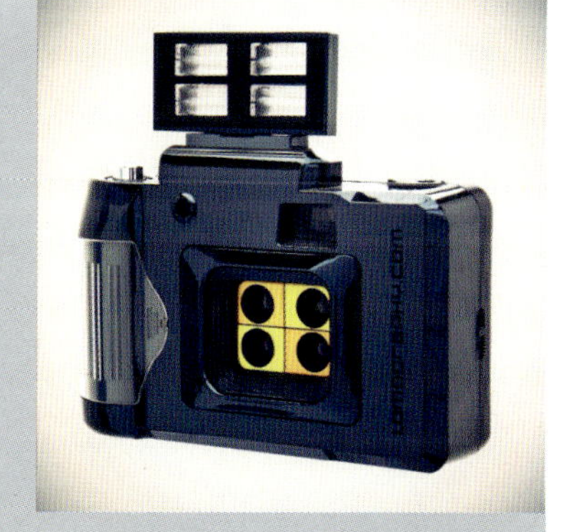

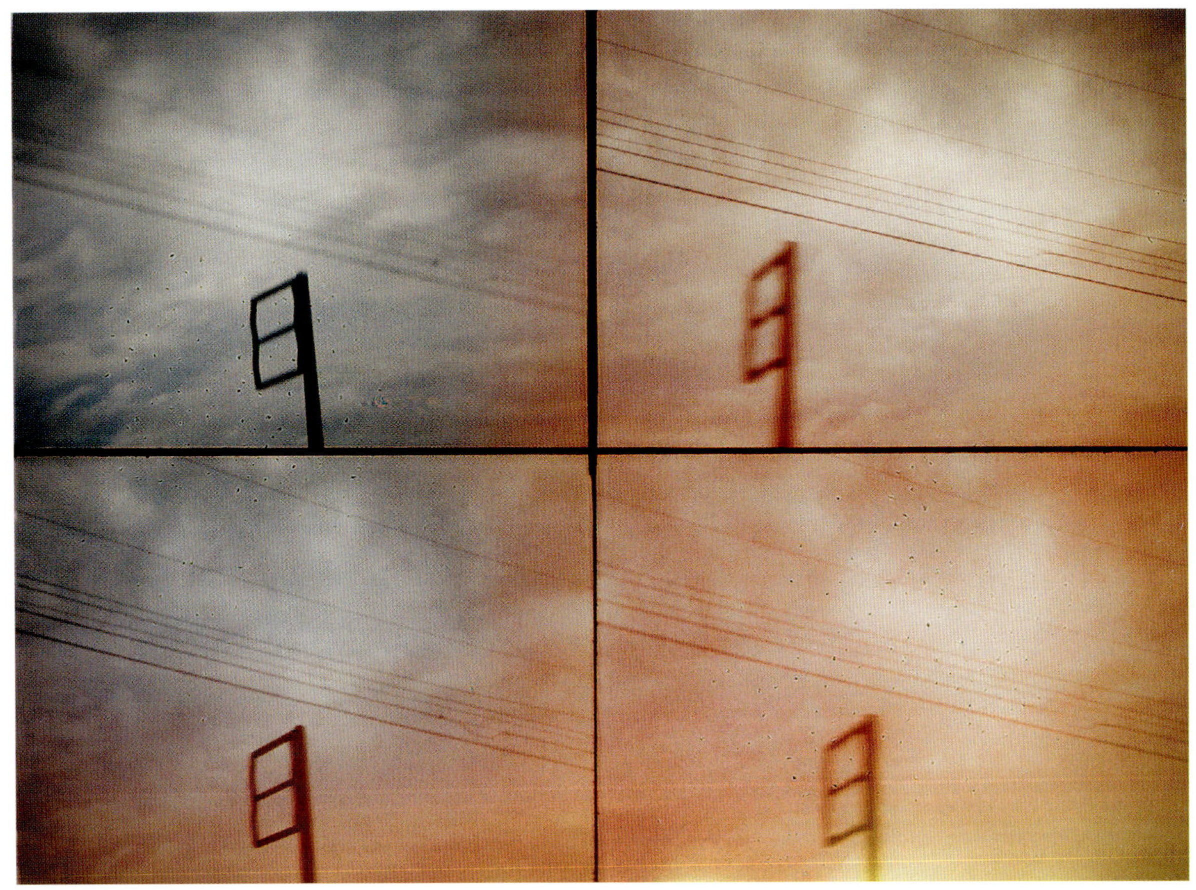

CAMERA: Lomography Actionsampler
FILM: Fuji Superia X-tra 400
EXPOSURE: Unknown

As with most plastic cameras, the Actionsampler is prone
to light leaks, but that just adds to the lo-fi effect.

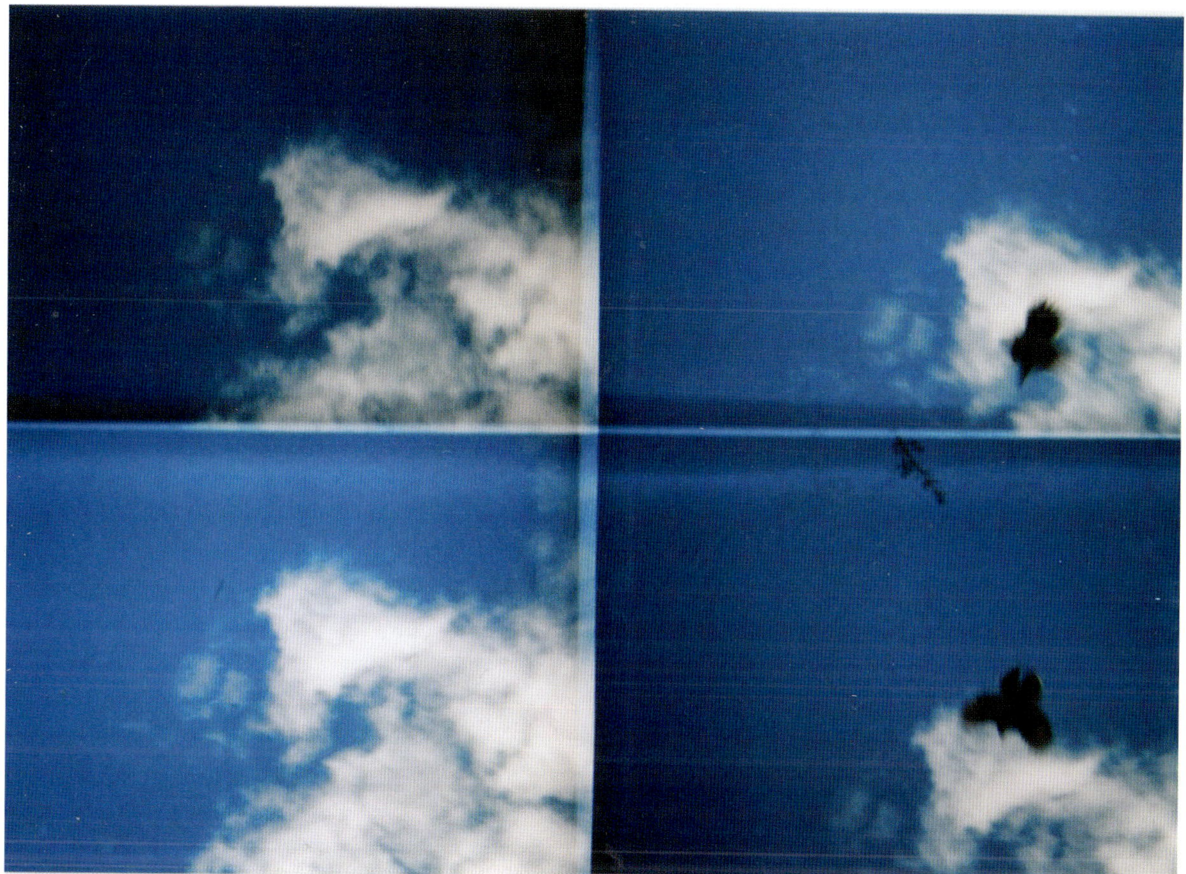

CAMERA: Lomography Actionsampler
FILM: Unknown
EXPOSURE: Unknown

A moving subject makes the perfect target for the
Actionsampler's quad lenses.

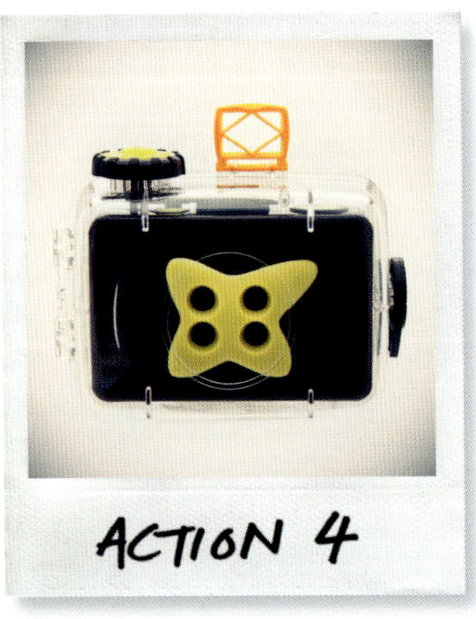

CAMERA:	Action 4
MANUFACTURER:	Unknown
FILM TYPE:	35mm
IMAGE FORMAT:	4 images on 36mm x 24mm frame
LENS:	28mm (x4)
FOCUS:	Fixed
APERTURE:	f/8
SHUTTER SPEED:	1/100 sec.
OTHER FEATURES:	Available with or without waterproof housing

The Action 4 comes from the same anonymous factory in China as the Twinkle 2 (see pages 116–117) and the Robot 3 (see pages 120–123), and delivers a four-shot sequence that is not dissimilar to Lomography's Actionsampler on the previous pages.

Indeed, it's interesting to note the physical similarities between this offering and the Lomography camera: the finger grip "bulge" front right; the design and position of the shutter release, frame counter, and rewind crank up top; and the overall size of the camera. Even the lenses fire in the exact same sequence.

Differences do exist though, and it's fair to say that the finish of the Action 4 isn't quite as "sexy" as that of the Actionsampler, and the single viewing frame is even less practical. The biggest difference, however, is the price: an Action 4 can cost up to 75% less than an Actionsampler, depending on where you get it from and whether you opt for the optional underwater housing (shown) or not.

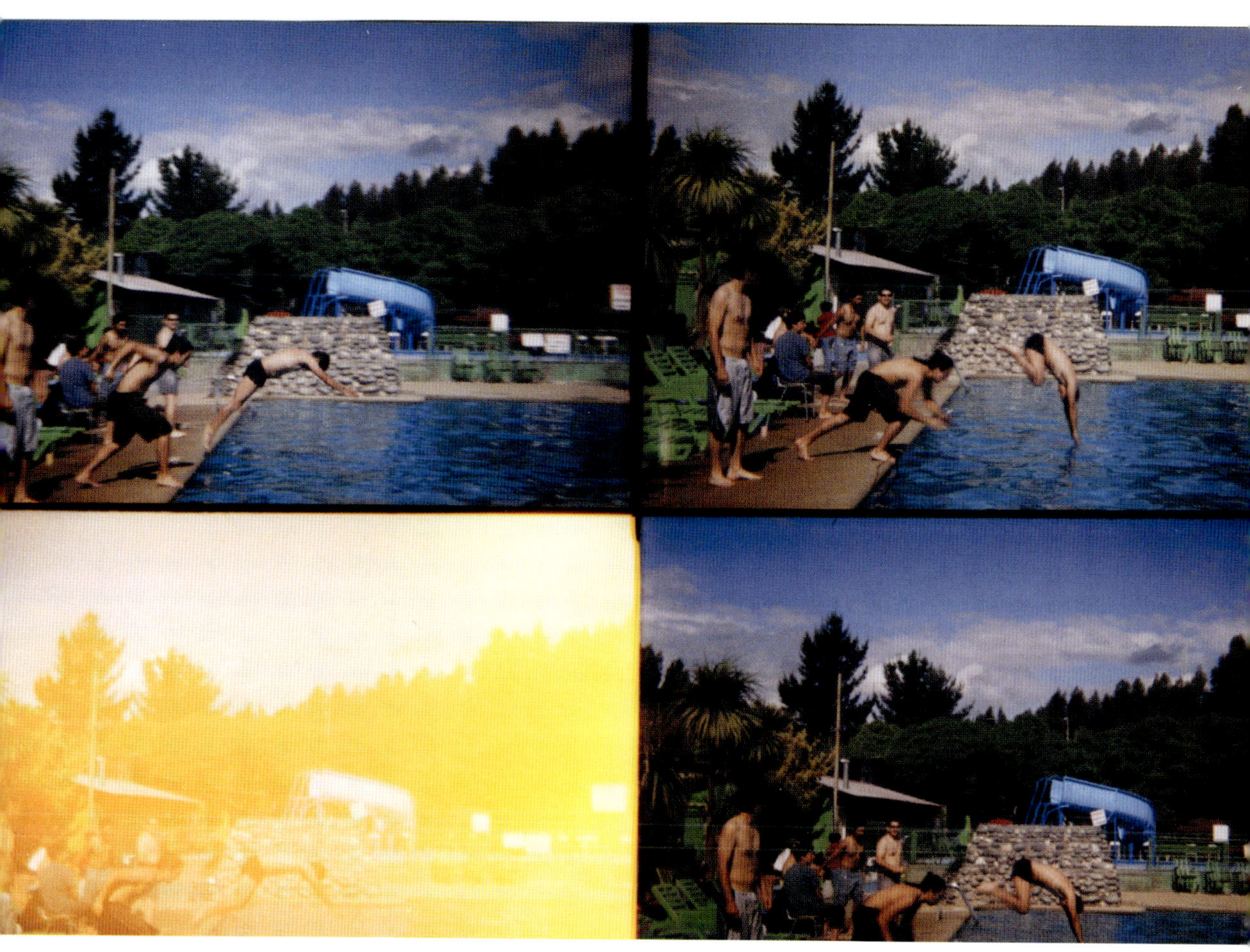

CAMERA: Actionsampler
FILM: Unknown
EXPOSURE: Unknown

Light leaking through one lens/shutter is a fairly
common occurrence with multilens cameras.

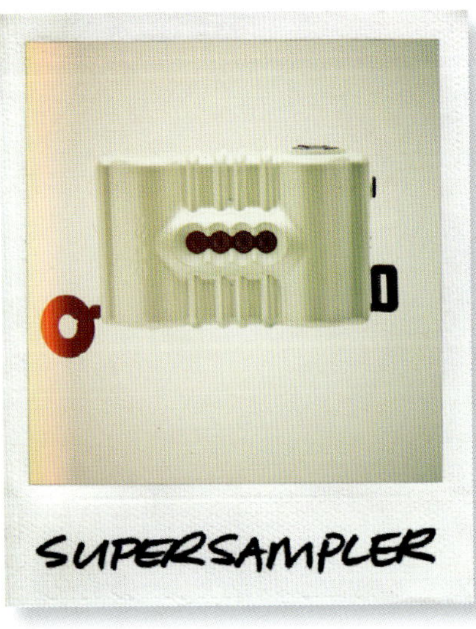

CAMERA:	Supersampler
MANUFACTURER:	Lomography
FILM TYPE:	35mm
IMAGE FORMAT:	Four panoramic images on 36mm x 24mm frame
LENS:	20mm (x4)
FOCUS:	Fixed (0.2m–Infinity)
APERTURE:	Fixed (f-stop not given)
SHUTTER SPEEDS:	4 photos in 2 sec. or 0.2 sec. (approx. 1/100 sec. per photo)
NOTES:	Multiple color options available

While the Actionsampler was the first camera to wear the Lomography name, the Supersampler was the first to be designed, rather than just marketed, by the company. As with the Actionsampler, the Supersampler is a multilens camera producing four sequential exposures on a single 35mm film frame. Yet whereas the Actionsampler arranges its exposures in a 2 x 2 grid, the Supersampler's stacked lenses create four mini-panoramas with each click of the shutter-release button.

Shooting from the hip is once again the order of the day, as the small rubber rectangle that's meant to serve as a viewfinder really is a cosmetic, rather than practical addition. However, unlike the Actionsampler, the Supersampler does provide you with a very small amount of control over your images, with a choice of taking your four-shot sequence across either 2 seconds or 0.2 seconds. This doesn't affect the individual exposure through each lens (this is fixed at roughly 1/100 sec.), but it does determine the overall time across which they are taken, which can have a significant impact on the final sequence if anything's moving in the shot.

Once you've made your exposure, a "rip-cord" at the bottom of the camera serves to wind on the film and ready the shutter for your next shot. It's a unique winding system, and one that is super-quick at moving your film to the next frame. It is also far more tactile than a traditional wind-on lever or notched wheel, but don't be too heavy-handed with it—broken Supersampler winding mechanisms have been widely reported.

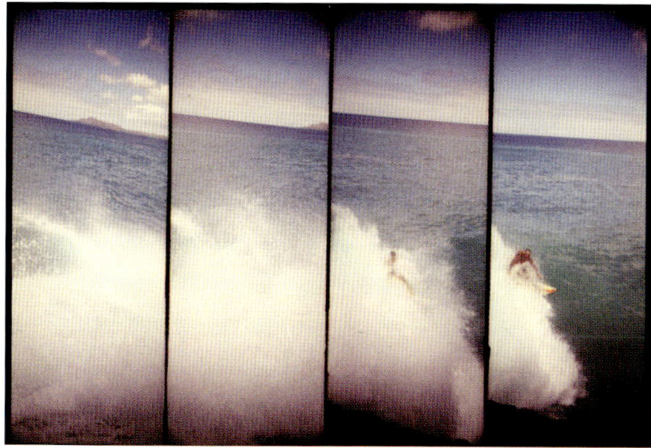

CAMERA: Lomography Supersampler
FILM: Lucky brand ISO 200
EXPOSURE: Unrecorded

A sequence of action shots can make one cool image.

CAMERA: Lomography Supersampler
FILM: Fuji Superia 200
EXPOSURE: 4 shots in 2 sec.

"Camera tossing" a Supersampler: press the shutter-release button, toss the camera into the air and let it capture four wildly different angles.

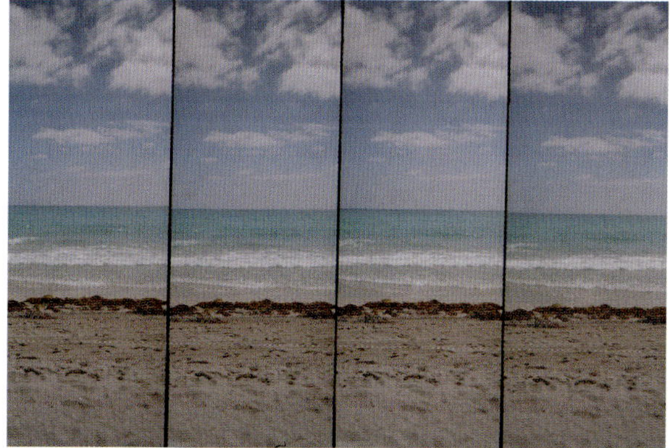

CAMERA: Lomography Supersampler
FILM: Kodak Gold 200
EXPOSURE: 4 shots in 0.2 sec.

Movement can also be subtle. Here the difference between the waves and the clouds separates the individual shots.

Keep it moving!

Movement is where Supersampler (like most sequential multilens cameras) comes into its own, but as well as photographing moving subjects, think about moving the camera while it shoots a sequence. You can even throw the camera into the air for a random, abstract result (a technique known as "camera tossing," see above right), but be sure to catch it when it comes back down—plastic cameras can break easily when they're dropped...

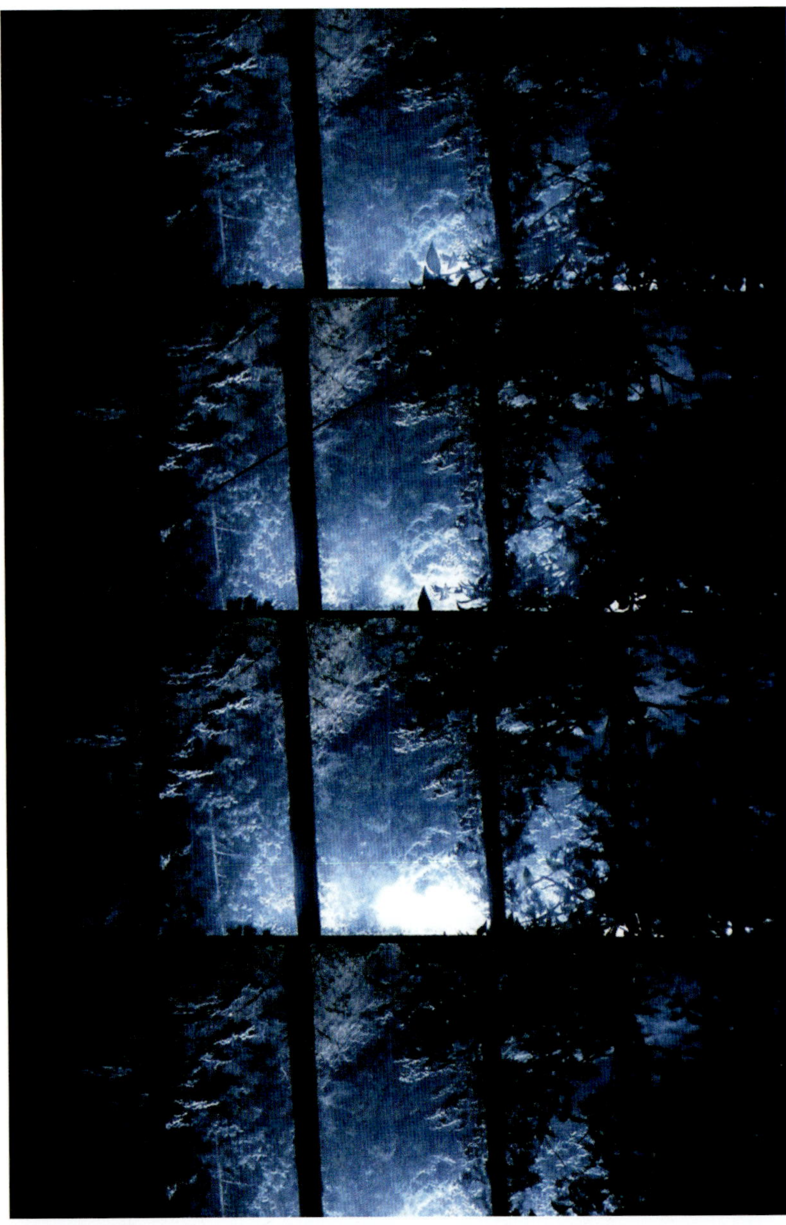

CAMERA: Lomography Supersampler
FILM: Fuji Superia 100
EXPOSURE: Unrecorded

The individual frames from the Supersampler can appear almost like stills from a widescreen movie.

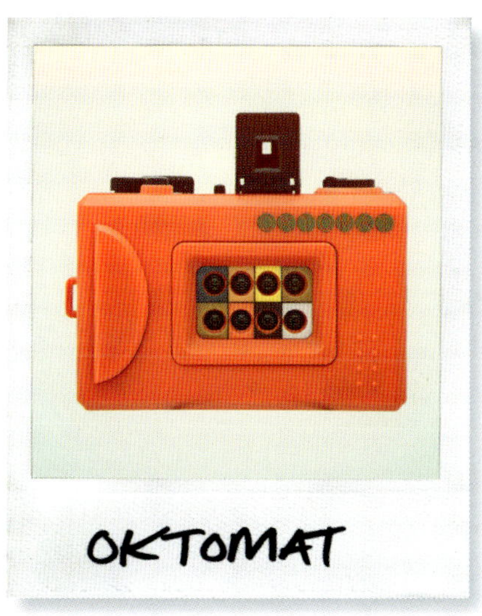

CAMERA:	Lomography Oktomat
FILM TYPE:	35mm
IMAGE FORMAT:	8 images on 36mm x 24mm frame
LENS:	Focal length not given
FOCUS:	Fixed
APERTURE:	f/8
SHUTTER SPEED:	8 photos in 2.5 seconds (1/100 sec. per photo)

If two, three, or even four lenses isn't enough to satisfy your multilens ambitions, then Lomography's Oktomat could be the answer you're looking for, with eight lenses conspiring to deliver multiple mini-images on a single 35mm film frame.

As with the Actionsampler (and Action 4), the Oktomat shoots a sequence of images across a fixed duration, exposing the area behind each lens for 1/100 sec. in an exposure process that lasts about 2.5 seconds overall. The top row of lenses fires first, flicking open and closed from left to right (as you look at the front of the camera) before the bottom row of lenses is fired from right to left to complete the sequence.

However, while the premise is great, many people have found the winding mechanism to be a bit fragile—sometimes you may find an overlapping frame or two (or more) as the film slips in the camera as you wind it on.

If you find yourself the victim of unintentional multiple exposures, don't give up. Take your time when you next load up. After you've loaded the film, tighten the rewind crank (without pressing the rewind button!) to add tension to the film. Then, keep an eye on the rewind crank after you take a shot and wind on—if it rotates in time with you stroking the wind-on lever, your film is advancing as it should. If not, or the movement is jerky, the film isn't moving freely. Try adding tension with the rewind crank, and if that doesn't work, try unloading the film and reloading it (or load a new film). Alternatively you can just shoot and see—who knows, one of your overlapping frames could be a stunner!

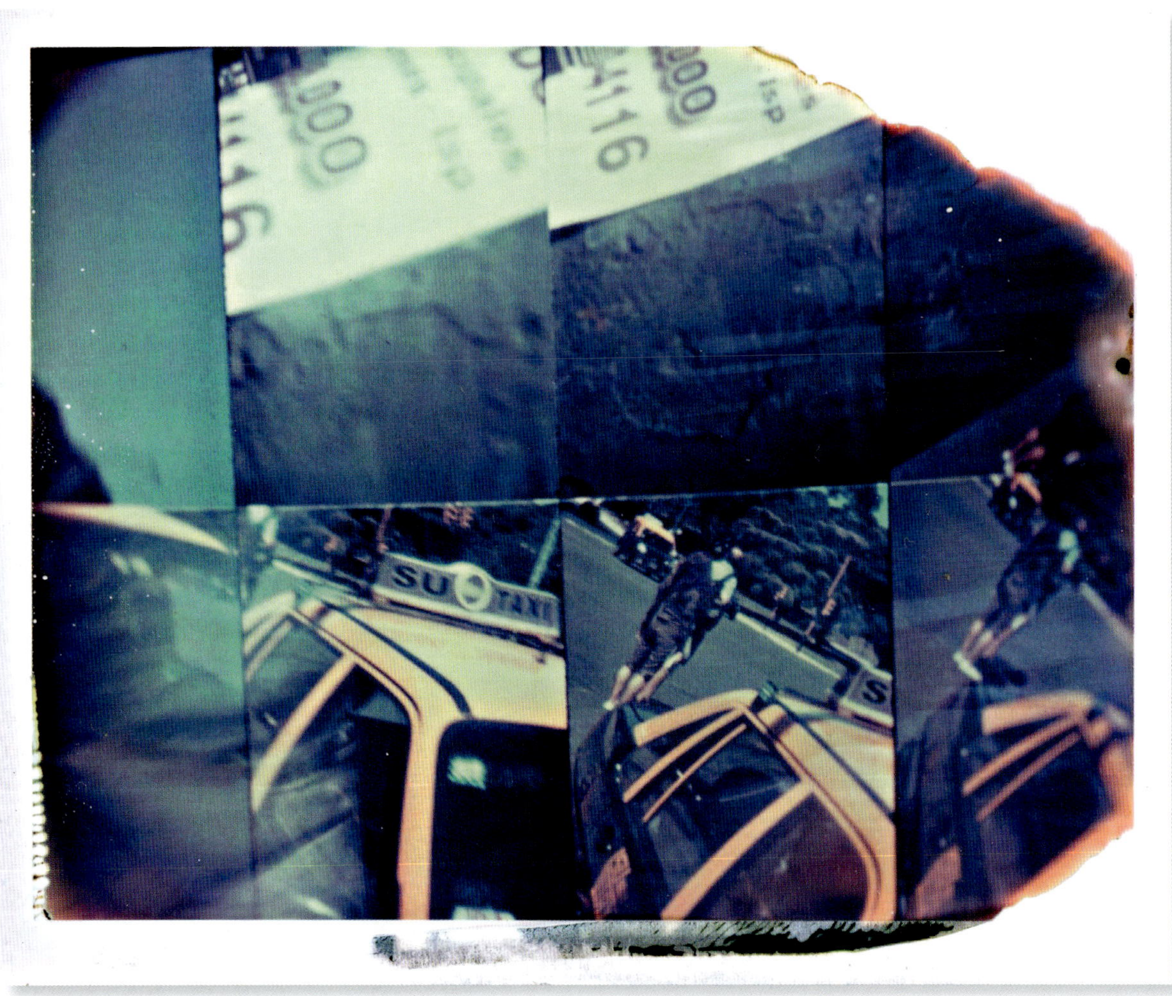

CAMERA: Lomography Oktomat
FILM: Fuji Provia/Polaroid 669
EXPOSURE: 8 images, each at 1/100 sec @ f/8

The original exposure from an Oktomat has been
copied onto expired Polaroid film, adding another
layer to the image.

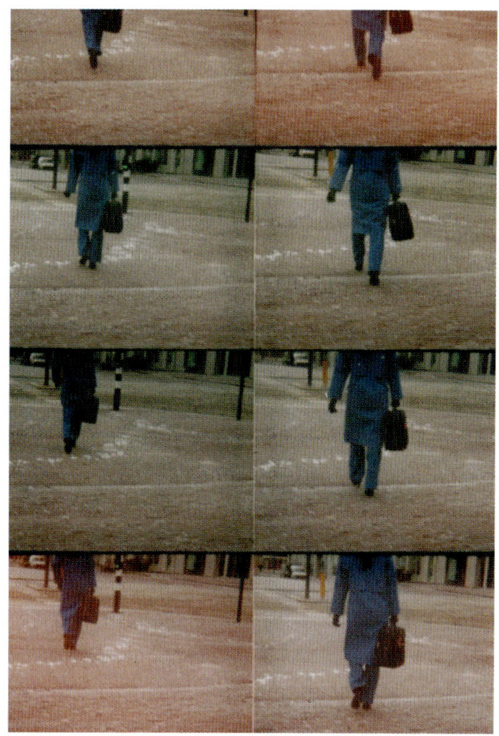

CAMERA: Lomography Oktomat
FILM: Fuji Superia X-tra 400
EXPOSURE: 8 images, each at 1/100 sec @ f/8

An air hostess swaps the skies for the road on her long walk home.

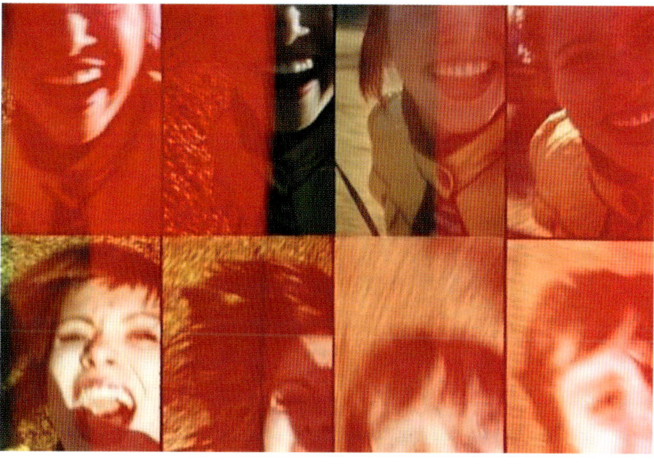

CAMERA: Lomography Oktomat
FILM: Kodak Gold 200
EXPOSURE: 8 images, each at 1/100 sec @ f/8

The only "special effect" here is the light leak which caused the beautiful red tinting.

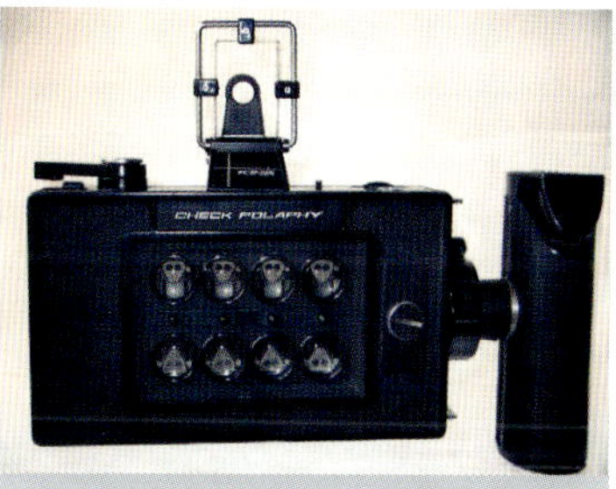

Okto originals

Although the Oktomat is something of a unique offering today, the eight lens design has been seen before. In the 1960s, Photogrammetry Inc. of Maryland, USA, manufactured the eight-lens Graph-Check camera, while Asanuma & Co. Ltd's King Check Polaphy camera (also known as the King Sequence 8, shown) was available in the 1970s. Both cameras allowed eight sequential exposures to be made on 4 x 5 inch Polaroid film, with multiple aperture settings and the ability to adjust the overall sequence duration. These cameras occasionally make an appearance on Ebay, and are a fantastic option if you're looking for some serious eight-lens action. Be warned though, the price is commensurate with their classic, collectible status.

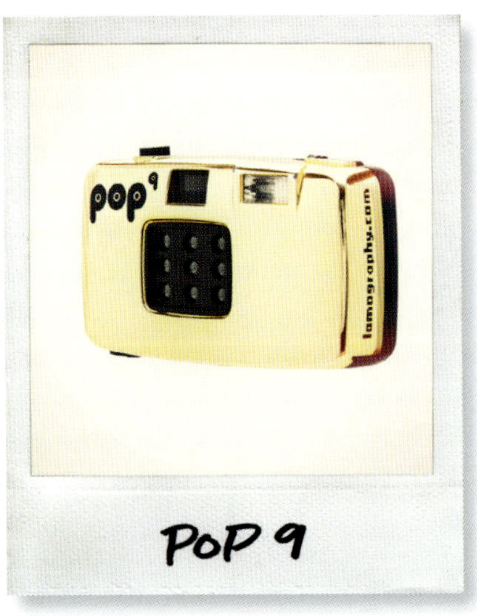

PoP 9

CAMERA: Pop9
MANUFACTURER: Lomography
FILM TYPE: 35mm
IMAGE FORMAT: 9 images on 36mm x 24mm frame
LENS: 24mm (x9)
FOCUS: Fixed (0.8m–Infinity)
APERTURE: f/11
SHUTTER SPEED: 1/100 sec.
OTHER FEATURES: Built-in flash

The premise behind Lomography's Pop9 is simple: press the shutter-release button once and the camera's nine lenses will simultaneously expose an identical image onto a single 35mm film frame, producing a 3 x 3 repeat grid that Warhol would have been proud of.

Be warned though, the small fixed aperture (f/11) and relatively fast shutter speed (1/100 sec.) mean that you need plenty of light and/or a high ISO film to get the best results. The built-in flash can help in close shooting situations, but it's easy for images to appear drab and underexposed on cloudy days, or overly grainy if you use very fast film.

Apart from deciding whether to turn the flash on (or off), there is little else to worry yourself with, as once your film is loaded the Pop9 is a pure plastic point-and-shooter in every respect. Indeed, perhaps the most pertinent decision is whether to buy it in a sleekly understated black finish or in outrageously ostentatious gold.

CAMERA: Lomography Pop9
FILM: Fuji Superia X-tra 400
EXPOSURE: 1/100 sec. @ f/11

Nine different colored gel filters were taped together in a grid to expose each of the Pop9's images with a different color.

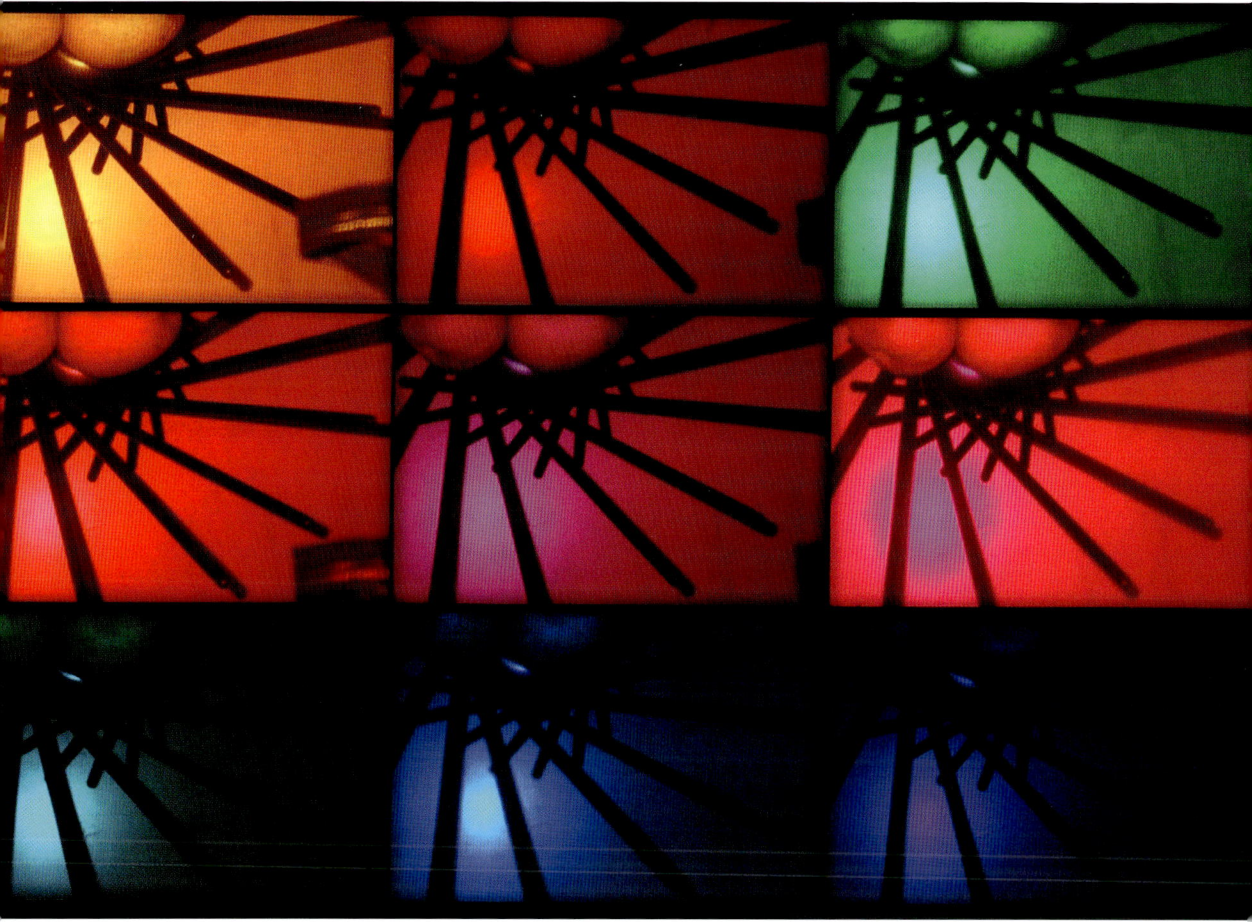

Color art

The space around the lenses on the front of the Pop9 is just big enough to allow you to add tiny colored filters to enhance your "pop art" pictures. The best quality (if that's your biggest concern) will come from cutting tiny squares from optical gel filters, but colored candy wrappers can work just as well.

Film swaps take the lo-fi idea of the "happy accident" to a whole new level by encouraging photographers to shoot a roll of film and then send it to someone else to expose again before it's processed, essentially producing multiple exposures that can be separated by a few miles, or a few thousand miles. In either case, it's not until the film has been processed that the photographers get to see the results of their collaboration, and while there might be a fair few duds on a roll, there are just as likely to be a few photographic gems.

The easiest place to start your film swapping experiments is with friends and family, perhaps setting some loose "ground rules" in an attempt to encourage some interesting exposures: maybe one of you will shoot in an urban environment and the other in a rural location, for example, or one of you shoots architecture and the other portraits to add a layer of contrast in terms of the subject(s). Alternatively, you might decide to shoot similar subjects so your exposures share a common theme, or you could just photograph whatever the heck you want and leave everything to chance—it might work, it might not.

The latter option is far more likely to be the case if the person you swap your film with lives hundreds or thousands of miles away, and this is where film swaps can get real interesting. Swapping your film with someone from a different country or continent can result in a literal "culture clash," producing images that are a fusion of different styles, and subjects that would otherwise be impossible—at least in any practical sense—to create deliberately. It's not difficult to find someone to swap your film with, either, as Facebook and Flickr host numerous film swapping groups with members from around the world; that roll of film you shoot today could be traversing the globe tomorrow.

Although you can use any film format for a swap, 35mm is the most commonly used, as it can be rewound in-camera without any hassle, and used in a wide variety of cameras. All you need to do is make sure that the first person to expose the roll doesn't rewind the film fully into the cassette. With the majority of cameras this means rewinding the film until you hear a click and the film goes loose, and not rewinding any further. This should leave the leader out of the cassette, ready to be reloaded and reshot, no matter who it is sent to, or where on the planet it ends up.

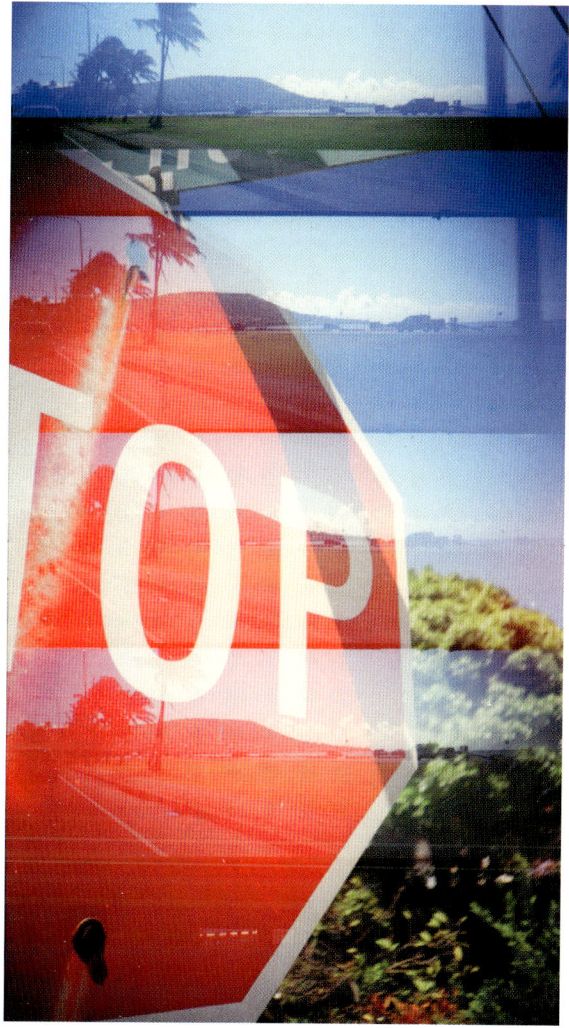

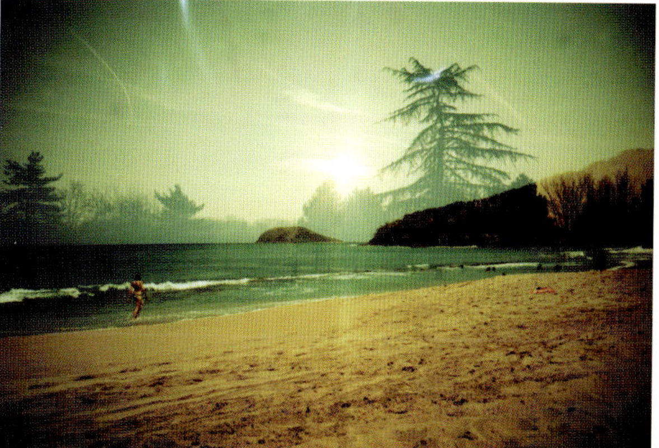

CAMERA: LOMO LC-A
FILM: Agfa CT Precisa 100 (cross-processed)
EXPOSURE: Various

Photographers living more than 4,000 miles apart exposed this film: first in Paris, and then in Guadeloupe.

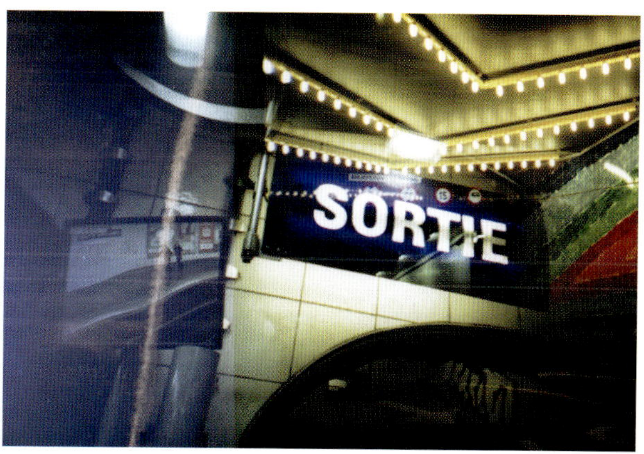

CAMERA: LOMO LC-A
FILM: Agfa CT Precisa 100 (cross-processed)
EXPOSURE: Various

This film was swapped between photographers in France and Switzerland.

CAMERA: LOMO LC-A/Lomography Supersampler
FILM: Agfa Vistacolor 200
EXPOSURE: Various

One roll of film exposed through two different cameras: a fun way to get some very creative random shots, without sending your film to anyone else.

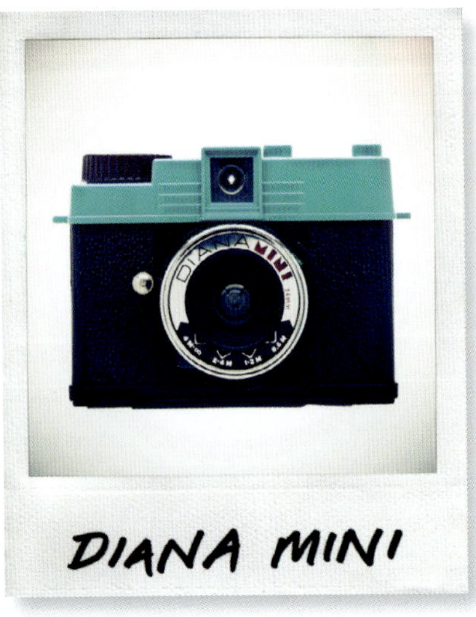

CAMERA: Diana Mini
MANUFACTURER: Lomography
FILM TYPE: 35mm
IMAGE FORMATS: Half-frame (17mm x 24mm)
Square (24mm x 24mm)
LENS: 24mm focal length
(35mm equivalent focal length
for half-frame format)
(30mm equivalent focal length
for square format)
FOCUS: Four settings (0.6m, 1–2m,
2–4m, Infinity)
APERTURES: Sunny (f/11), Cloudy (f/8)
SHUTTER SPEEDS: N (1/60 sec.), B (Bulb)
OTHER FEATURES: Cable release socket
Tripod mount
Compatible with Diana flash

Not content with reviving the original medium format Diana in 2007, Lomography decided to add a 35mm Diana model—the Diana Mini—to its plastic camera lineup in 2009. The logic is simple: medium format film is not for everyone, as it can occasionally be difficult to source (especially if you need a roll in a hurry); hard to get processed; and it's also expensive when you're getting just a dozen frames on a roll.

By comparison, 35mm film is easier to get hold of and have processed, and you also get a lot more shots per roll. This is especially true with the Diana Mini because Lomography has not only enabled it to emulate the square-format images produced by the bigger Diana, but with the flick of a switch the Diana Mini is transformed into a half-frame camera, shooting up to 72 17mm x 24mm sized images on a 36 exposure roll of film. The "magic" is achieved through the use of a built-in mask that switches formats quickly and easily, even mid-roll so that you can mix-and-match square and half-frame images. You can also overlap your frames to create an "endless panorama."

In keeping with the Diana F+, the Diana Mini offers a modest amount of exposure control, with two aperture settings and a choice of a fixed, 1/60 sec. shutter speed and Bulb. As the plastic lens is fixed, there isn't a pinhole mode and you're obviously stuck with a single focal length, but a great deal of care has gone into making sure that the image quality this lens delivers lives up to its predecessors: shoot square and you will be rewarded with softly focused, darkened corners to your shots, with an overall diffuseness that is reminiscent of

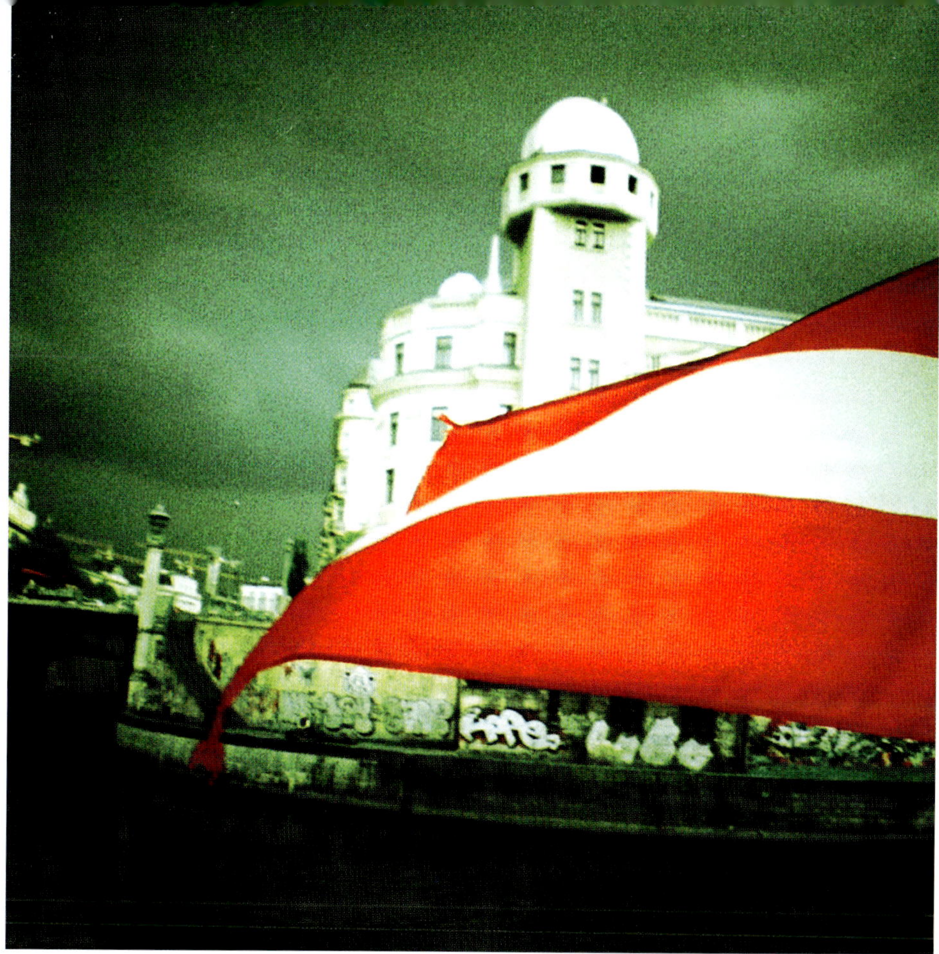

Winding woes

The ability to switch from square to half-frame formats with the flick of a switch is one of the Diana Mini's most exciting features, but it is also its weakest point. The gearing of the wind-on mechanism is changed to compensate for the different frame size when you switch from one format to the other, but this can cause the camera to "lock up." As a result, Lomography recommends covering the lens with the lens cap and firing a "blank" frame before you change formats. There are also several online guides that will show you how to affect a permanent fix, although this does require you to dismantle and "hack" your camera.

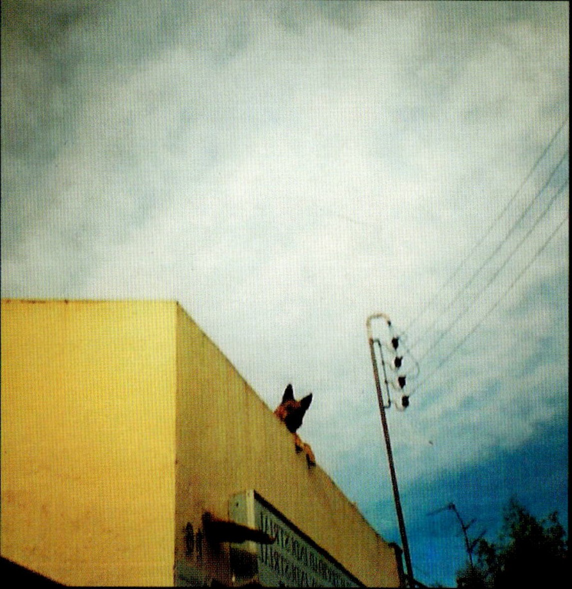

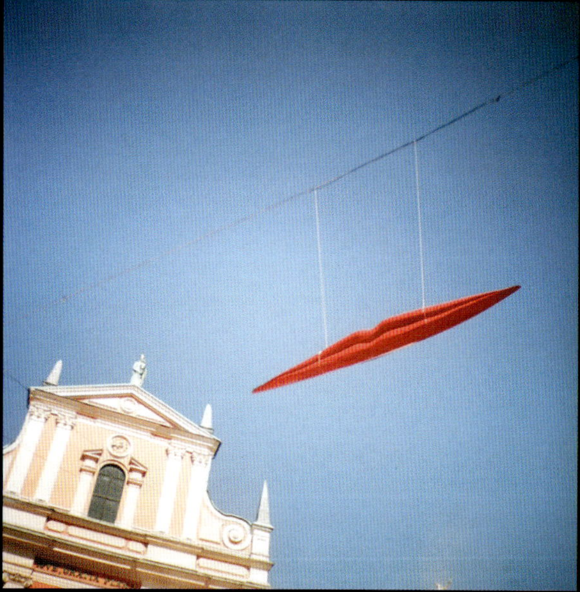

CAMERA: Diana Mini
FILM: Kodak Gold 200 (expired)
EXPOSURE: 1/160 sec. @ f/8

CAMERA: Diana Mini
FILM: Unknown
EXPOSURE: 1/160 sec. @ f/11

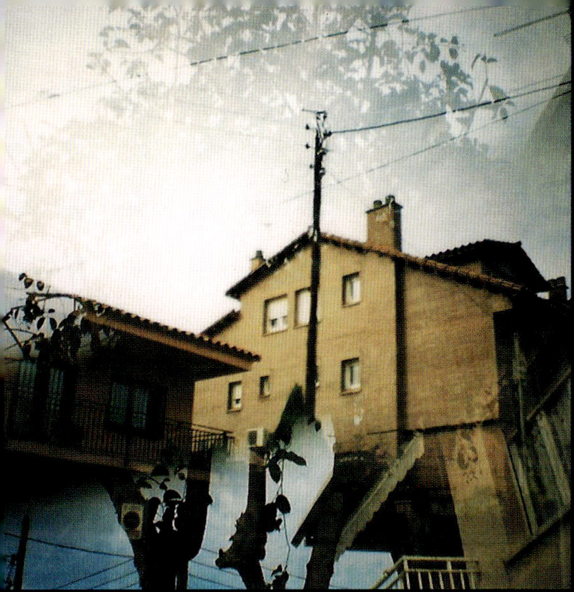

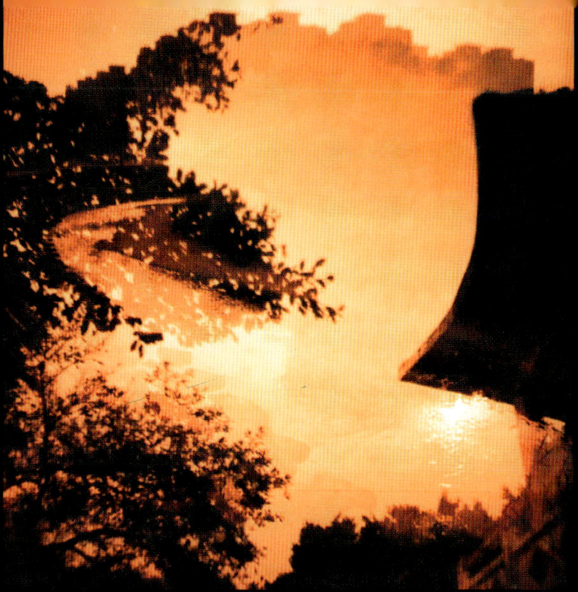

CAMERA: Diana Mini
FILM: Kodak Gold 200 (expired)
EXPOSURE: 1/160 sec. @ f/8

CAMERA: Diana Mini
FILM: Lomography Redscale
EXPOSURE: Two exposures at 1/160 sec.

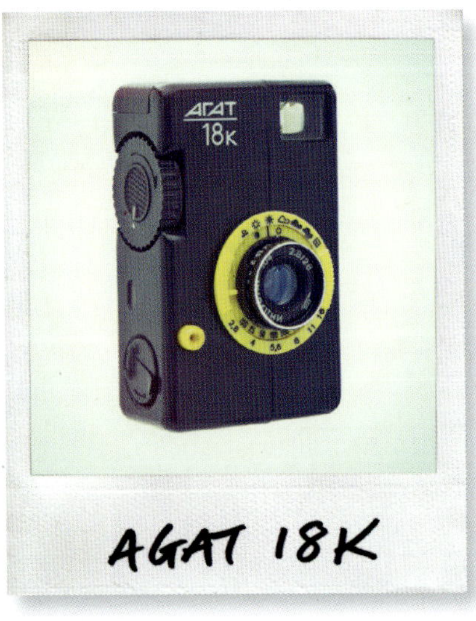

AGAT 18K

CAMERA:	Agat 18k
MANUFACTURER:	BelOMO
FILM TYPE:	35mm
IMAGE FORMAT:	18mm x 24mm
LENS:	28mm
FOCUS:	0.9m–Infinity (continuous)
APERTURES:	f/2.8, f/4, f/5.6, f/8, f/11, f/16
SHUTTER SPEEDS:	1/60–1/500 sec. (linked directly to aperture)
OTHER FEATURES:	Standard hotshoe Tripod mount

The half-frame Agat 18k, and its predecessor, the Agat 18, were produced by the Belarus Optical & Mechanical Enterprise, primarily for the domestic Soviet market. The 18k expanded the ISO and shutter speed range of the 18, and added a threaded shutter-release button.

While the 18 and 18k are similar, they are very different to most other 35mm cameras. Exposures are made using a "semi-programmed" system. You set the ISO and manually choose the aperture based on weather symbols (or the f-stop value), and the camera chooses the shutter speed. This may sound like Aperture Priority, but the remarkable part of this is that the cameras set the shutter speed without using any type of lightmeter. Rather than measure the light, each aperture is linked to a shutter speed, so if you set the aperture to f/2.8, the Agat 18k uses a 1/64 sec. shutter speed, while an aperture of f/8 sets 1/155 sec., and f/16 is matched to 1/256 sec. This is strange, but the system is surprisingly capable once you have mastered it, and there are even marks on the lens for introducing deliberate over- or underexposure.

Despite being designed as a low-cost, plastic-bodied snapper, the Agat 18k can deliver excellent results—certainly when compared to other plastic cameras. Part of the credit for this goes to the glass Industar 104 triplet lens, which is definitely up to the job of creating sharp shots, but don't imagine that this means the camera is "perfect": the dubious quality of the lens coating can result in spectacular lens flare in direct light, and light leaks are common thanks to the camera's "split" design.

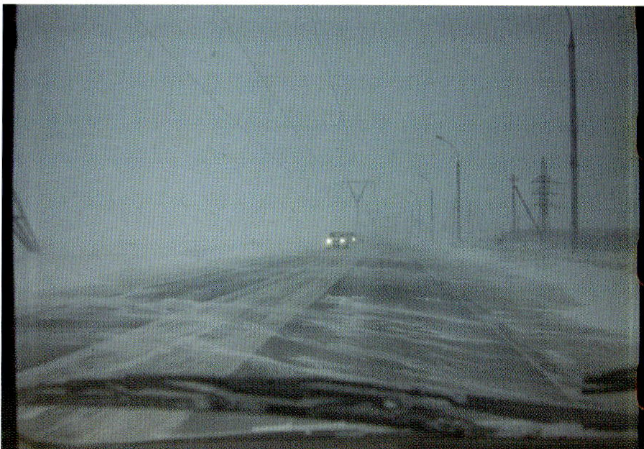

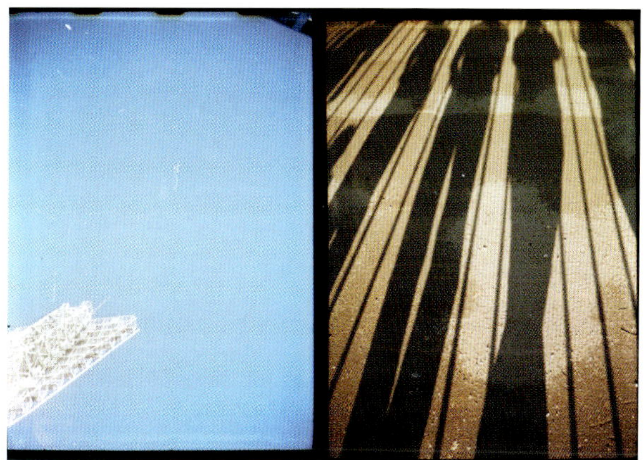

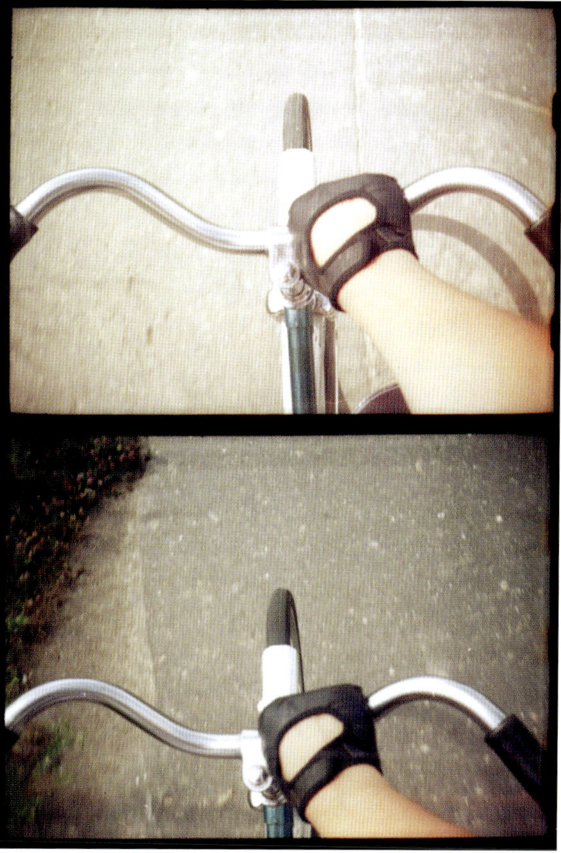

Top:
CAMERA: Agat 18
FILM: Unknown negative film (expired)
EXPOSURE: Unrecorded

Being fully mechanical means that the Agat 18 will work in almost all conditions, including a blizzard, as this shot demonstrates.

Above left:
CAMERA: Agat 18
FILM: Unknown
EXPOSURE: Unrecorded

With 72 shots fitting on a "36 exposure" roll of film there's every chance you'll end up with a pair of seemingly disparate images that work well when seen together.

Above:
CAMERA: Agat 18
FILM: Unknown
EXPOSURE: Unrecorded

A wide range of aperture settings and shutter speeds gives you full control over the Agat 18's exposures.

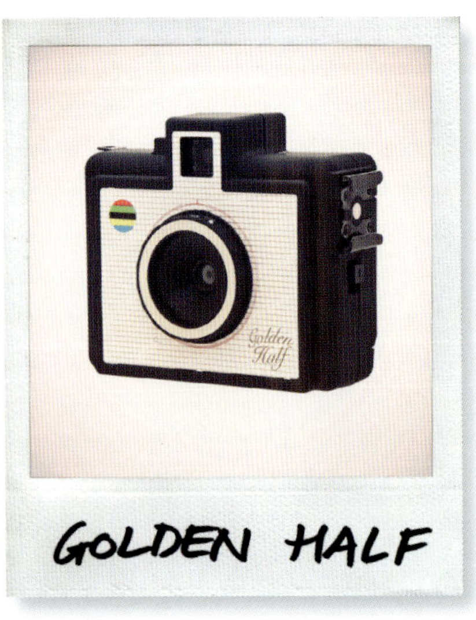

CAMERA: Golden Half
MANUFACTURER: Superheadz
FILM TYPE: 35mm
IMAGE FORMAT: 18mm x 24mm
LENS: 22mm
FOCUS: Fixed   (1.5m–Infinity)
APERTURES: Cloudy (f/8), Sunny (f/11), Flash (f/11)
SHUTTER SPEED: 1/100 sec.
OTHER FEATURES: Hotshoe
                   Tripod mount

At a glance Superheadz' Golden Half is reminiscent of some of the early Kodak Instamatic cartridge cameras and their many derivatives, thanks to its near-square, minimalist stance and central viewfinder. But in the hand its semi-rubberized covering hides any plastic from sight, and the diminutive proportions reveal that this is clearly a small-format shooter.

As its name suggests, the Golden Half is a half-frame camera, but unlike the Diana Mini or Agat 18 it has very few "tricks" up its sleeve: it only shoots half-frame images, and aside from its two aperture settings (three if you count the Sunny f/11 and Flash f/11 settings separately), it's pure point-and-press.

The only other potential distraction is the hotshoe if you want to fit a flash when the light levels drop, or add a burst of creative fill flash. But why use flash when you can celebrate that most filmic of creations: grain? The restrictions placed on your exposures by the typical plastic camera small aperture/fast shutter speed combination mean that you have to rely on relatively fast, grainy film to start with.

The smaller frames mean that printing your shots at any given size requires greater enlargement than "full frame" 35mm and this also enhances the apparent grain. So instead of fighting it, load up with fast film, print the results big, and worship the grain!

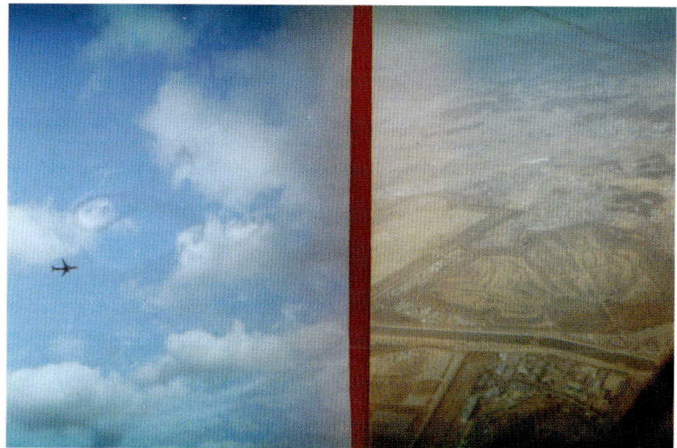

CAMERA: Golden Half
FILM: Kodak Ultramax 400
EXPOSURE: 1/100 sec. @ f/8

These contrasting frames provide two different angles that tell the same story: together they work perfectly.

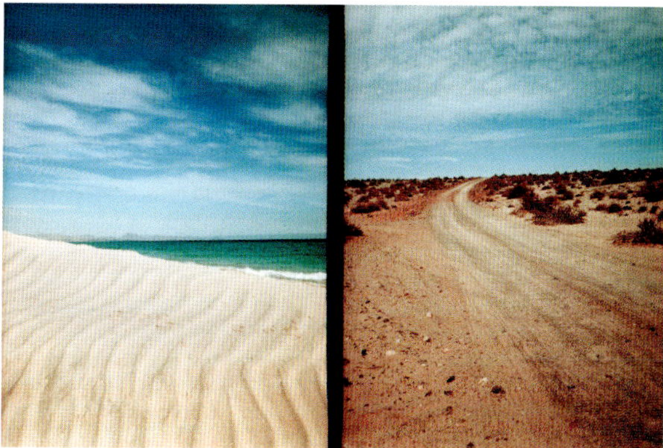

CAMERA: Golden Half
FILM: Ferrania Solaris 200 (expired)
EXPOSURE: 1/100 sec. @ f/11

The two aperture settings on the Golden Half provide a small amount of control over exposure, which is useful if you find yourself shooting in moderately variable conditions.

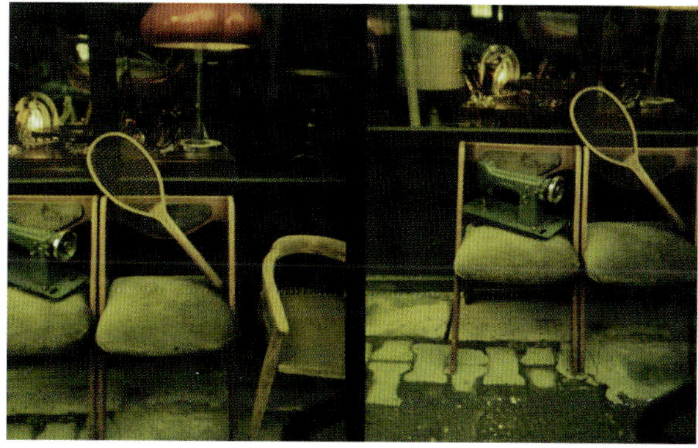

CAMERA: Golden Half
FILM: Rollei Crossbird 200 (cross-processed)
EXPOSURE: 1/100 sec. @ f/8

Small and light, the Golden Half is a great camera to carry with you all the time.

Minimizing grain

If you want to keep grain to a minimum in your half-frame shots, consider each pair of demi-frames as a potential diptych, with one acting as a contrasting or harmonious foil to the other. When your dynamic duo is enlarged it will be no different to enlarging a "full frame" 35mm shot.

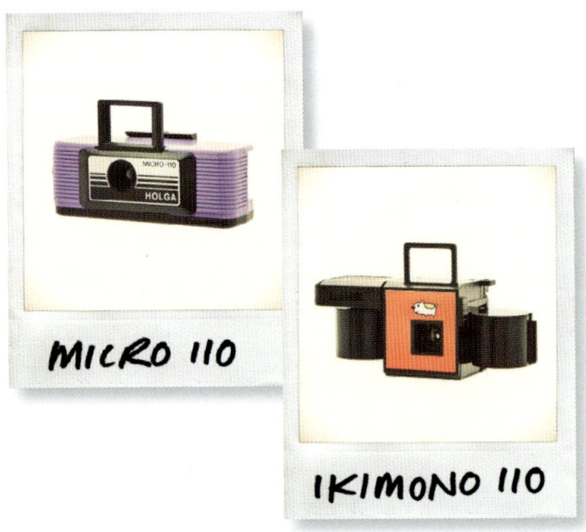

CAMERA:	Micro 110
MANUFACTURER:	Holga Limited
FILM TYPE:	110
IMAGE FORMAT:	13mm x 17mm
LENS:	25mm
FOCUS: Fixed	(1m–Infinity)
APERTURE:	f/8
SHUTTER SPEED:	1/125 sec.

CAMERA:	Ikimono 110
MANUFACTURER:	SuperHeadz
FILM TYPE:	110
IMAGE FORMAT:	13mm x 17mm
LENS:	Focal length not given
FOCUS:	Fixed
APERTURE:	f/11
SHUTTER SPEED:	1/100 sec.

With their reliance on miniature, cartridge-based film, 110 format cameras do not need to be big or bulky in the way that most other cameras do, which is great if you want a real "go anywhere, drop it in your pocket snapper."

In addition to their small size, 110 cameras are also capable of producing stunningly unique images thanks to their tiny, grain-enhancing frames (a mere 13mm x 17mm), a reliance on expired film stocks (no 110 film is currently being made), and a generally low build quality: no one has produced "high end" 110 cameras since Pentax and Minolta in the format's heyday. As a result, 110 images are more prone than any other to suffer from color shifts, unpredictable film "defects," and striking lens flare.

As Holga's Micro 110 and Superheadz' Ikimono 110 prove, you can have all of these lo-fi effects for a minimal price, but don't expect these cameras to stretch your photographic skills: both are pure point-and-shoot, with a fixed lens, fixed focus, a fixed aperture, and a fixed shutter speed.

In fact, the biggest decision you will have to make is which camera you prefer—the widely available, fixed-bodied Micro or the discontinued, slightly more scarce Ikimono—and in which color (both are/were available in a wider range of colors).

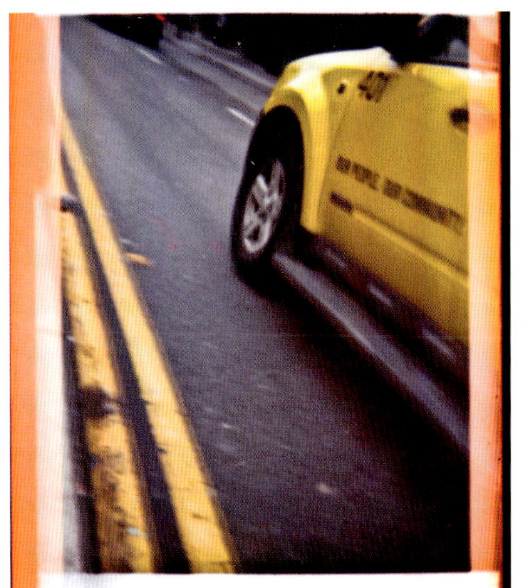

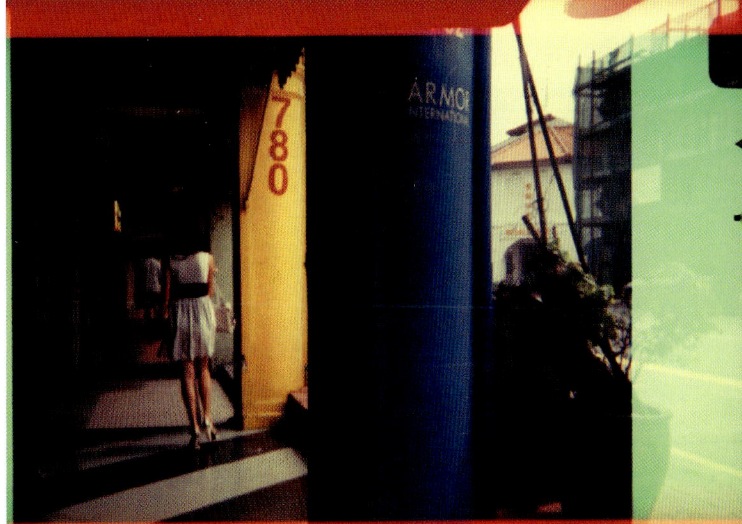

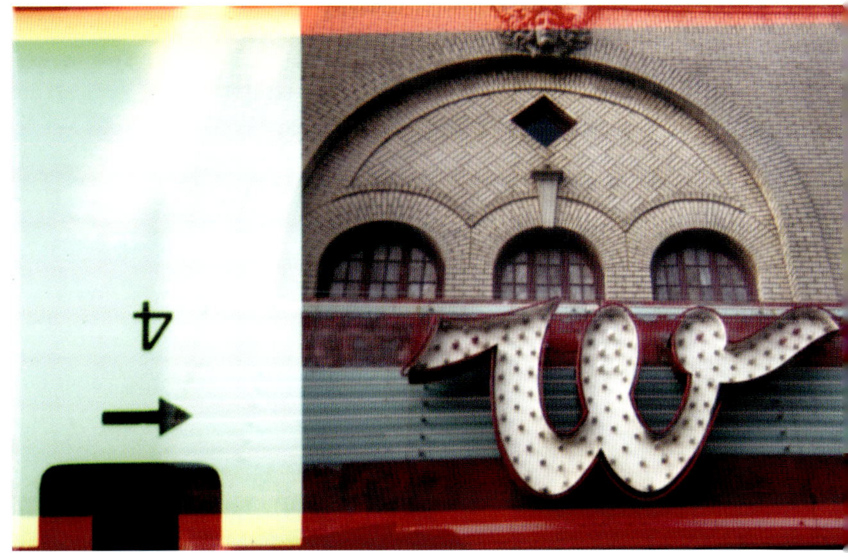

Above:
CAMERA: Ikimono 110
FILM: Kodak 200
EXPOSURE: 1/100 sec. @ f/11

The Ikimono 110 comes with a keychain attachment, so there's no excuse for leaving it at home!

Top right:
CAMERA: Holga Micro 110
FILM: Fuji Superia 200
EXPOSURE: 1/125 sec. @ f/8

The Holga Micro 110's 25mm lens is the equivalent to a "standard" lens in 35mm SLR terms, giving a similar angle of view to our eyes.

Right:
CAMERA: Ikimono 110
FILM: Fuji Superia 200
EXPOSURE: 1/100 sec. @ f/11

The edges of a 110 frame add to the distinct "shot on film" look.

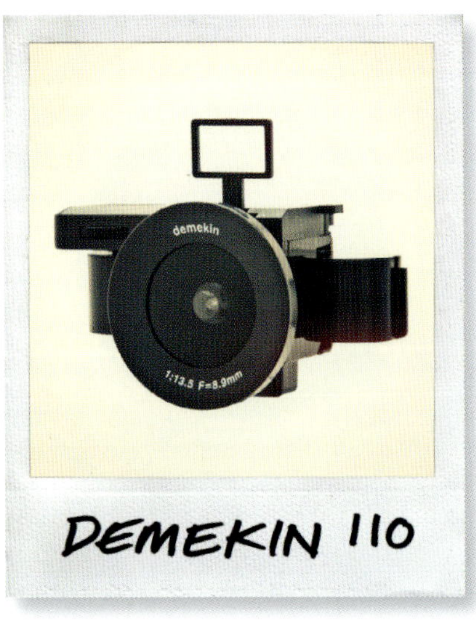

DEMEKIN 110

CAMERA: Demekin 110
MANUFACTURER: SuperHeadz
FILM TYPE: 110
IMAGE FORMAT: 13mm x 17mm
LENS: 8.9mm
FOCUS: Fixed (1m–Infinity)
APERTURE: f/13.5
SHUTTER SPEED: 1/100 sec.
OTHER FEATURES: Tripod mount

If you love super-wide angles then your plastic camera choices are few and far between. The extreme 10mm lens on the Fisheye No. 1 or No.2 is one option, but if you don't want circular images then the 22mm lens on either the Ultra Wide & Slim or La Sardina is your next widest option—there's nothing in between. At least there isn't if you stick to 35mm cameras: if you're willing to "downsize" to 110 format film, then the Demekin 110 could be the ideal inbetweener.

This diminutive camera follows in the footsteps of the Ikimono 110, in that the Demekin 110 folds open and "wraps around" a 110-film cartridge (rather than having the film loaded into it in a more conventional fashion) and it relies on a single shutter speed and aperture for its exposures. However, there is one glaring difference between the two—the Demekin has a (comparatively) gargantuan disc of a lens on the front.

This lens is clearly what makes the Demekin "special," as the 8.9mm focal length delivers an angle of view that is equivalent to an ultra-wide 18mm focal length in "full frame" 35mm terms. Strictly speaking this is a fisheye lens, and the extreme distortion does suggest a circular image in the style of the Lomography Fisheye. This is curtailed, however, so while the corners of your images will darken significantly, and any would-be straight edges toward the edges of the frame will curve like crazy, the frame itself just about retains a more traditional rectangular shape, rather than succumbing to the circular image of the "true" fisheye.

The Demekin 110's fisheye lens does not produce circular images, an aspect that some people prefer.

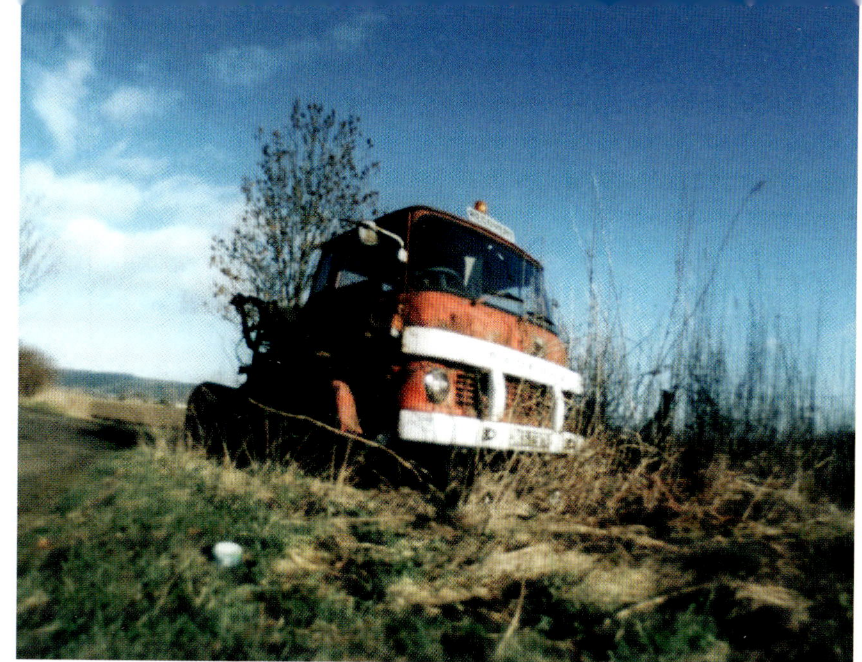

The ultra-wide 8.9mm lens translates to 18mm in "full frame" camera terms, which is perfect for shots containing an extreme wideangle perspective.

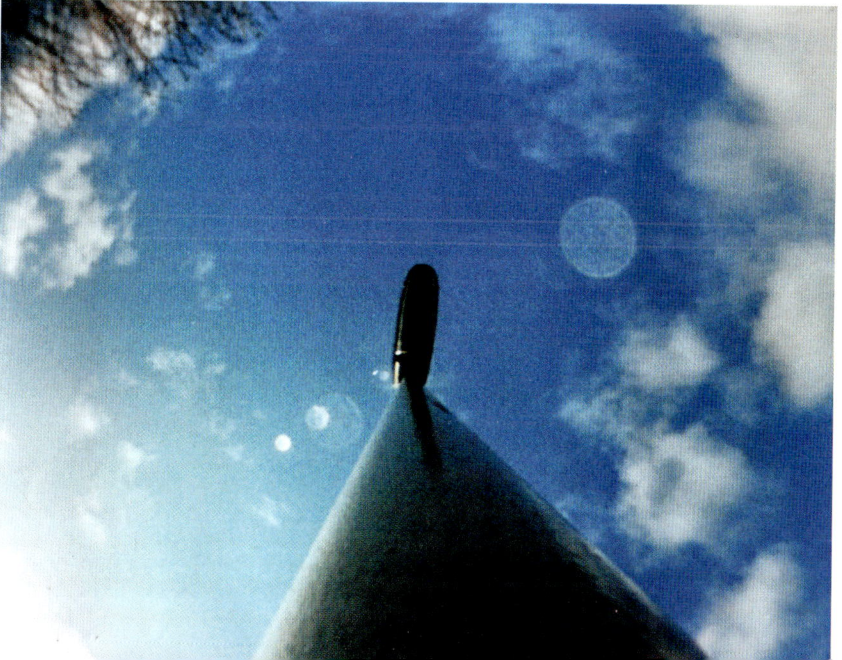

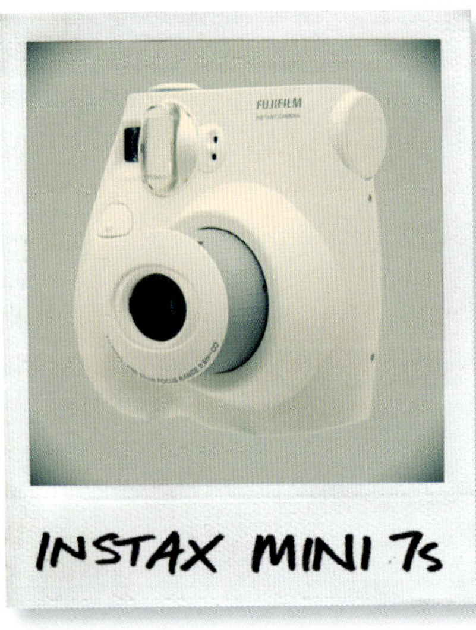

CAMERA:	Instax Mini 7s
MANUFACTURER:	Fujifilm
FILM TYPE:	Instax Mini
IMAGE FORMAT:	62mm x 46mm
LENS:	60mm
FOCUS:	0.6m–Infinity
APERTURES:	f/12.7, f/16, f/22, f/32
SHUTTER SPEED :	1/60 sec.
NOTES:	Built-in flash

The Mini 7s is the entry-level model in the Instax Mini line-up, but don't for a second think that the word "mini" refers to the size of the camera—the 7s' beautifully curvaceous body measures a chunky 4.7 x 4.8 x 2.8 inches (119.5 x 121.5 x 70.5mm), so it's certainly not in the "pocket camera" class.

Part of the reason for its size is that the camera uses Fuji's Instax Mini instant film, so you're effectively loading it with unexposed prints, and that takes up space. With the Mini 7s (and indeed all of the Instax Mini cameras), the film cartridge is easy to load: just open the film compartment in the camera and line up the yellow marks on the camera and cartridge. After that you simply need to pull out the lens to switch the camera on, and you're good to go.

Unlike its more advanced stablemates, the Mini 7s offers four manually selected exposure settings—Indoor, Cloudy, Fine, and Clear—which equate to apertures of f/12.7, f/16, f/22, and f/32 respectively. To help you pick the right one there's a "green light" selection system: a green light indicates which setting the camera thinks is right for its fixed, 1/60 sec. shutter speed and it's up to you to set the exposure dial in the right position. What this means is that you can intentionally set the wrong option,

CAMERA: Fuji Instax Mini 7s
FILM: Instax Mini
EXPOSURE: Unrecorded

Photographs taken with an Instax Mini camera often work well if they are presented as a series, or single, larger collage.

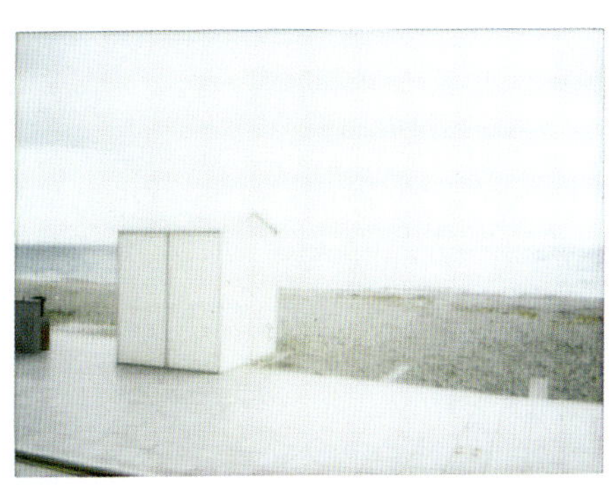
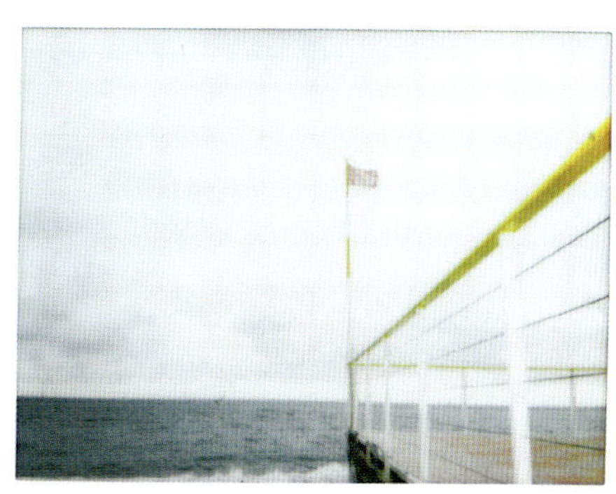
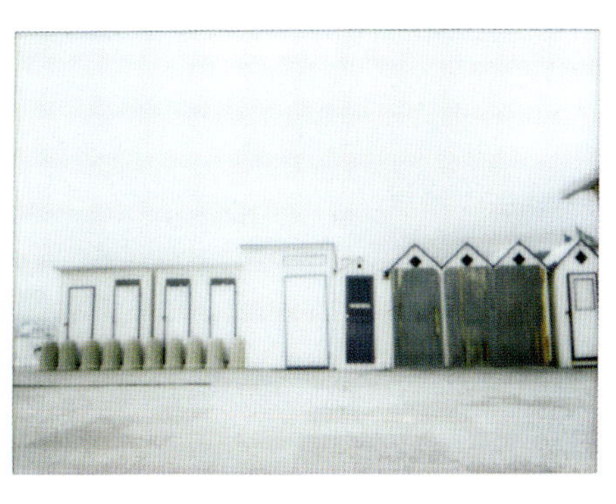
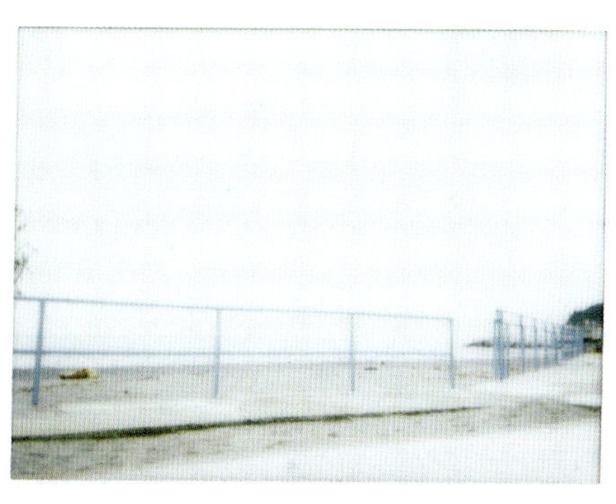
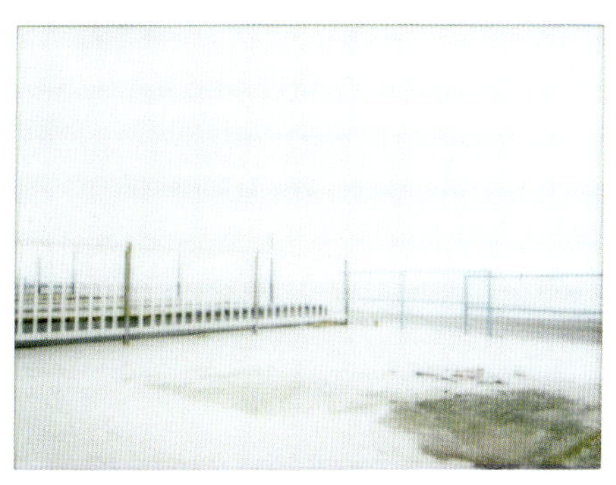
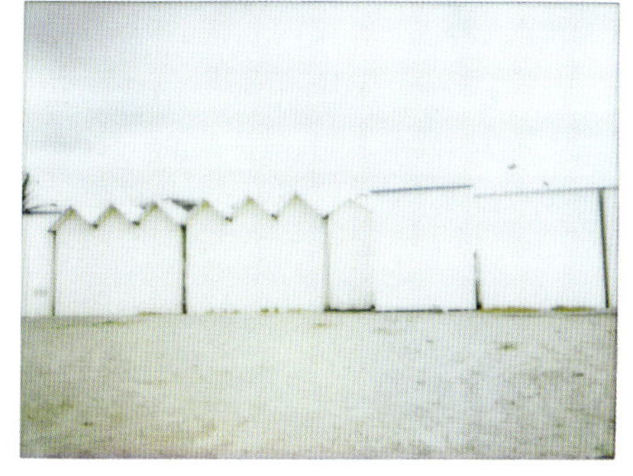

giving you a rudimentary form of exposure control across a 4-stop range.

Having pressed the shutter-release button, your 62mm x 46mm print is ejected smoothly from the camera. It takes just a couple of minutes for the image to process fully, and it does this in the "magical" way that only instant film achieves; with your shot emerging slowly from an initially blank window. Going from exposure to print in such a relatively short space of time makes the shooting experience with an Instax Mini much closer to digital imaging in terms of seeing your results, but try not to get carried away: the costs can quickly add up if you also employ a "shoot first, think later" digital mindset.

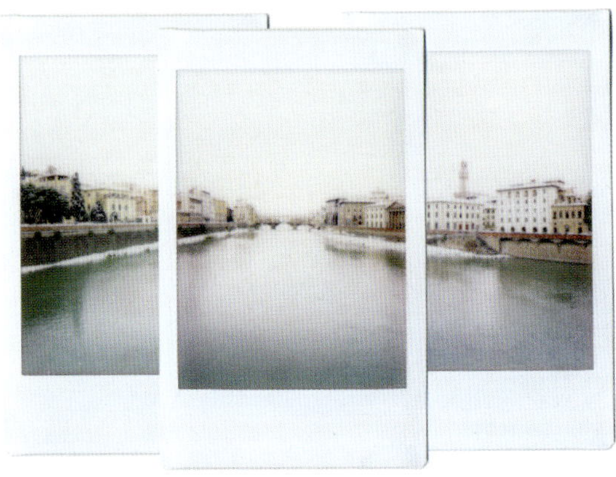

CAMERA: Fuji Instax Mini 7s
FILM: Instax Mini
EXPOSURE: Unrecorded

These three shots were scanned one by one and assembled digitally. Almost no other post-processing was applied

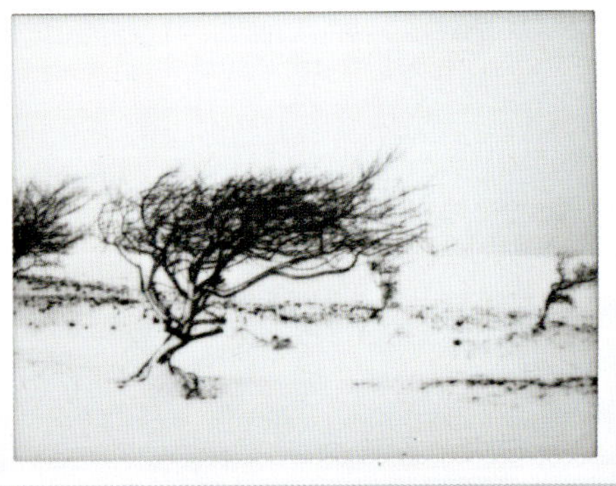

CAMERA: Instax Mini 50s
FILM: Instax Mini
EXPOSURE: Unrecorded

Fuji's Instax Mini 50s is auto-only when it comes to the exposure, but you can apply exposure compensation to compensate for overly dark or light subjects.

Mini film

Instax Mini film has just one option: 10-shot cartridges of glossy, color, ISO 800 instant print film. You want black-and-white shots? Or a matte finish? Then you'll have to scan your Instax prints and reprint them—it's the only option. You want a slower or faster film? Tough!

CAMERA: Instax Mini 25
MANUFACTURER: Fujifilm
FILM TYPE: Instax Mini
IMAGE FORMAT: 62mm x 46mm
LENS: 60mm
FOCUS: 0.5m–Infinity
APERTURES: Automatic (max. f/12.7)
SHUTTER SPEEDS: 1/400–1/3 sec.
NOTES: Exposure compensation (±2/3EV)
Two shutter-release buttons
Removable close-up lens
Built-in flash

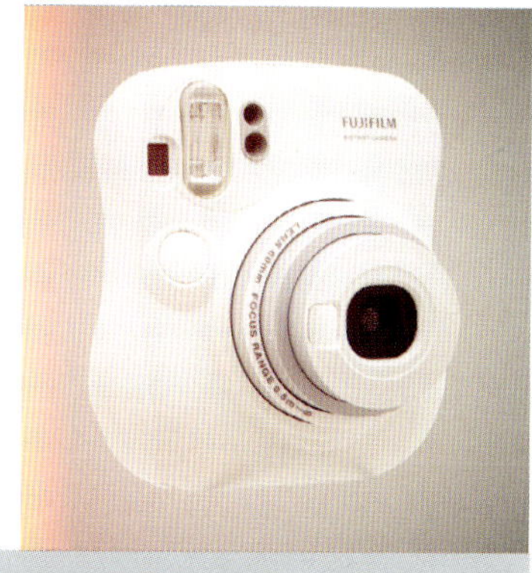

Instax Mini 25

Although it's a more "advanced" model than the Mini 7s in Fuji's eyes, the Instax Mini 25s doesn't offer quite the same control as its low-end brother: the ±2/3-stop of exposure compensation is welcome, but automatic aperture and shutter speed selection restrict the level of manual control.

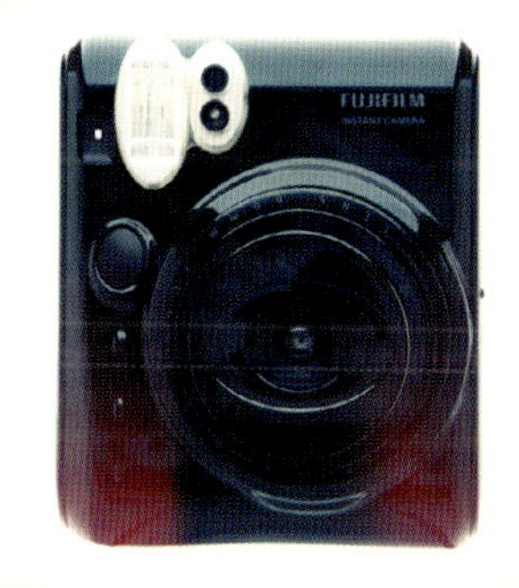

CAMERA: Instax Mini 50s
MANUFACTURER: Fujifilm
FILM TYPE: Instax Mini
IMAGE FORMAT: 62mm x 46mm
LENS: 60mm
FOCUS: 0.6m–Infinity
APERTURES: Automatic (max. f/12.7)
SHUTTER SPEEDS: 1/400–1/3 sec.
NOTES: Self timer (10 sec. delay)
Exposure compensation (±2/3EV)
Removable close-up lens
Tripod mount

Instax Mini 50s

If Lomography's Colorsplash (see page 96) wouldn't look out of place being used by a Stormtrooper, then the Instax Mini 50s would clearly be Darth Vader's photographic weapon of choice. However, while the "piano black" finish looks awesome, a self timer is the only real difference between the Mini 50s and the less expensive Mini 25.

Chapter 4:
DIGITAL PLASTIC

A life less **analog**

There are some staunch plastic camera and lo-fi enthusiasts who refuse resolutely to acknowledge digital photography, preferring instead to adhere to a "film or nothing" message. I guess you could argue they're kind of right—surely the very idea of high-tech, electronic capture being used to create lo-fi images is totally contradictory? As I said in the introduction, there's a reason why there are no digital cameras in this book.

However, while the two may be at near-opposite ends of the technology scale, there is still room for both when it comes to image making—even if your end result is to create a decidedly lo-fi effect.

As you'll see in this chapter, if you're using an interchangeable lens camera—a digital SLR or mirrorless compact system camera—your options start with a new lens, but this isn't the only choice: there's always software, plug-ins, and apps if you want to get a lo-fi look after you've taken your shots, or to affect photographs that you've already taken.

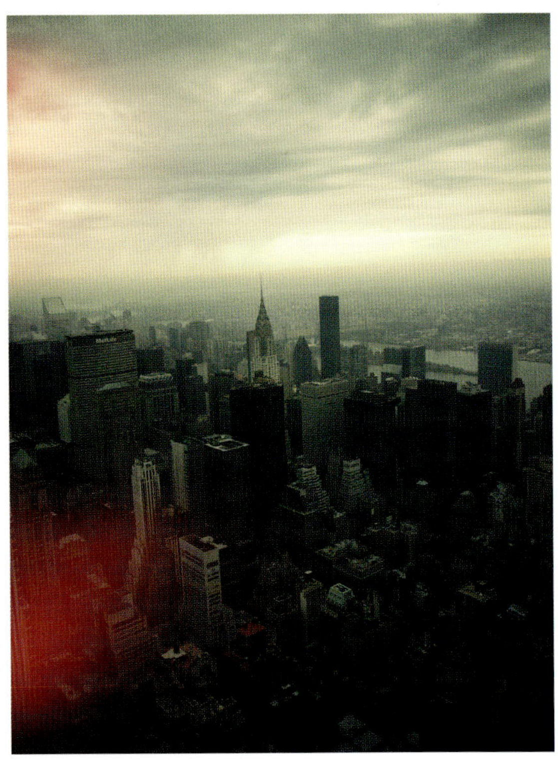

Above: This shot of the New York skyline received a lo-fi treatment courtesy of ToyCamera AnalogColor software.

Facing page: Software can be used to emulate many lo-fi characteristics, including sprocket holes and light leaks.

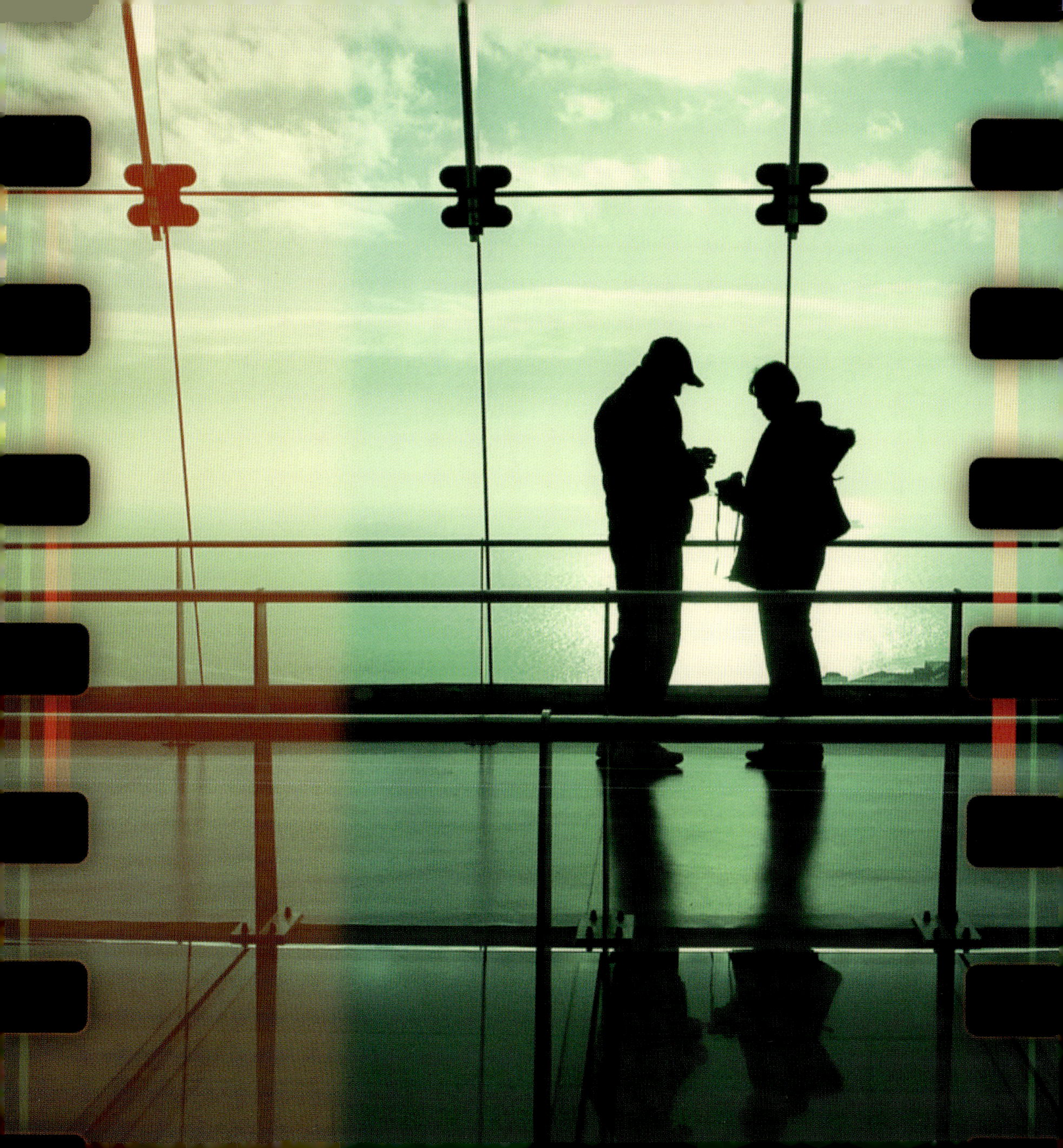

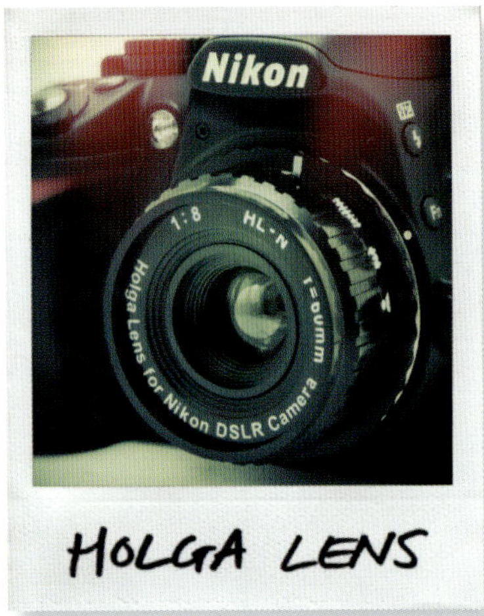

HOLGA LENS

With such enthusiasm for Holgas, it was only a matter of time before the first "ready made" Holga lenses for digital cameras appeared. The first version failed to truly satisfy photographers looking to combine the "raw" Holga aesthetic with the convenience of digital imaging: the problem was, the plastic lenses simply weren't "Holga-ry" enough.

Following initial feedback, the design was revisited and a new Holga lens was released in 2011. As with the original Holga cameras, the lens uses the same zone focus system and has the same 60mm focal length, although this doesn't give the same wide-angle view as it does on a medium format Holga: on a camera with a full-frame sensor it will be a slightly longer-than-standard focal length, while the camera's focal length magnification factor needs to be taken into account if you're fitting it to a camera with an APS-C sized sensor (or smaller).

There is also a fundamental change when it comes to the aperture. With a medium format Holga the aperture is housed in the camera body, but this obviously isn't the case with a digital SLR (or similar) camera. Instead, the Holga lens has a fixed aperture of f/8. With some cameras this will still allow TTL (through-the-lens) metering in Aperture Priority or Manual mode, but others will require something of a trail-and-error approach to getting the exposure right.

These are minor points, though, since apart from the differences in focal length and aperture the current Holga lens definitely lives up to the reputation of its analog counterparts. Vignetting and focus fall-off are exhibited on all digital sensors, from full frame all the way down to the diminutive Micro Four Thirds format. In addition there's a typically Holga-esque diffusion across the image as a whole, and when you throw in chromatic aberrations and flare it all adds up to a genuine Holga vibe. The only thing missing are the light leaks!

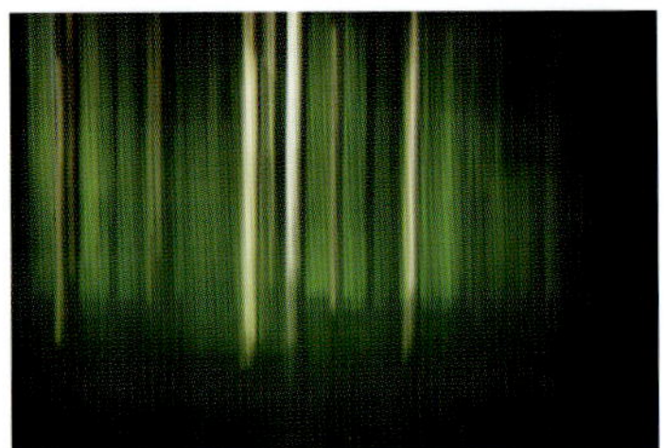

Although the aperture is given as f/8, it's actually significantly smaller, great for exploring movement with long exposures.

Add-ons

As with the original medium format Holga, you can use the slide-on wideangle, telephoto, and macro adapters—as well as the supplementary close-up lenses—with the digital SLR Holga lens. The wideangle adapter may prove especially useful for cameras with a sub full-frame sensor, as it will help to cancel out the camera's focal length magnification factor.

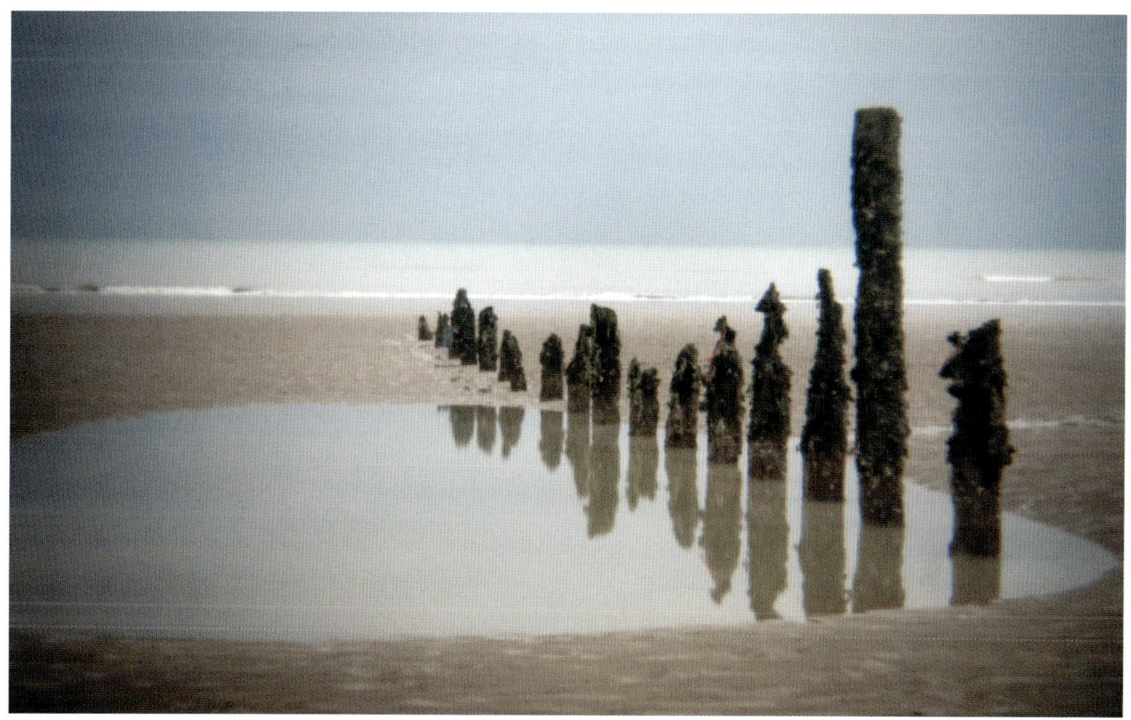

Heavy vignetting typifies the Holga lens, even when it's used on a digital SLR camera with an APS-C sized sensor, as it was here.

Compatibility

The Holga lens is available in the following digital camera mounts: Canon EF, Nikon F, Olympus (Four Thirds SLR and PEN), Panasonic Lumix G, Pentax K/Samsung GX, Samsung NX, Sony (Alpha SLR and NEX).

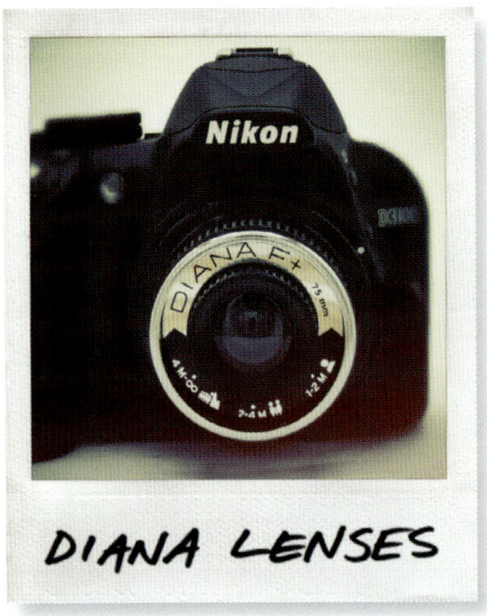

DIANA LENSES

While the Holga lens shown on the previous pages demonstrates that the lo-fi aesthetic can, to a certain degree, make the transition from analog to digital, the same cannot be said of the Diana lenses seen here. I'm not saying there's anything wrong with the lenses themselves, but there is a fundamental issue with their implementation and they just aren't quite so convincing.

Unlike the Holga lens (which has been designed and tailored specifically for use on small format cameras), Lomography has simply produced an adapter that enables its existing Diana+ lenses to be attached to Canon or Nikon SLRs (film or digital). This is great in principal, but the sensor in a digital SLR (or a frame from a 35mm SLR) is significantly smaller than the 52mm x 52mm images produced by the Diana+. As a result, all of the "good stuff" that you'd normally see at the edges of a medium format frame— the vignetting, focus fall-off, and chromatic aberrations—is effectively cropped out of the shot when you fit the lens to a small-format (35mm/full-frame or smaller) SLR camera.

This means that you end up with images that appear to have been taken with a "soft" lens, rather than shots that are heavily stamped with the signature traits of a Diana+. This is more pronounced on cameras with APS-C sized sensors than it is with full-frame or 35mm SLRs: on a cropped-sensor camera there is little to no trace of vignetting or focus fall-off.

So while the idea of using Diana lenses on your digital SLR might appeal, you could well be disappointed if you expect the same lo-fi results. Sure, the results do have a soft-focus charm and the adapter's not massively expensive (although you will need a Diana+ lens as well), but if it's a hardcore lo-fi look that you're after, it's just not there and a Holga lens will give you a much stronger result. Alternatively, you could just buy a Diana+ instead, or a few rolls of film if you already own one.

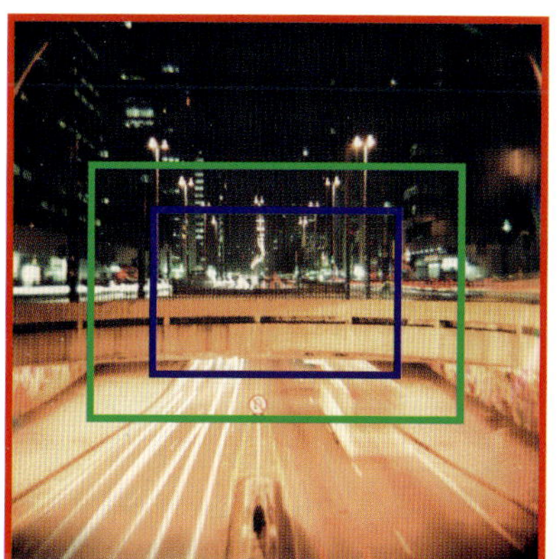

Rather than displaying all of the classic characteristics of a medium format Diana camera, a standard Diana lens simply provides a soft-focus effect when fitted to a digital SLR.

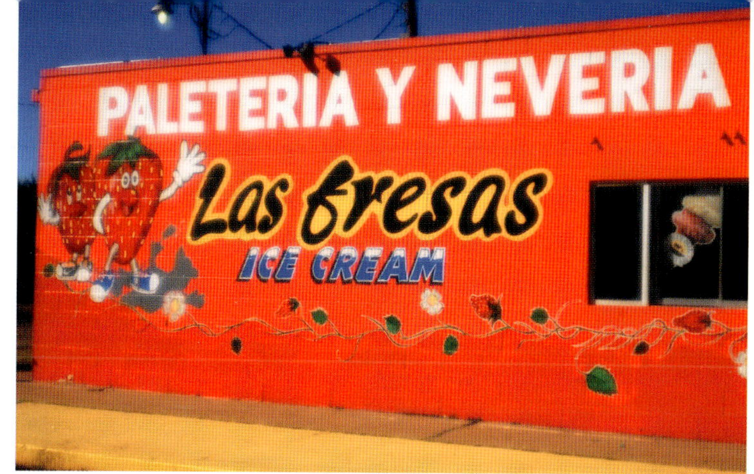

— Diana+ (52mm x 52mm)

— Full frame sensor/35mm film (36mm x 24mm)

— Nikon DX/APS-C sensor (nominally 23.7mm x 15.6mm)

Left: The image circle projected by a Diana lens only just covers the film frame, which explains the fall off in exposure and focus at the corners. However, use the same lens on a smaller format sensor and these characteristic lo-fi traits just aren't recorded.

Image circle

All lenses project a circular image (known as the "image circle"). This is usually slightly larger than the medium it's projecting an image onto, whether that's medium format film, 35mm film, or a digital sensor. As a rule, the performance at the edge of the image circle is weakest—so this is where you get the strongest vignetting, focus fall-off, and chromatic aberrations—while the performance at the center is better, with improved sharpness and illumination.

Expensive, pro-spec lenses are designed to minimize edge artefacts, while less sophisticated, lower cost lenses (such as those found in many plastic cameras) tend to emphasize such "defects"—which is great for lo-fi enthusiasts!

As the illustration above shows, using the same lens on different camera formats can make a dramatic difference to the end result: while a medium format Diana+ will produce stunning lo-fi images with corner shading and focus fall-off, a digital SLR with a full-frame sensor or an APS-C sized sensor would record a far "cleaner" image from the center of the image area.

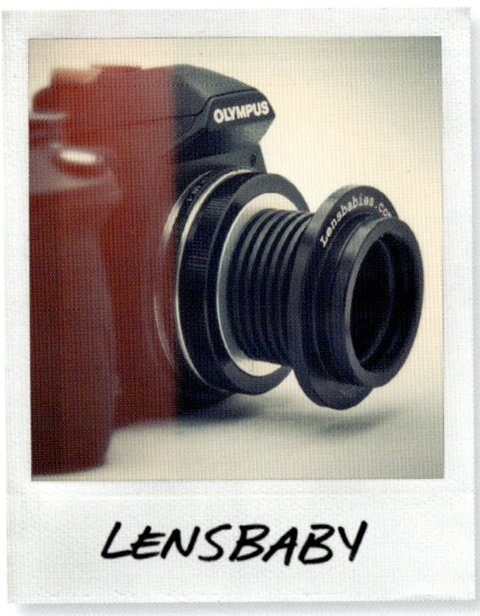

Unlike the Holga and Diana lenses, the Lensbaby doesn't originate from an analog plastic camera, but given the unique look that it produces and its almost cult status, it seems only right that it appears here.

The original Lensbaby (shown here) appeared in 2004 and has spawned a number of variants, with the range now including the Muse, Control Freak, Composer, and Composer Pro models. Although each of these is different to the others, the fundamental premise remains the same: a Lensbaby produces a zone of focus known as the "sweet spot" (the size of which is controlled by the aperture) and the lens' design allows the sweet spot to be moved around the frame. It's very much like having a "spot focus" lens that enables you to choose an area of sharpness, with everything else drifting into a hazy blur.

The key difference between the models is the way in which they operate, and in the most simplistic sense, the more you spend on your 'Baby, the more refined it will be. The base model—the Muse—is fully manual, like the original Lensbaby. You physically have to bend and squeeze the lens to move the sweet spot around the frame and gain something resembling sharp focus, and then hold it in position while you make an exposure. This is all fairly rough-and-ready, and does make your results somewhat unpredictable—a bit like using a plastic camera.

At the opposite end of the scale is the Composer (and now the Composer Pro), which combines a ball and socket design with manual focus adjustment for far greater precision and repeatable results. Between the two lies the Control Freak, which is manipulated in a similar fashion to the Muse, but can be locked in place for consistency, making it a great option for close-up or studio based shots.

However, the way in which your Lensbaby works is only part of the story, as you can also choose the lens that it houses. Originally, a Lensbaby had an uncoated single element lens and that was it. After a few years, a coated double glass element was introduced that offered sharper results, and this is now the "default" lens.

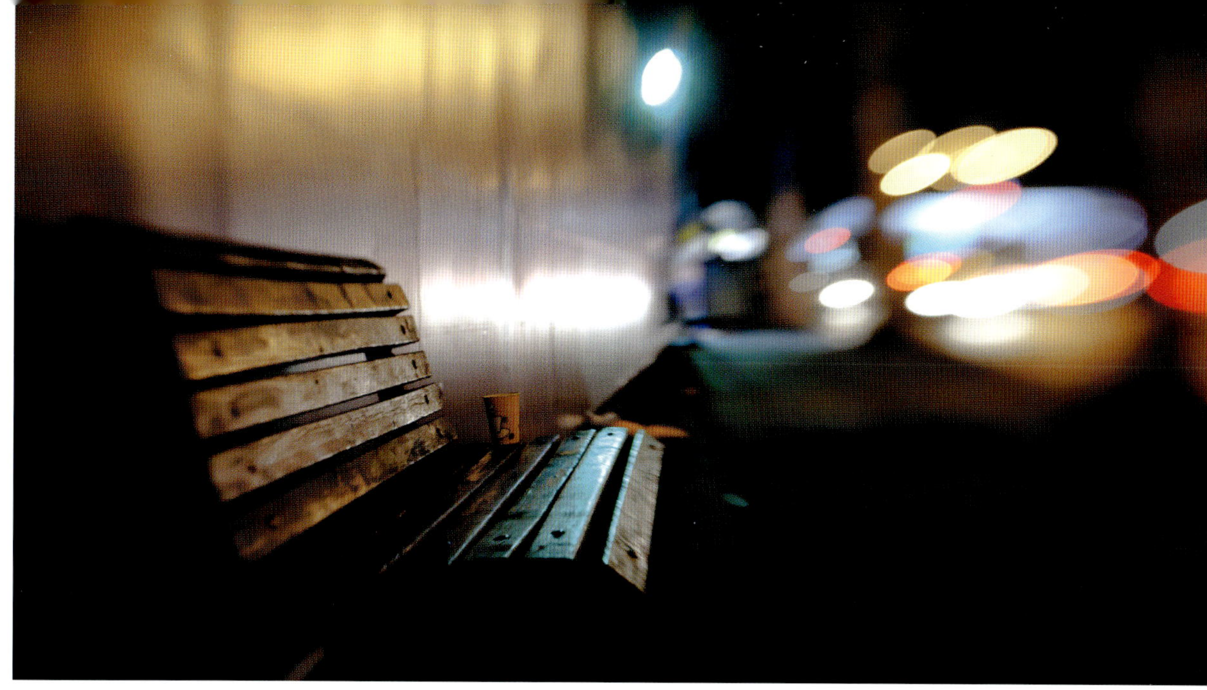

A Lensbaby allows you to place the focus on a precise area of a scene, with everything else melting away.

The single element lens is now an optional extra, and it has been joined by a further six lenses that can be switched for the standard double glass optic, providing a range of effects from fisheye to pinhole. The most recent addition being the 5-element "Edge 80" that gets rid of the sweet spot and transforms your 'Baby into a more traditional tilt lens. A range of lens accessories such as macro, telephoto, and wideangle converters expands your creative possibilities even further, but be warned: as with plastic cameras, Lensbabys are highly addictive, and the cost of buying multiple lenses and accessories can soon add up.

Lensbaby compatibility

The Muse, Control Freak, Composer, and Composer Pro are available in the following mounts: Canon EF, Nikon F, Olympus (Four Thirds SLR), Pentax K/Samsung GX, Sony (Alpha SLR and NEX). In addition, the Composer Pro is also available in these mounts: Olympus PEN, Panasonic Lumix G, Samsung NX, and Sony NEX.

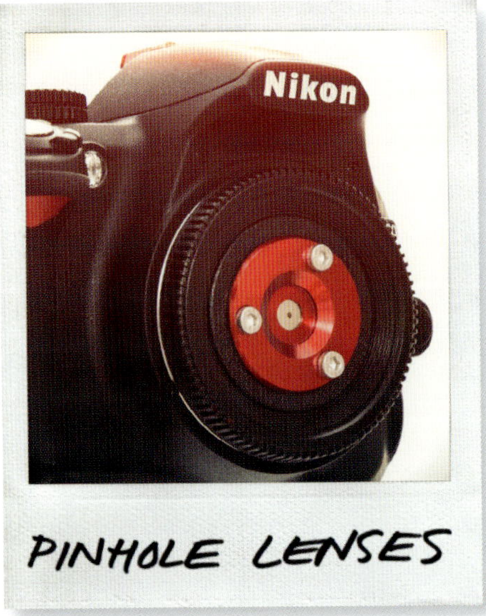

PINHOLE LENSES

With Holga making numerous pinhole cameras, and the Diana+ having a pinhole lens built in, there's a definite blurring (no pun intended) of the boundaries between plastic and pinhole cameras. This is perhaps because the two types of camera have many shared traits: often unpredictable results, light leaks, blur, softness, and a general overarching vibe that is contrary to the "cleanliness" of a typical digital image. However, this doesn't mean that pinhole imaging is the exclusive preserve of film photography, as there are countless pinhole lenses designed for digital (or film) SLRs, as well as the option to make your own.

There simply isn't the space in this book to go into detail on all of the pinhole options available, but if you're looking to shoot digital pinhole images, then a commercial pinhole lens such as the pinhole "cap" shown here (or a Holga pinhole lens) is the most straightforward option. Simply fit the lens to your camera as you would a body cap and you're ready to start shooting.

Alternatively, you can think about making your own pinhole cap using a hand-made pinhole lens and a body cap with a hole drilled in it. This is not going to be as "neat" as the commercial alternative, and it's definitely going to require a little more trial and error, but it does have one major advantage: you are free to use whatever size hole you want, and can make it in whatever material you like.

You would typically want to make a relatively small hole in metal (brass is great, but aluminum will work), but if you're making a lens yourself, why not experiment with larger and smaller pinholes—or maybe multiple pinholes—and make them in card, thick plastic, or some other material? Each one will create its own unique look (some, admittedly, will be better than others), but there's every possibility that you will stumble across a winning combination that simply does not exist anywhere else in the world.

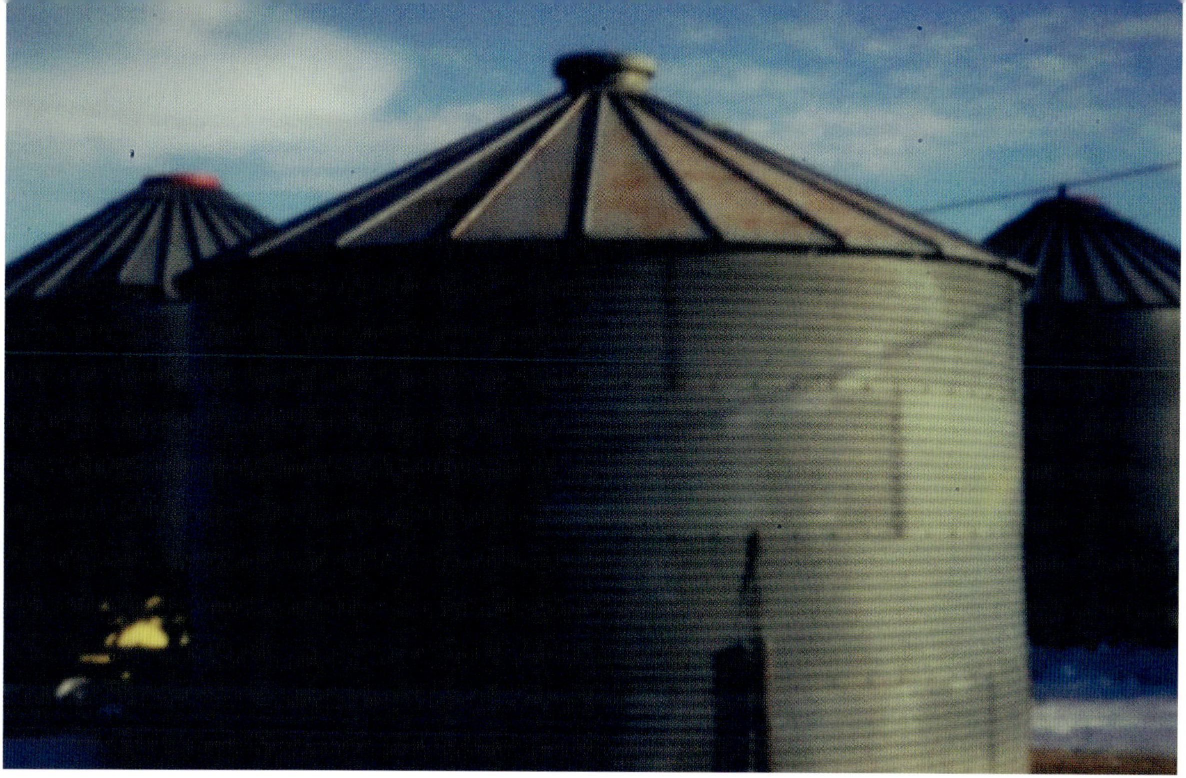

Both of these images were created using a homemade pinhole lens. The simplest solution is to drill a hole in a spare camera body cap, and then tape a piece of thick foil (or thin aluminum) with a small hole poked in it over the body cap hole.

Lo-fi **software**

Although shooting with a plastic camera is the ideal (and a lo-fi lens on a digital camera can be a reasonable second choice), there are countless software plug-ins and standalone programs that will attempt to recreate the lo-fi look with any digital image. These offer various levels of sophistication and automation, ranging from fully automated to fully manual, and they also vary widely in terms of how convincing the results are. The following pair—Poladroid and ToyCamera AnalogColor—are simply the two that I reach for most often.

Apps

In addition to programs for your desktop or laptop computer, there are countless apps available for smartphones and tablet PCs that promise to retrograde your tech and give it the unpolished allure of a lo-fi plastic camera. Some are better than others, and the list of apps is growing all the time, but the following will give you a "heads up" about what's out there:

AnalogColor: Simplified mobile version of ToyCamera AnalogColor as seen on the following pages.

Andigraf: Four lens options allow you to recreate the look of an Actionsampler, Supersampler, Oktomat, or Pop9.

Hipstamatic: Versatile app that allows you to switch virtual "lenses" and "film" for a wide range of lo-fi effects.

Instagram: Provides you with a choice of filtered effects, including a tilt-shift effect for "model world" style shots.

Lo-Mob: Adds a vintage look rather than a plastic camera effect, but some of the results will please lo-fi fans.

LOMO Camera: Apply LC-A, Redscale, or Black & White effects to your shots.

Polarize: Gives your image an instant Polaroid style border. The ability to write on the bottom of the frame in a "handwriting" font is a neat touch.

QuadCamera: Emulate an Actionsampler or Oktomat, with the added bonus of being able to set the delay between your shots.

SplitCam: Creates split images in a similar style to the film-based Split-Cam.

Toy Camera: Randomly applies one of eight pseudo toy camera effects to your image.

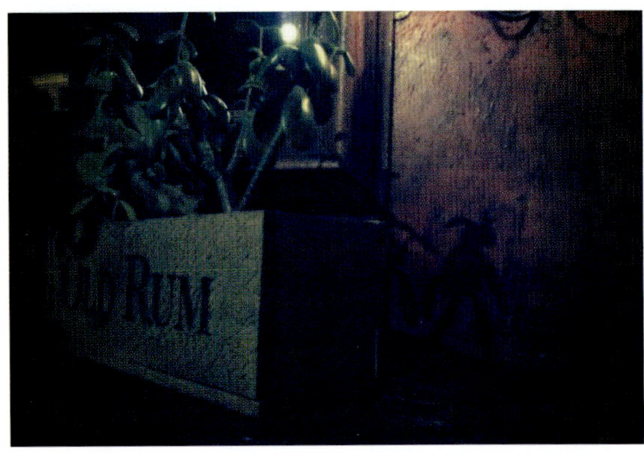

Image shot on a smartphone using **Toy Camera** app.

Poladroid

As the name suggests, Poladroid enables you to create digital Polaroid images in the style of the iconic SX70, complete with white frames and unpredicatable color shifts. Using the software is incredibly straightforward: simply activate the app; drag and drop a JPEG file onto the Polaroid camera icon that appears on your desktop; and after a suitably Polaroid-esque "click and whirr" your picture is ejected from the virtual camera.

Just like the real thing, it takes a few minutes for your instant image to emerge from the darkness, and when you've "taken" 10 shots, the virtual film cartridge is empty: you need to quit and "reload" the camera (program) before you can shoot again.

In keeping with the point-and-shoot Polaroid theme there is little control over the end result: the app's preferences allow you to introduce Blur (on or off), add Stripes (Photo or Paper), and set the Vignetting (Lite or Strong), but that's it in terms of image manipulation. Everything else is fully automated, from the crop (all images are cropped to fit the classic Polaroid proportions), through to the output of a JPEG image measuring 1392 x 1692 pixels that's perfectly proportioned for printing at the original Polaroid size. It's hard to complain though—Poladroid is 100 percent free.

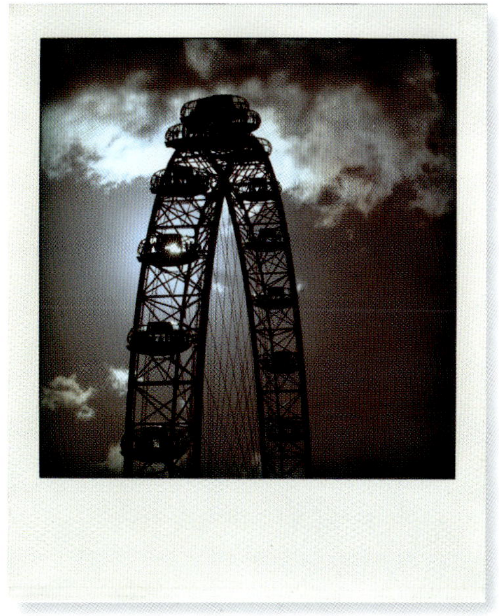

Poladroid is fully automated, so there's no control over the final appearance of your image. However, you can reprocess them until you get a result you like.

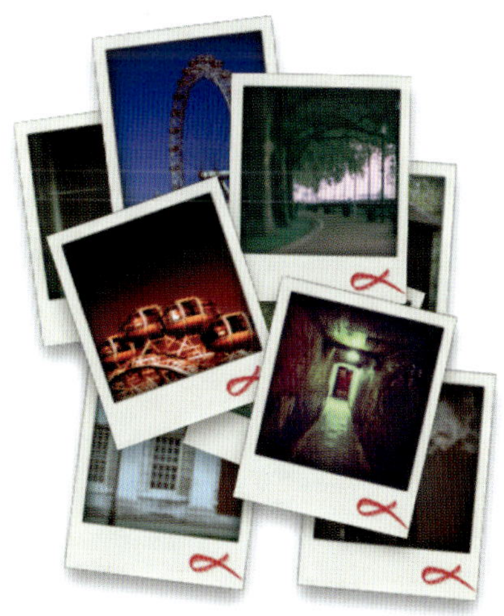

ToyCamera AnalogColor

While Poladroid works in a fully automated fashion to give your images a single analog look (and does it fairly well), ToyCamera AnalogColor (TCAC) brings far more to the image-editing party. For the modest price of ¥1050 (approx. $13/£8) you get a range of tools that will enable you to create a near-infinite number of lo-fi style images, ranging from Polaroid-esque shots (similar to those produced by Poladroid) through to "fake" sprocket shots.

TCAC only works with JPEG images (so if you shoot Raw you'll have to convert your files first), but this doesn't prevent it from producing some great quality results. The program's preset options provide you with a wide range of "one-click" automated image styles that basically set the sliders and processing options for you.

All of these options can be fine-tuned, so you really do have absolute control over your

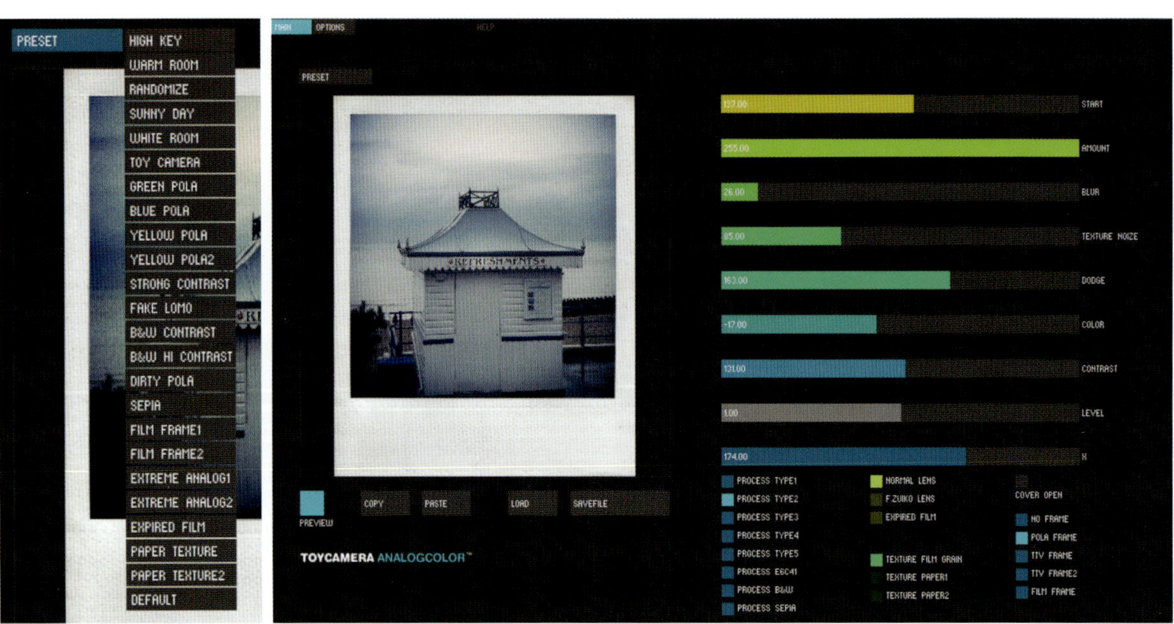

Preset: Choose from the list of presets to apply a predetermined combination of processing parameters, as well as setting the process type, lens, texture, and frame effect. You can use any of the presets "as is," or use it as a starting point: you are free to make any changes you like.

Processing Parameters: The sliders allow you to set key parameters for your image, or fine-tune a preset, while the buttons beneath enable you to choose different color processes, lens types, textures, and border effects, as well as introducing light leaks to your digital lo-fi shot.

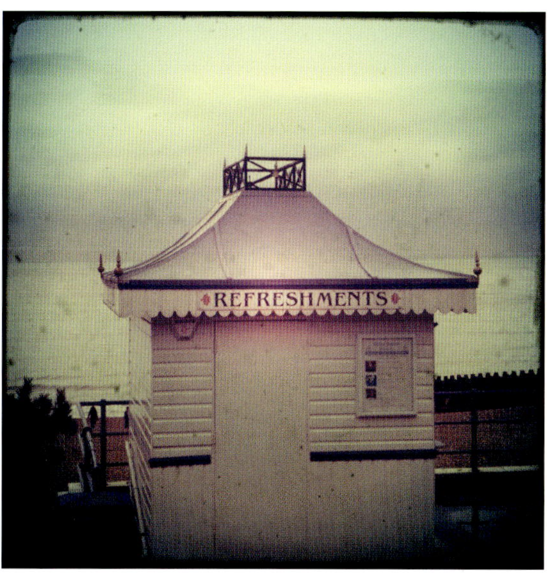

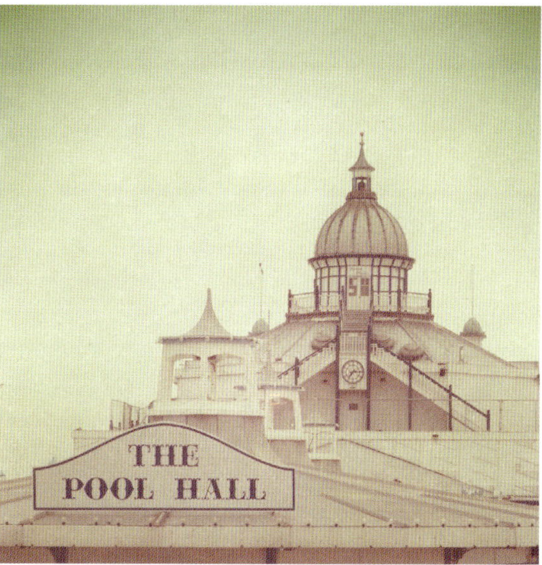

Above:
The starting point for this lo-fi shot included applying a
TTV (Through The Viewfinder) frame...

Above right:
...while a coarse paper texture and muted colors formed
the basis for this faded image.

Right:
ToyCamera AnalogColor's 35mm film sprockets come
complete with frame numbers and other markings,
making them very convincing.

images. You can also create and save your own
lo-fi processing combinations to reuse on future
shots. Unless you need to use any selection
tools or want to retouch parts of your picture,
you may find that once you've got TCAC you
don't need to use your regular image-editing
program as much as you used to.

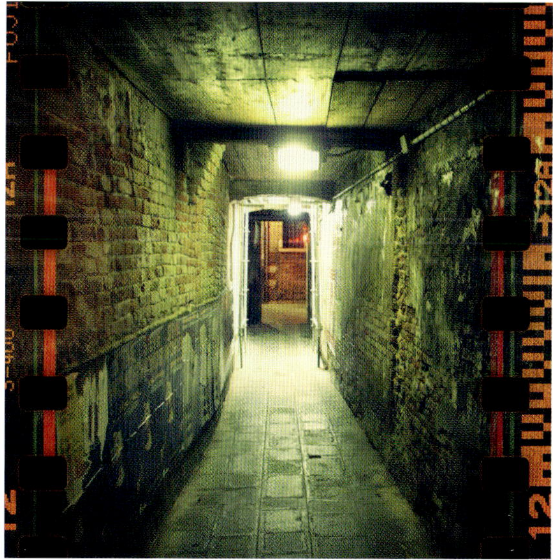

Digital lo-fi FX

ToyCamera AnalogColor is great at creating a range of lo-fi looks, and Poladroid does a good job of giving you an "instant image" look with minimal effort (or expense), but if you aren't afraid to "get your hands dirty" (at least as much as that's possible with a computer) then you can also create a pseudo lo-fi and/or plastic camera look using an image-editing program such as Photoshop (including Elements), PaintShop Pro, or Gimp.

The advantage of working this way, rather than using an "off the shelf" lo-fi image creator, is that you will have access to a much wider range of tools. This means you have greater choice and freedom when it comes to customizing your results, as well as the option to work "non-destructively" on layers.

The ability to change an image (and undo and redo any such changes) means you're not going to be subscribing to the "happy accident" ethos of plastic cameras. This removes any serendipity from your shots, and it's easy to create "polished" digital images that undermine the exercise. As you'll see on the following pages, you can create a relatively authentic result that can be honed to match your vision.

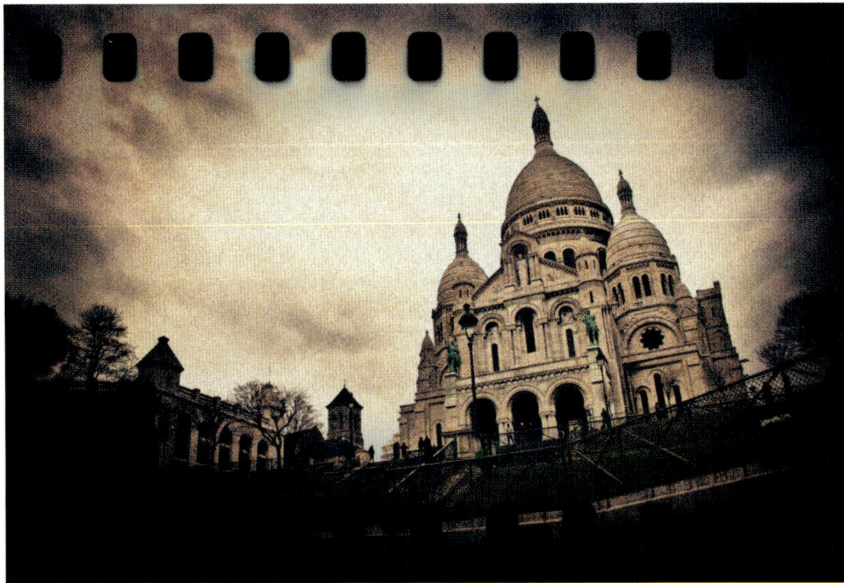

Your regular image-editing software package will most likely have all the tools you need to transform your high-tech digital shots into wonderfully lo-fi images.

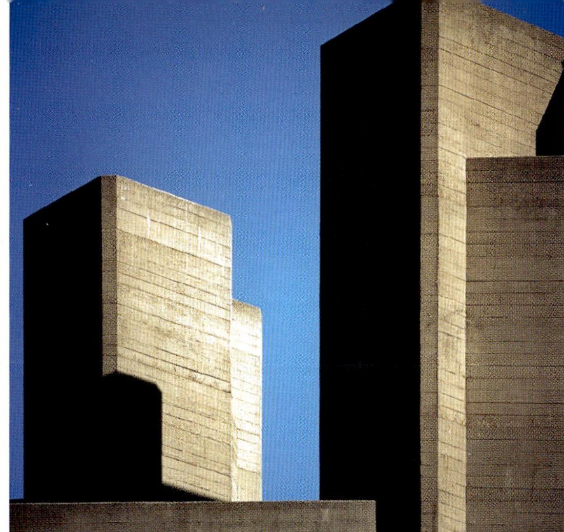

Grain

Nothing screams "shot on film" as loud as grain. Most editing programs have at least one "film grain" filter. Not all are successful, and some have even less appeal than digital noise. However, with a couple of filters and a contrast tweak, you can produce something that's far more convincing.

1. Noise doesn't compare to grain, but ironically that's the starting point for a film grain effect. In Photoshop, head to Filter>Noise>Add Noise. Set Distribution to Gaussian, check the Monochromatic box, and then dial in the Amount—5–15% is usually enough, but it depends on the size of your image.

2. With the base noise added, transform it into "grain." Select the Gaussian Blur filter (Filter>Blur>Gaussian Blur): set the Radius no higher than 1.0 pixel so that it softens the noise, but not image detail.

3. Adding noise (or grain) reduces the overall contrast, so open the Levels dialog (Image>Adjustments>Levels) and set the black and white slider values to 5 and 250 respectively to put the "bite" back into your image. That's it—you're done!

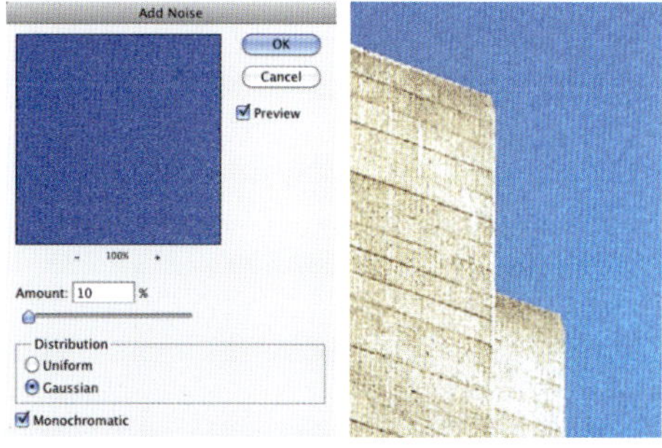

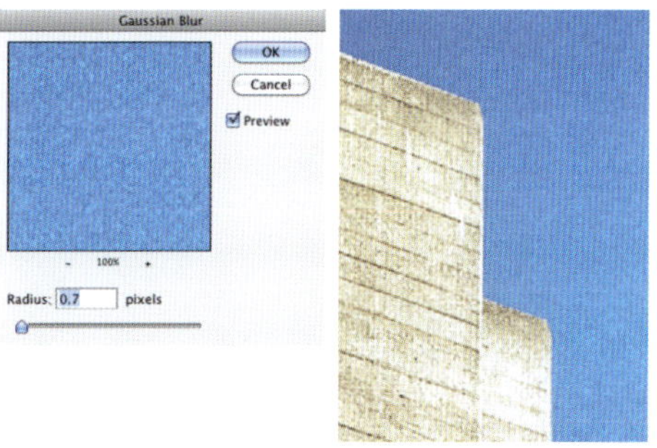

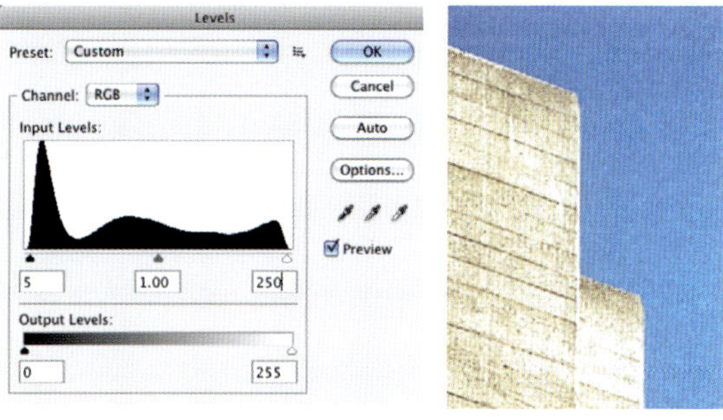

Vignettes

Vignetting—or "corner shading"—is an integral part of the lo-fi aesthetic, whether it's a gentle and subtle darkening of the corners of the frame, as with the Lubitel 166, or the severe fall-off in exposure exhibited by the Diana. A lot of editing programs will allow you to add a vignette to your images, often using sliders to control the size and density of the shading. This is fine, but your vignettes can start to look a little bit regimented—something that definitely doesn't apply when you add your digital vignette manually.

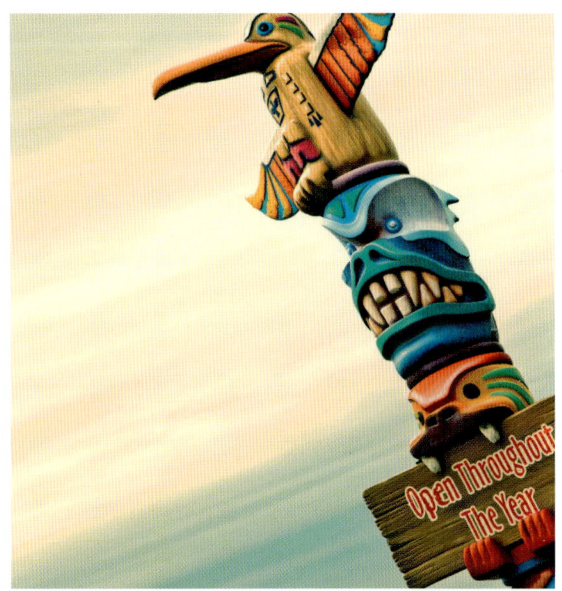

1. Because I want a one-of-a-kind vignette I'm using Photoshop's freehand Lasso Tool to define the areas I want to darken. However, rather than select the corners, draw the selection around the area of the image you want to preserve.

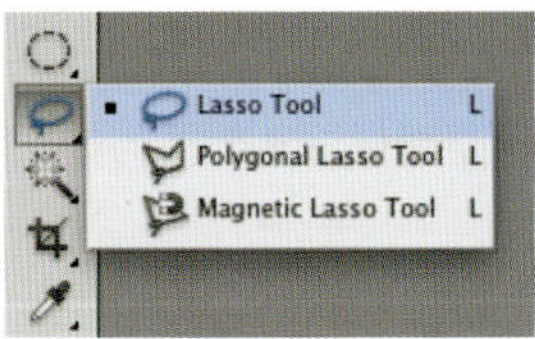

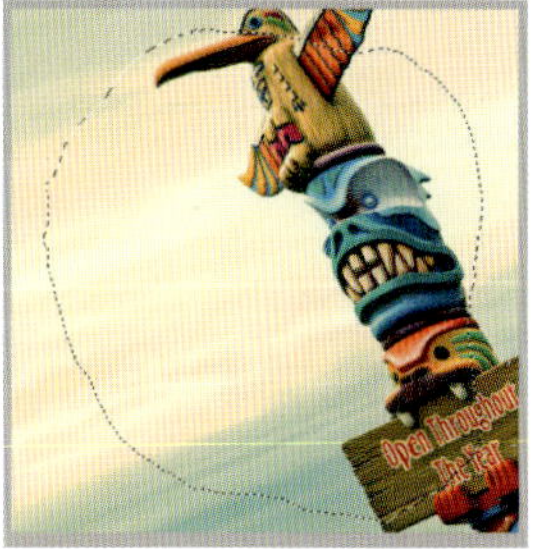

2. Flip your selection using Select>Inverse so the corners are now selected and then press Q to enter Photoshop's Quick Mask mode. It will depend on your Quick Mask Options whether the edges or center of the image is masked, and the color of the mask (I have my preferences set to Selected Area with a red mask at 50% Opacity).

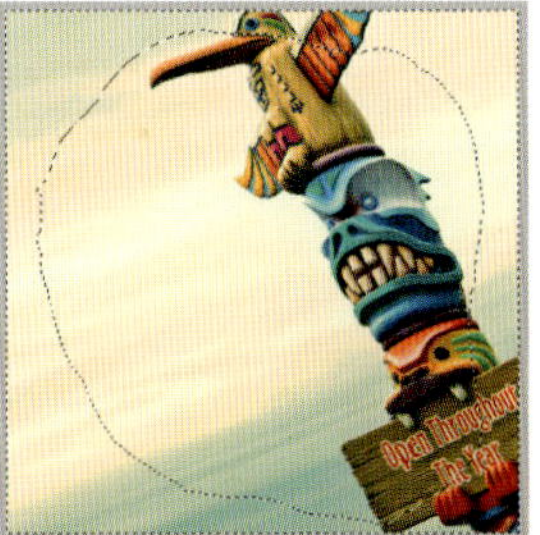

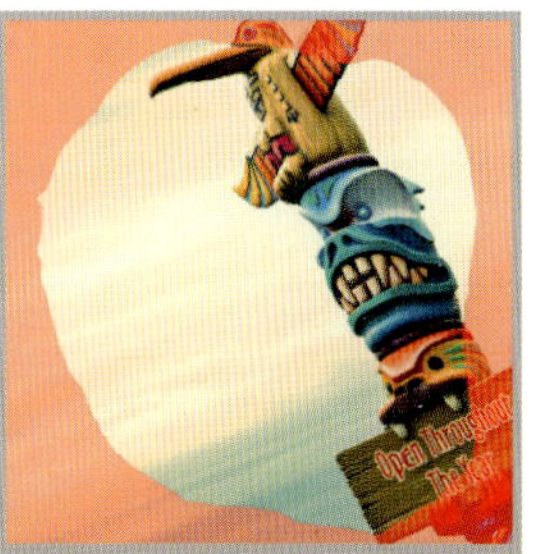

3. Blur the mask using the Gaussian Blur filter. The Radius you set will depend on the size of your image and how "hard" you want the vignette to be. A higher Radius gives a softer transition, while a lower Radius will make the edges of the vignette stand out more. Here I've gone for a Radius of 200 pixels.

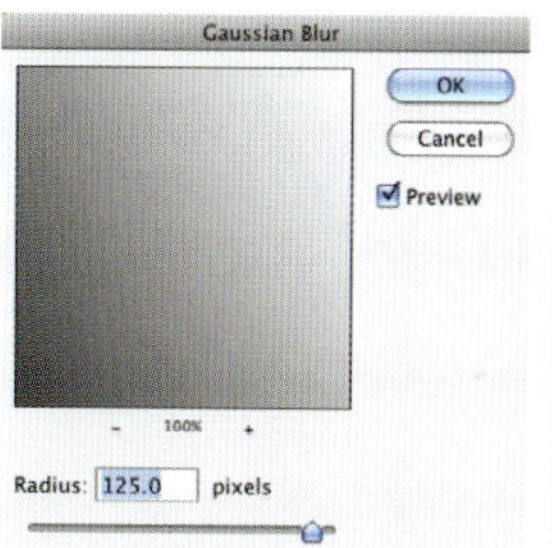
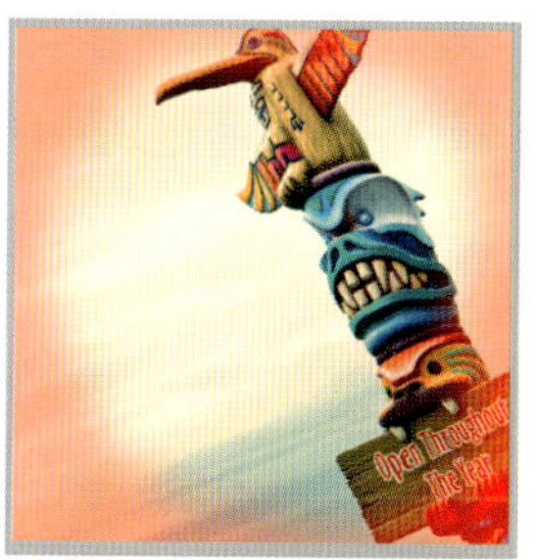

4. Press Q again to switch from Quick Mask to Standard Mode (the "marching ants") and then copy (Edit>Copy) and paste (Edit>Paste) the selected corners into a new layer.

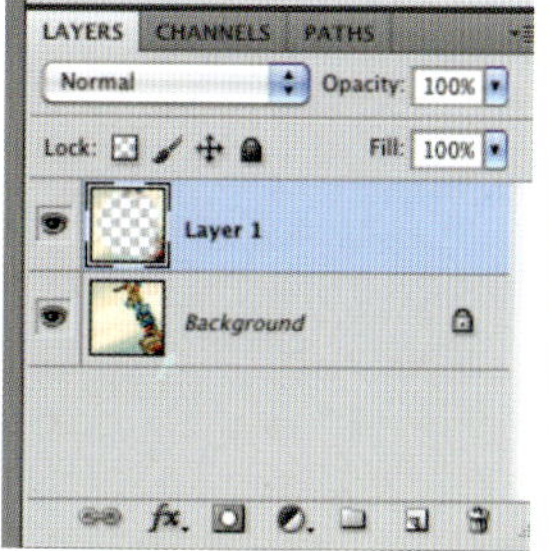
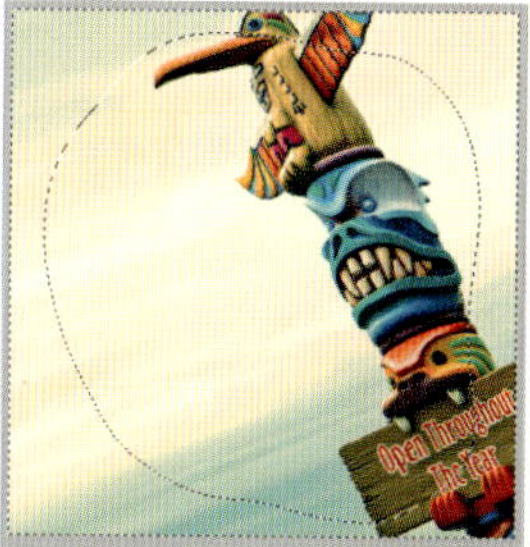

5. You can now use one of your software's exposure tools (Levels, Curves, or Brightness/Contrast, for example) to darken the corners layer and create your handcrafted vignette. You can also experiment with layer blending modes, the opacity of your vignette layer, and use additional color and contrast tools until you get the result that you want.

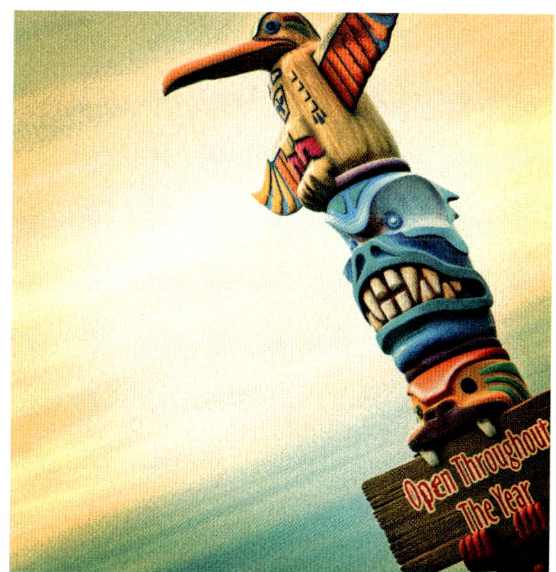

Focus **fall-off**

In addition to vignetting, the lens on a plastic camera will often struggle to maintain sharpness across the frame, with edges and corners—and sometimes even the center of the image—gaining a softness that's distinctly lo-fi. Recreating this with your editing program relies on a process that largely echoes that of adding a vignette, but don't be tempted to combine the two: the result will be more convincing if your vignette and focus fall-off aren't perfectly aligned with each other.

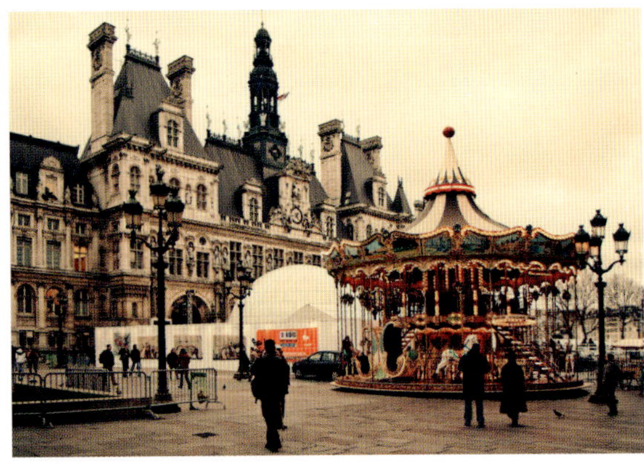

1. Follow steps 1–4 of Vignetting on the previous pages, using the freehand Lasso Tool, Quick Mask mode, and Gaussian Blur filter to select the corners and edges that will be defocused. Then copy your selection into a new layer.

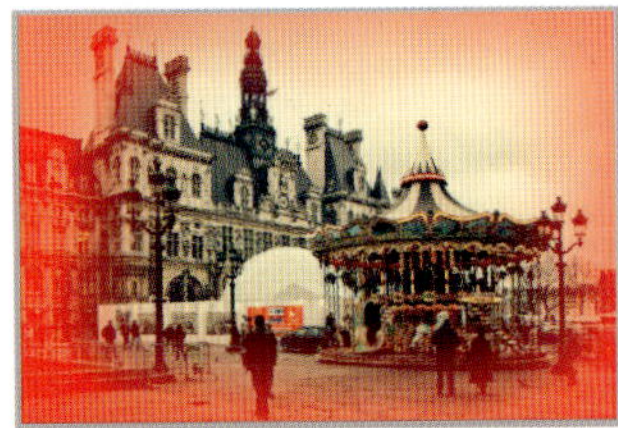

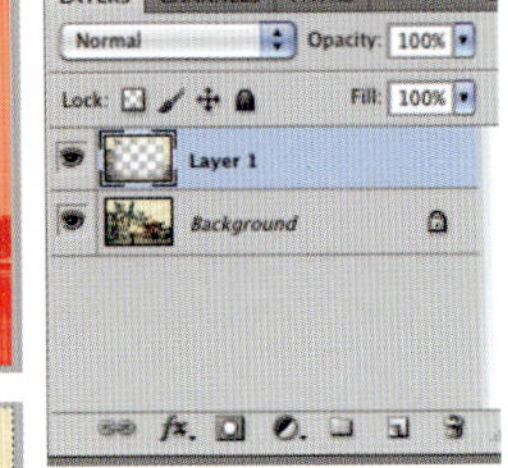

2. You could use Photoshop's Lens Blur filter (Filter>Blur>Lens Blur) to defocus the edges of the frame, but this is a bit sophisticated for the lo-fi look, so I use the Gaussian Blur filter instead. Simply dial in the Radius that gives you the blur you're after: anything from a mild, LOMO LC-A style softness, through to the heavy blur of a medium format Holga or Diana.

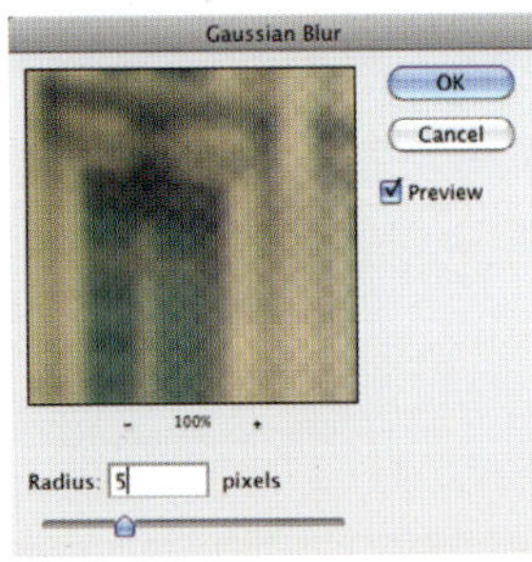

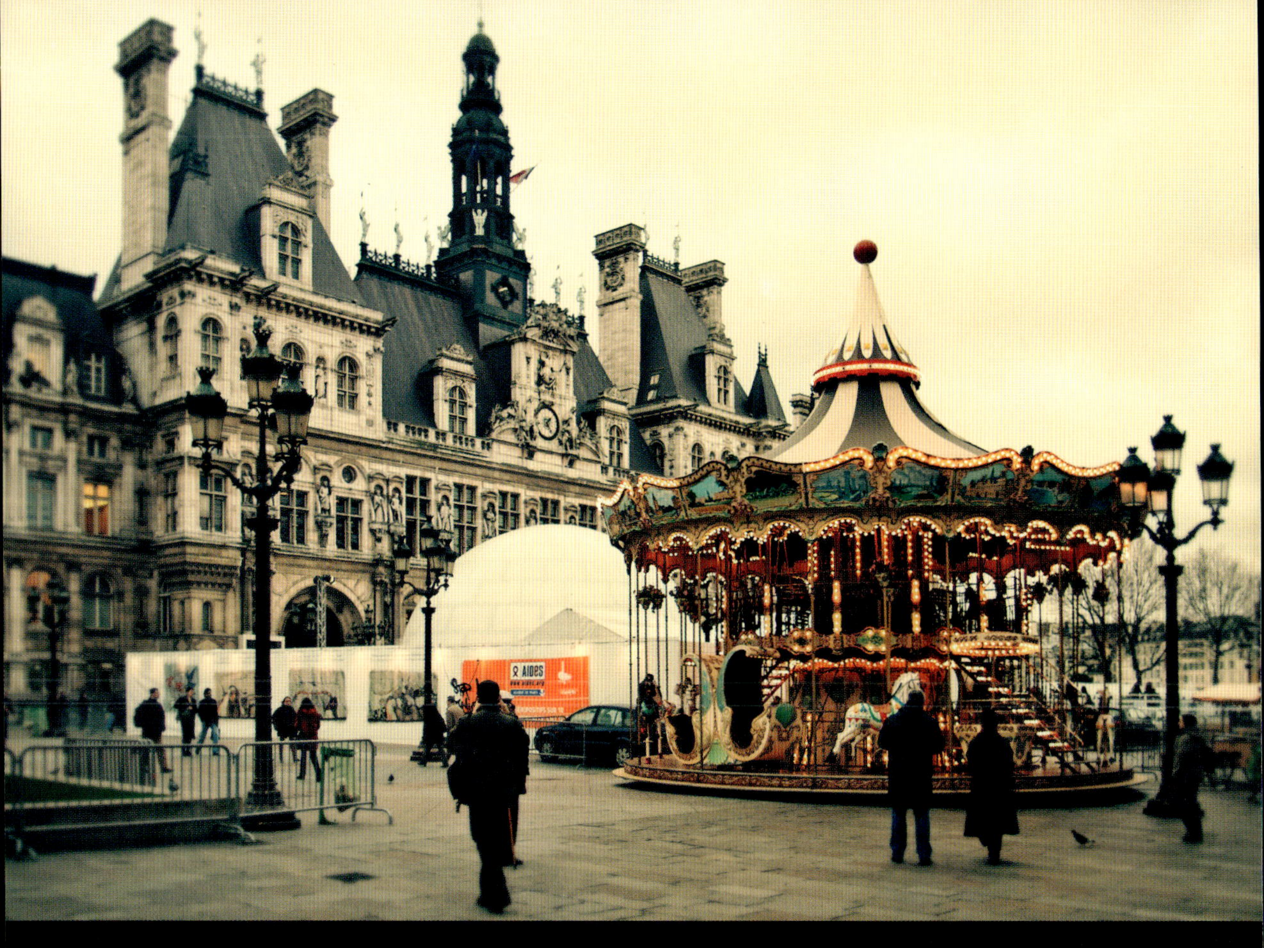

Sprocket **shots**

In earlier chapters you saw how you can create "sprocket shots" using a medium format camera loaded with 35mm film, or a camera such as the Blackbird, Fly or Sprocket Rocket. But you don't need to have shot using one of these cameras to celebrate the distinctive edges of 35mm emulsion, or indeed used film—you can add "fake" sprocket holes to your digital images.

You need two things: first, the image you want to add the sprocket holes to and, second a "blank" film frame. This could be a scan or photograph of a piece of exposed and processed 35mm film (you'd replace the image that's already there) or you could look online for something suitable.

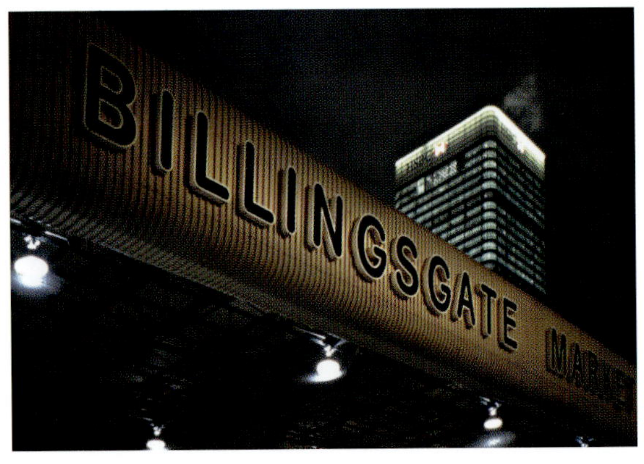

1. The first step is to prep your film frame. The aim is to keep any frame numbers or marks around the edges of the film, with sprocket holes for authenticity. Start by copying your film to a new layer (Layer>Duplicate Layer) and then delete the original Background layer. This will enable you to edit your film on a transparent background.

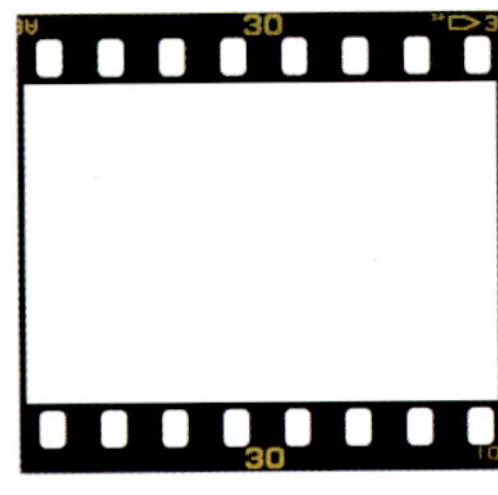

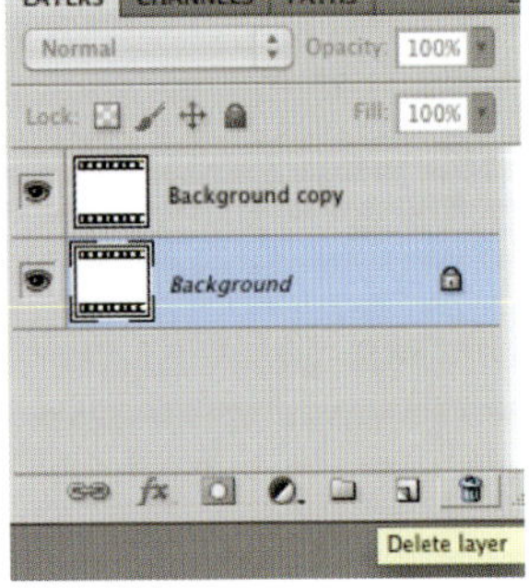

2. To preserve the numbers at the edge of the frame, copy them to a new layer. There are numerous ways of doing this, but if they're all the same color, as they are here, using Color Range (Select>Color Range) is a good option. When the Color Range dialog opens, click on one of the numbers to determine the color and set the Fuzziness slider to its maximum. Click OK to make the selection and copy and paste (Edit>Copy/Edit>Paste) the selected numbers to a new layer.

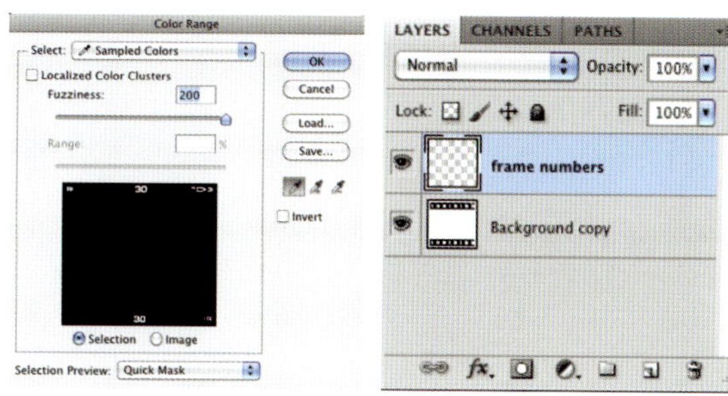

3. The sprocket holes are next on the list. This frame has already had the image removed and replaced with white, so I'm using Color Range again, this time to select the white areas of the film before copying and pasting them into another new layer. Your film image will not appear to have changed in any way at this stage.

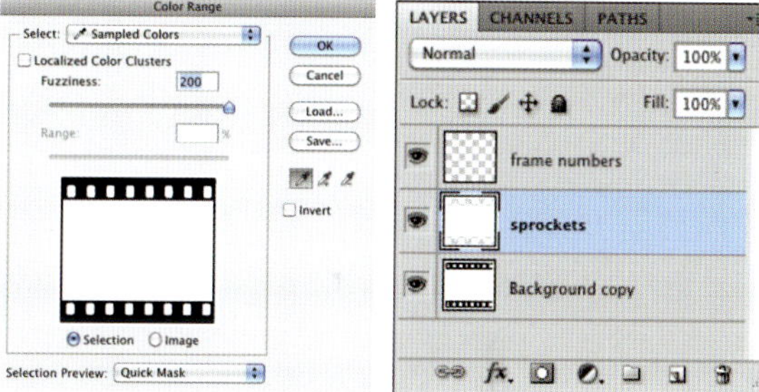

4. With the sprocket holes and frame numbers isolated on their own layers, delete the Background copy layer by selecting the layer and clicking on the Trashcan at the bottom of the Layers palette. You should now have your white sprocket holes, colored numbers, and a checkerboard grid indicating transparent areas in the image.

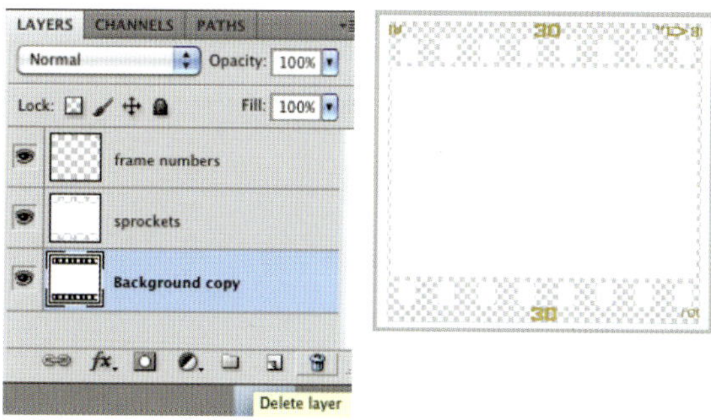

5. The last step before adding your image is to remove the center of the frame—the white rectangle in this example. Because of its shape I'm simply going to select it with the Rectangular Marque tool and use Edit>Cut to delete it.

6. It's now time to bring in your main picture, either by copying and pasting it into your film image, or dragging it from one image window to the other. Position it at the bottom of the layers stack in the Layers palette, and use the Move tool and Scale tool (Edit>Transform>Scale) to fit it in your film frame

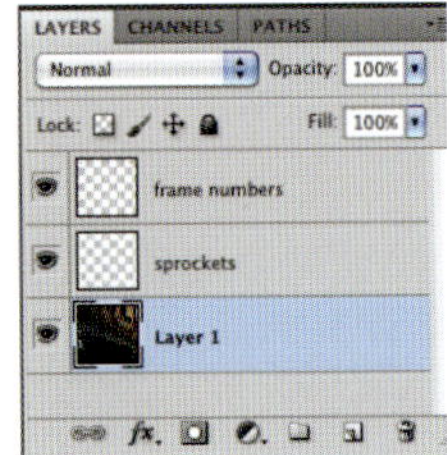 

7. To finish up, convert the white sprocket holes to black by selecting the sprocket layer and inverting it (Image>Adjustments>Invert). With this shot I've also increased slightly the scale of the sprocket holes to exaggerate them for creative effect.

False sprockets

Although you will only get the sprocket shot look from using a 35mm film frame, the same technique can be used to create faux medium format (or large format) shots as well. Using a medium format frame is particularly effective when combined with a square image and the vignetting and focus fall off techniques mentioned previously, to create a pseudo Diana or Holga style result.

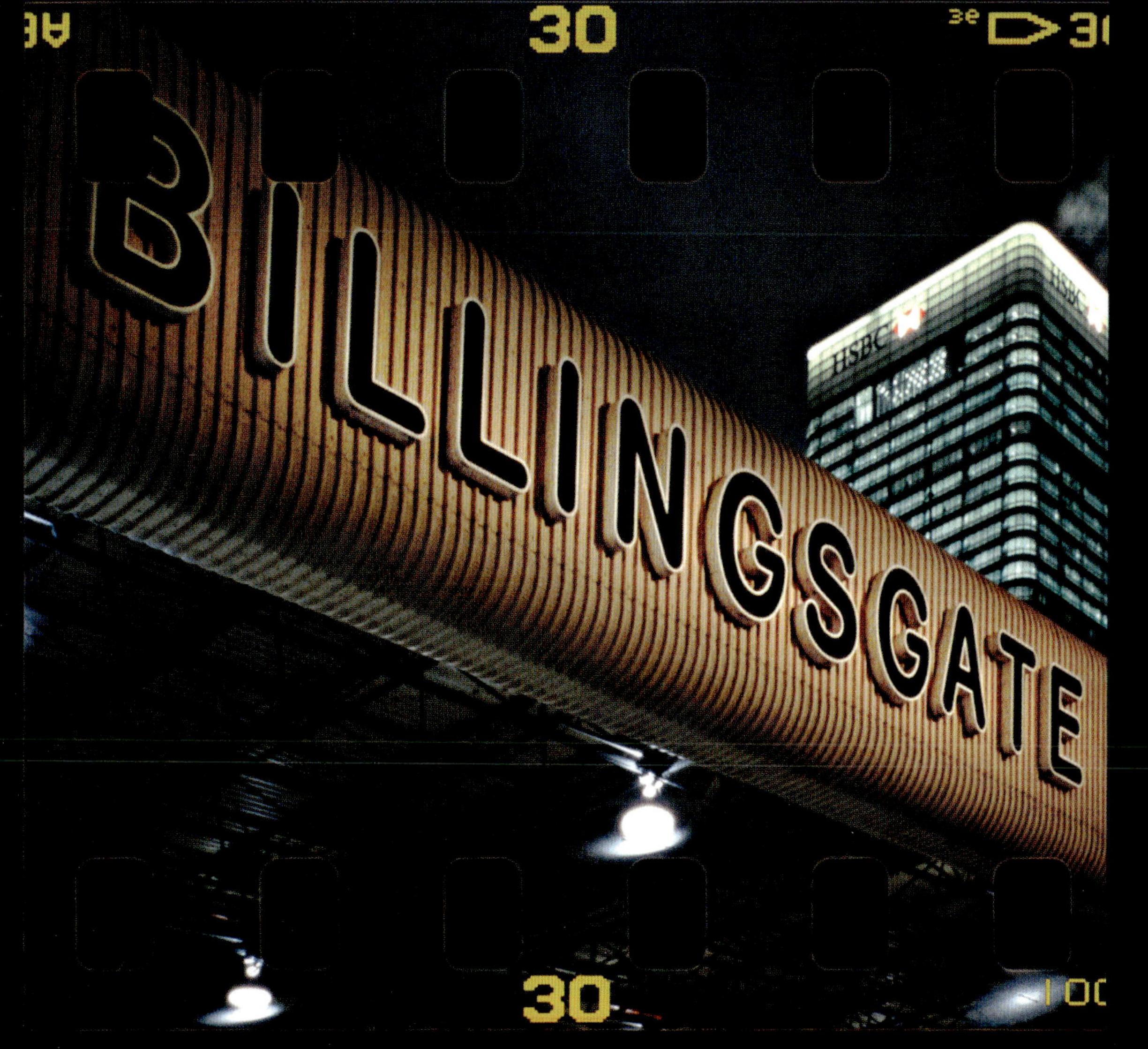

BILLINGSGATE
HSBC

Cross-processing

The practicalities of cross-processing film used to be fairly straightforward: all you needed to do was ask your lab to process your film through the "wrong" chemistry (slide film through the C41 chemistry designed for negative film, or running negative film through the E6 transparency process). However, your local "wet" lab might not be that local any more, as digital print stations increasingly replace chemical lines. Of course, there is the option to send your film off and get it cross-processed—Lomography offers precisely that service, for example—but it takes time, and great results aren't always guaranteed when you "abuse" your film in this way.

Digital post-processing neatly sidesteps all of these pitfalls, allowing any image to be treated with a cross-processed look (and if you don't like it you can revert back to your original picture and try something different). However, it's fair to say that it also removes any sense of surprise or anticipation from the process.

1. The most versatile method for creating a cross-processed look is to use Curves. Start by adding a Curves Adjustment Layer (Layer>New Adjustment Layer>Curves) and switch from the RGB curve to the Red channel using the dropdown menu. The curve shown here uses two additional control points, while the top right point has been dragged to the left to add an overall pink color-cast to the highlights.

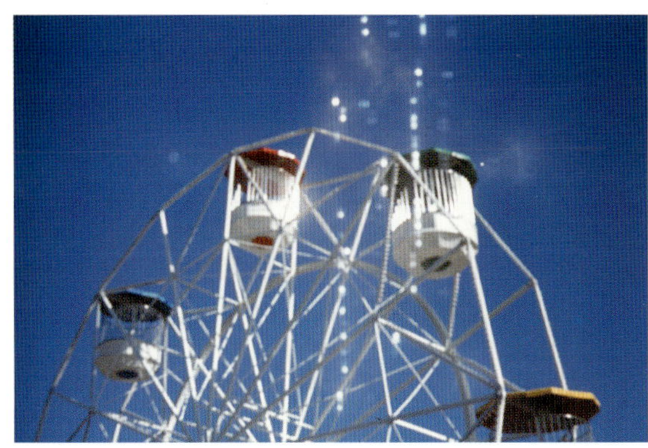

This shot was taken using a fake Leica camera that wasn't particularly light-tight, hence the "sparkles" in the center of the image.

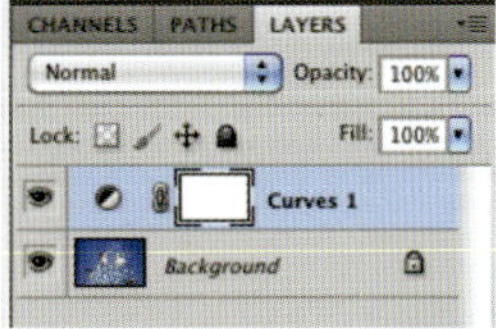

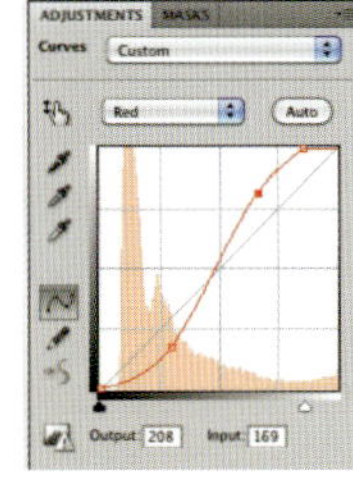

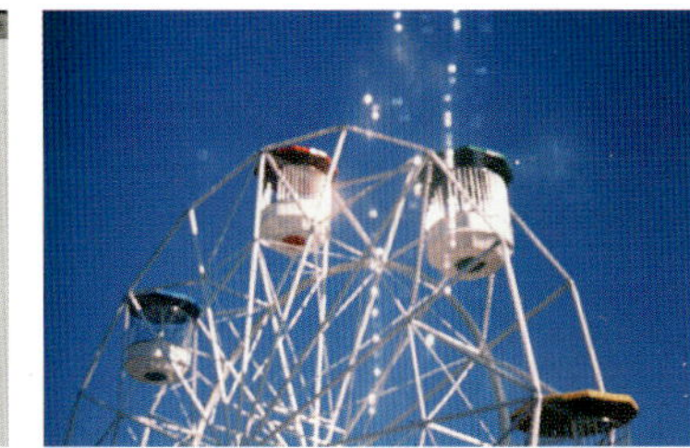

2. Next, select the Green channel and adjust this curve as well. Again, two control points have been added—one to the lower left to hold the shadow areas, and one to the right, which increases the amount of green in the highlights.

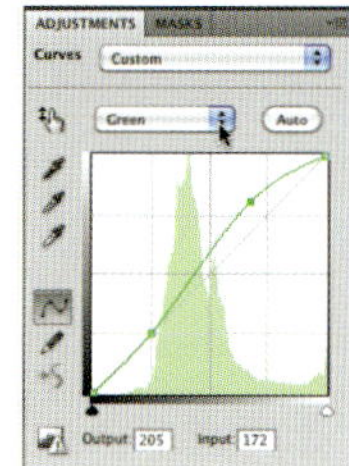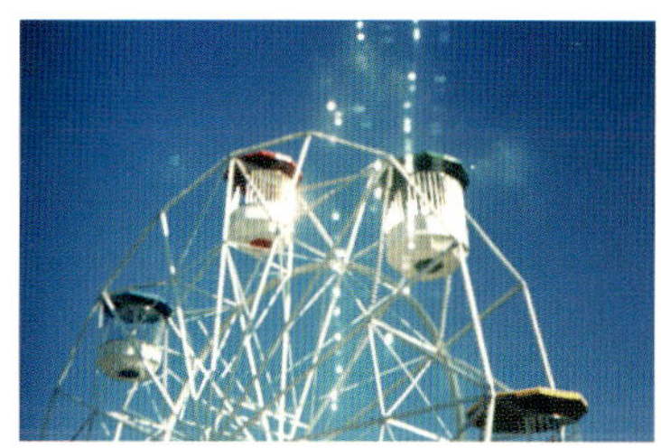

3. The final curves adjustment is to the Blue channel, but no additional points are needed here. Instead, the lower left control point has been raised (increasing the amount of blue in the shadows), while the top right point has been lowered (decreasing blue/increasing yellow in the highlights).

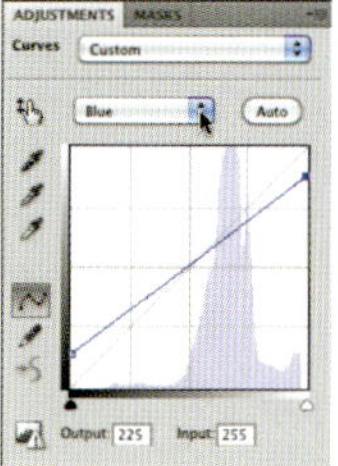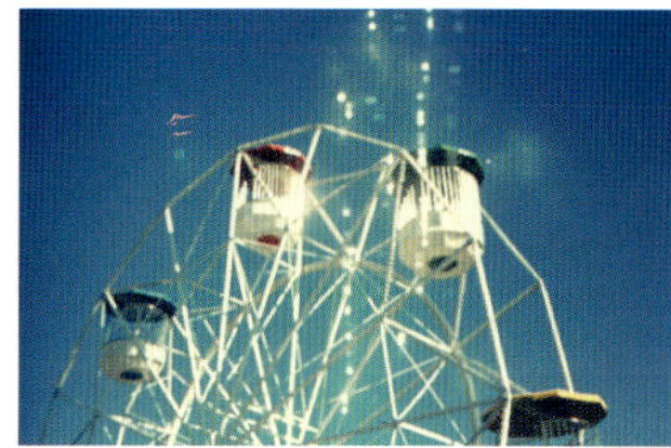

4. With the color-work done, the effect can be fine-tuned, starting with a contrast tweak. Create a new Curves adjustment layer for this and change its blending mode to Luminosity. It's important to use a new layer, as this will prevent your adjustments having any effect on the color. You can now adjust the contrast using the main RGB curve. I've used anchor points to hold the upper (highlight) end of the curve; raise the mid-point to lighten the midtones; and lower the bottom end of the curve to produce the characteristically dark shadows.

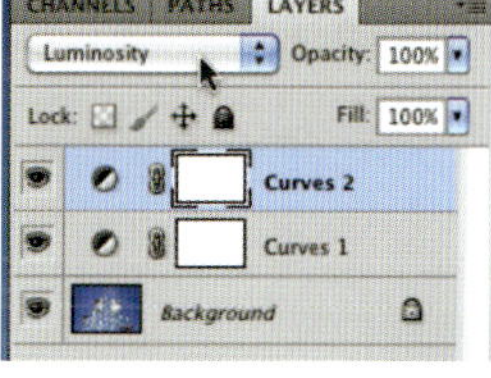
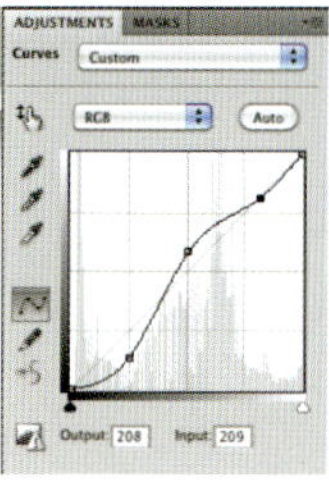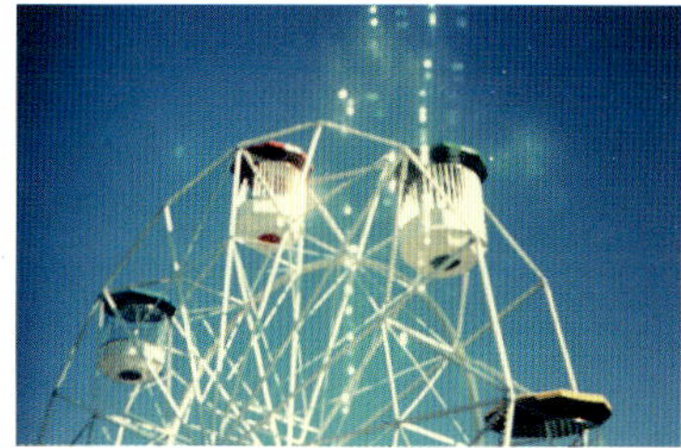

5. This next step is optional, but adds an overall yellow tint that is often found when you cross process some film types. Create a fill layer (Layer>New Fill Layer>Solid Color) and choose a yellow hue from the color picker. Once this has been applied, set the layer's blending mode to Color, and reduce the opacity—5–15% is usually enough.

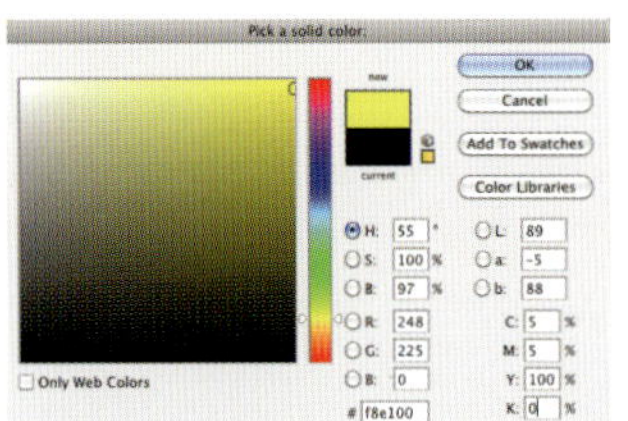
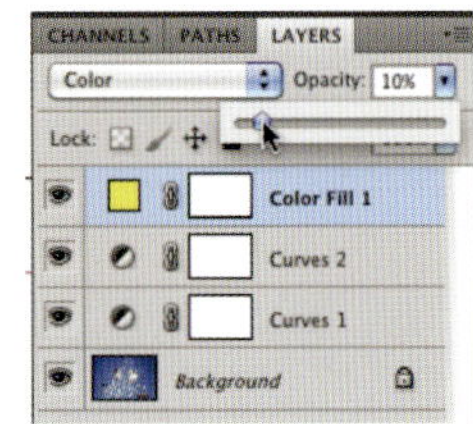

6. To finish up, I've added grain (see page 175) and dropped in some sprocket holes (see pages 180–183) before making a couple of minor levels and curves adjustments to fine-tune the image.

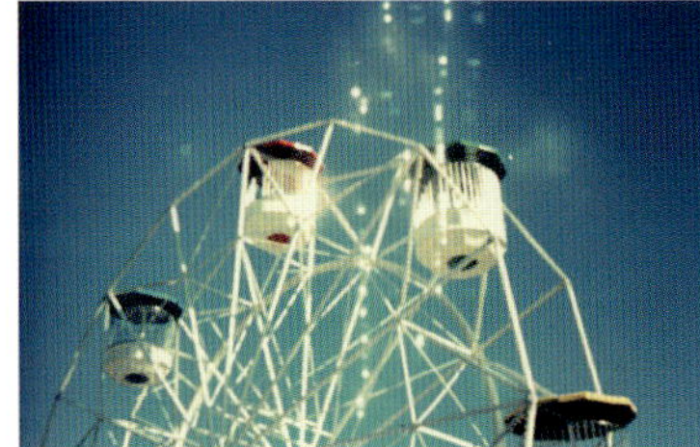

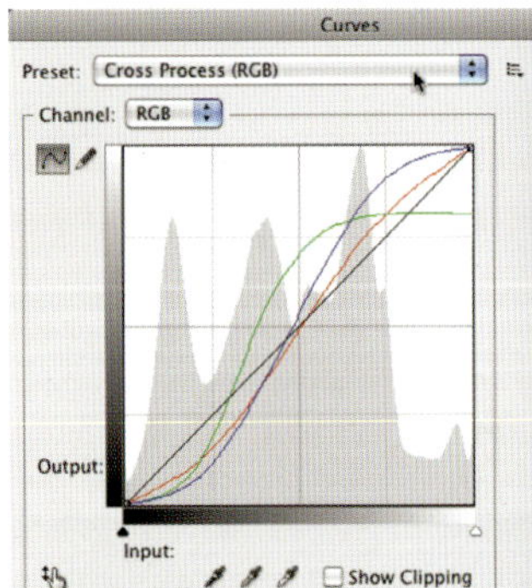
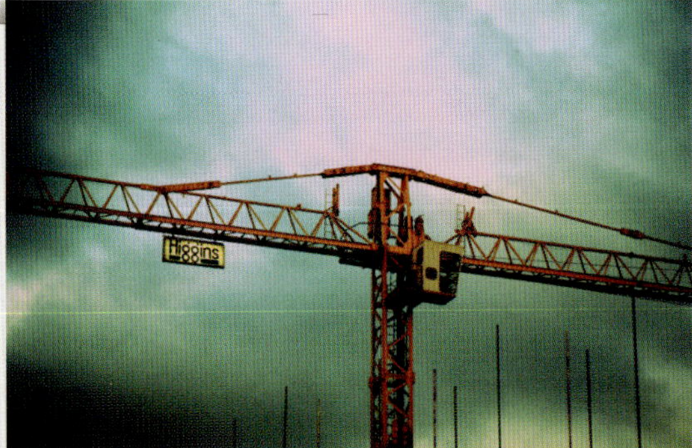

Instant cross-processing

Photoshop's Curves dialog has a dropdown menu offering a number of preset curve adjustments, including a Cross Process option. So why not just use that and save yourself a heap of work? Well, as shown here, the Cross Process preset certainly changes the color of an image, but it's an unusual take on the technique, and one that is perhaps best left alone.

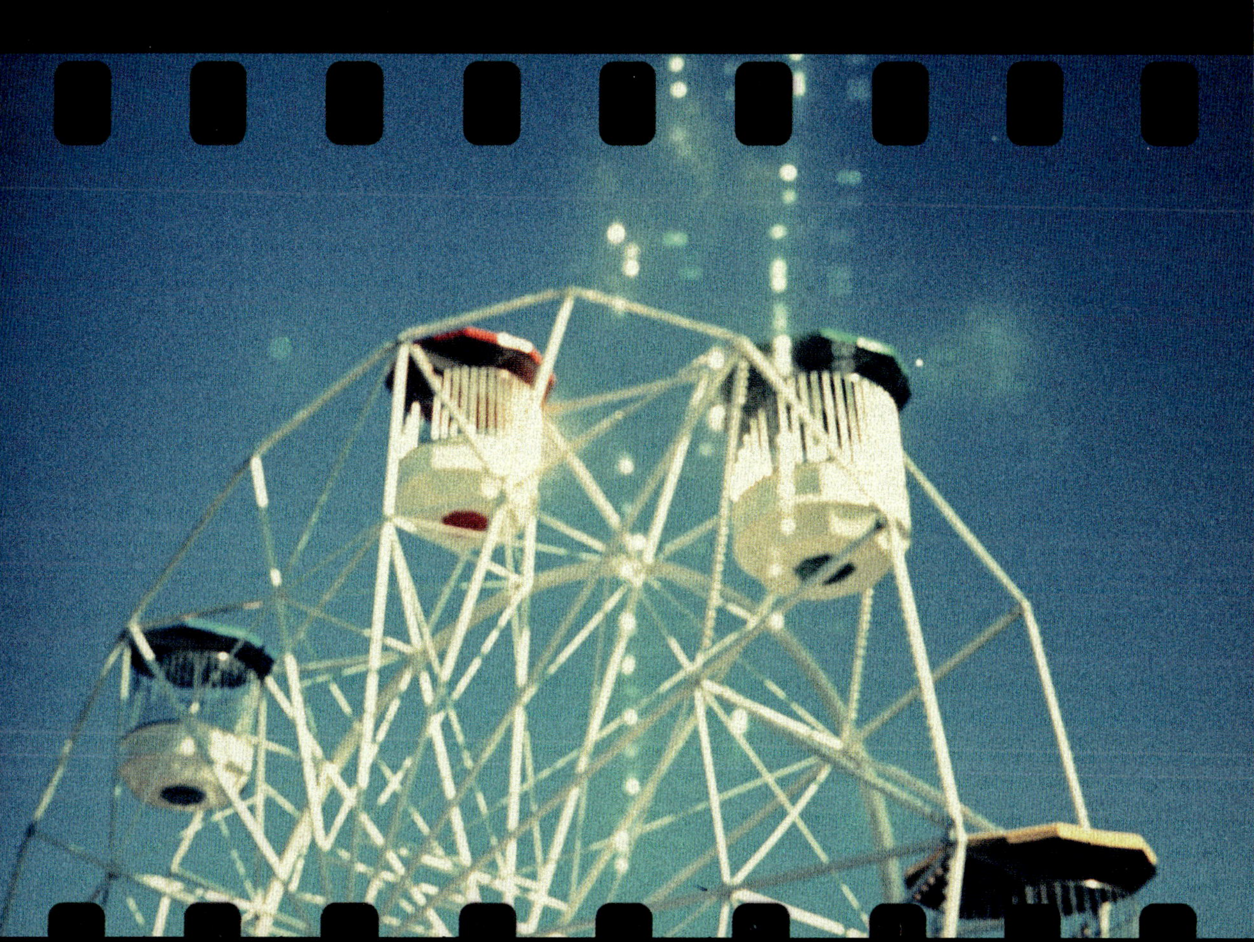

Redscale

In the previous chapter you saw how you can get the redscale look using "readymade" redscale film or rolling your own. But you may simply want to take one camera out with you—perhaps digital, or loaded with regular color film, rather than redscale. There's nothing stopping you from faking the redscale look post-capture, as shown in the following steps.

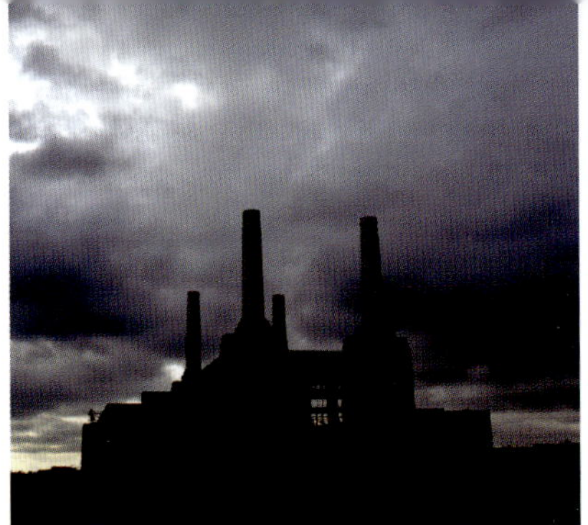

1. As with cross-processing, the key to the redscale effect is the Curves tool, so open your image and add a Curves adjustment layer by choosing Layer>New Adjustment Layer>Curves from the menu or clicking on the Adjustment Layer button at the bottom of the Layers palette and selecting Curves.

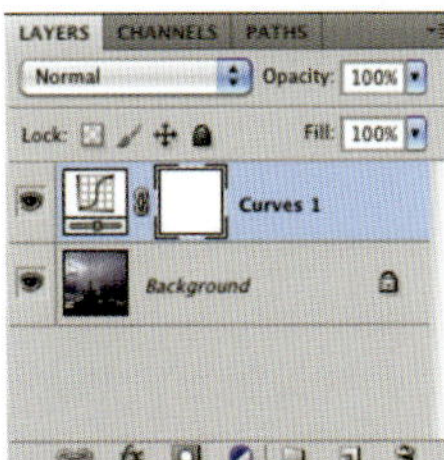

2. In the Adjustments palette, switch from an RGB curve to Red, using the dropdown menu. To introduce some red to the shadows of your image raise the far left anchor point on the curve by dragging it upward. Then, add a second anchor point approximately ¼ of the way in from the left and drag this point upward as well.

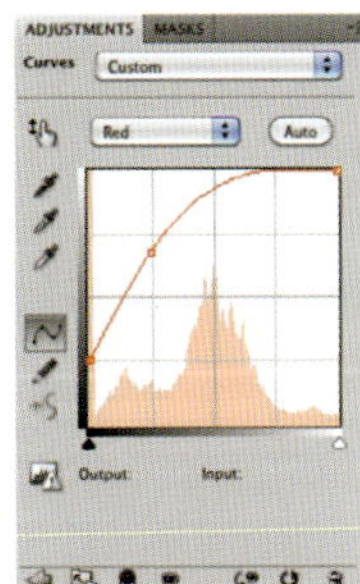
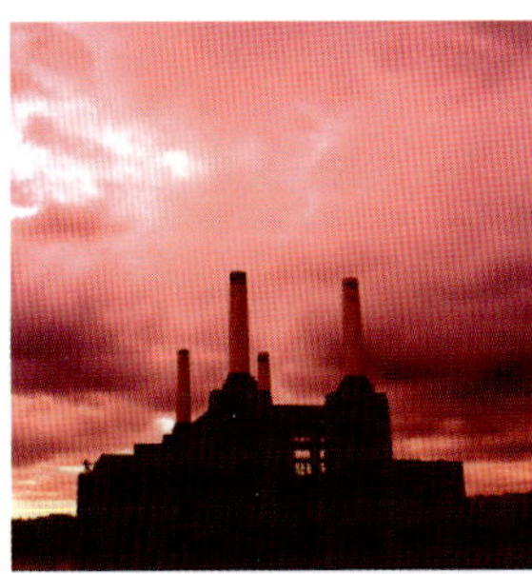

3. Switch to the Green channel (again using the dropdown menu toward the top of the Adjustments palette). This time add two anchor points to the curve, and drag them downward to decrease the green in your image and boost the magenta tones.

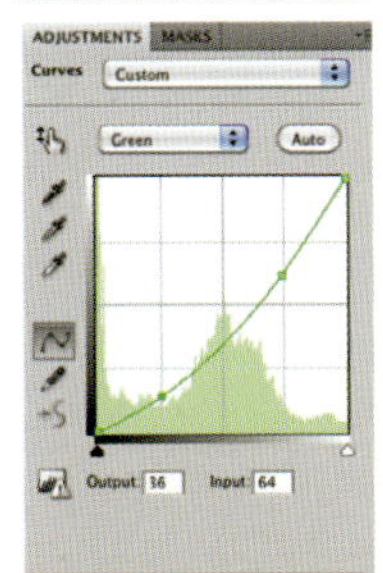
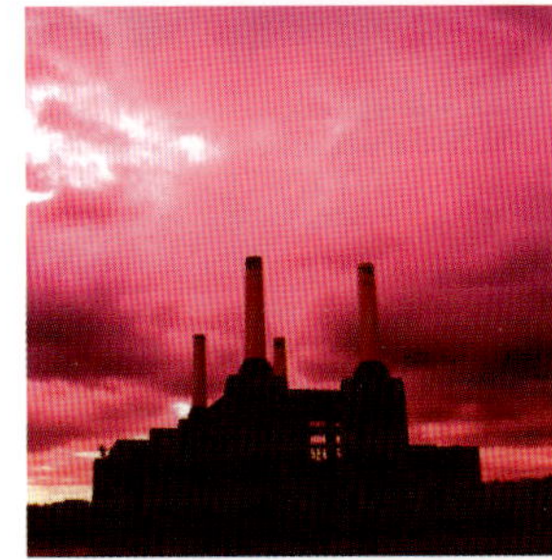

4. The third curve adjustment is to the third color channel: blue. Having selected the blue channel from the dropdown list, click on the top right anchor point and drag it straight downward. This will reduce the amount of blue in your photograph (effectively increasing the yellows), immediately giving you a vibrant, characteristic redscale look.

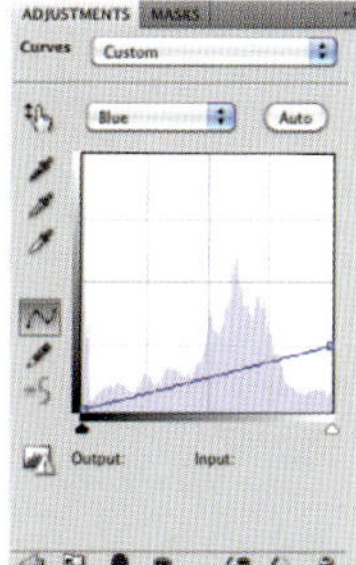

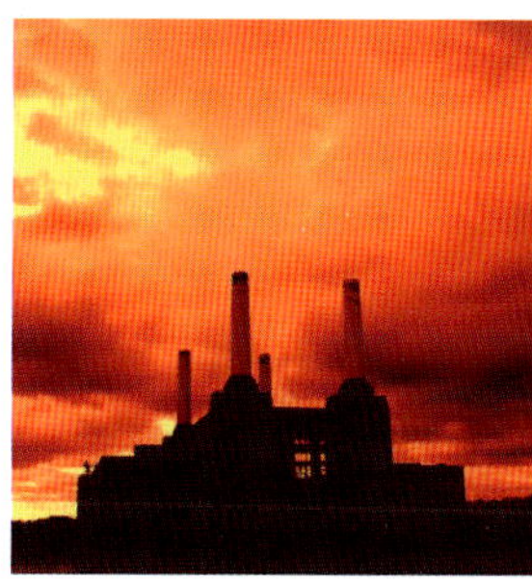

5. Now return to the "master" RGB curve by selecting RGB from the dropdown list and adjust the overall contrast of the image—in this example, I've raised the master (black) curve to lighten the image overall and reduce the color intensity slightly. Remember, you can also go back to the individual color curves to fine tune them as well.

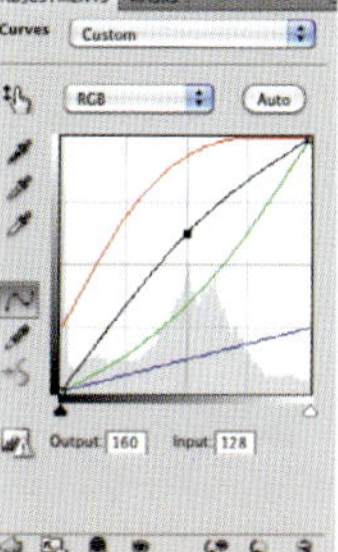

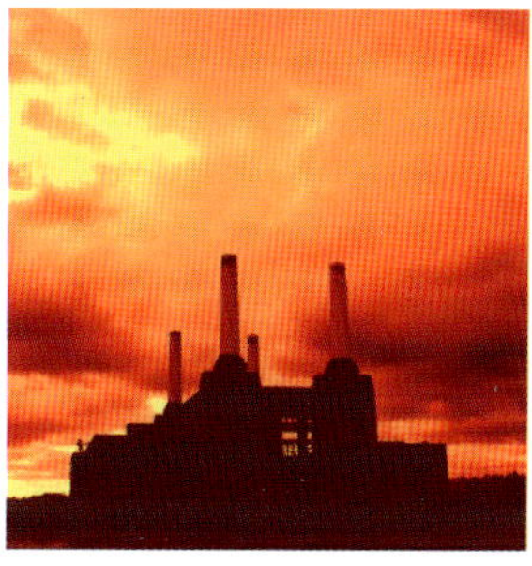

6. To finish up, consider adding a small amount of grain as outlined on page 175; Lomography and Rollei redscale films are all medium-to-fast, ISO 400–800 emulsions, so a bit of grain is to be expected. With this shot I also reduced the saturation by a small amount.

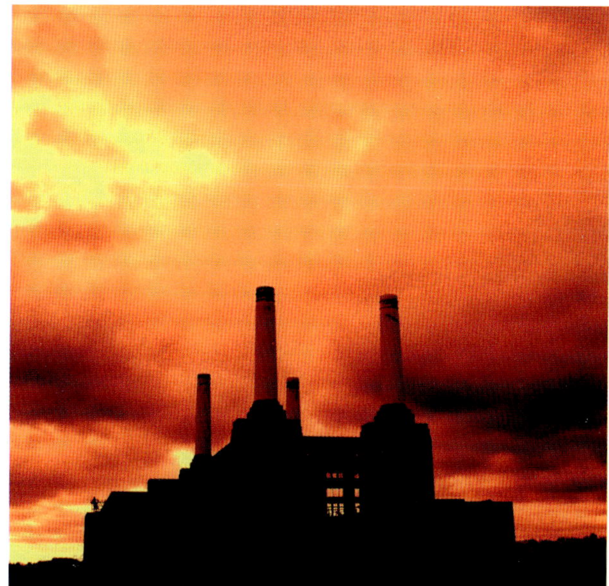

Picture **credits**

All product photography by Chris Gatcum, with the following exceptions:

(Kandor Candid) 105
John Kratz
www.flickr.com/kratz

(Dick Tracy) 109
John Kratz
www.flickr.com/kratz

(King Check Polaphy) 135
Holger Schult
www.camerasdownunder.com

Lo-fi Polaroid/color effects by Chris Gatcum using ToyCamera AnalogColor.

With thanks to the following photographers for contributing images to this book:

Katrin Adam 147 (top r)
www.impression-expression.de

Ximena Alzugaray 129
www.flickr.com/dementosa
www.lomography.com/homes/ximenalzugaray

Thanawat Amnueypornsakul 38 (r)
www.flickr.com/vikkies

David Åsbrink 55
www.flickr.com/tveljus
www.tveljus.se

Richard Barnard 79 (top l, r)
www.flickr.com/ftwentytwo

Darin Barry 25 (r), 60
www.flickr.com/darynbarry

Roberto Barraez D'Lucca cover; 134
www.flickr.com/rahul3

Bruce Berrien 12–13, 47 (both)
www.flickr.com/bruceberrien

Victor Bezrukov 165
www.flickr.com/s-t-r-a-n-g-e

Abe Bingham 109 (r)
www.flickr.com/8838

Michele Boccamazzo 135 (top l)
www.flickr.com/micboc
www.micboc.com

Adrian Boliston 36, 37
www.flickr.com/boliston

Joel Bombardier 33, 40 (bottom r & back flap)
www.flickr.com/bombardier

Tristan Bowersox 167 (both)
www.flickr.com/9516941@N08

Jenni Callard 71, 105 (top l)
www.flickr.com/ipdegirl

Yisheng Chang 143 (r)
www.flickr.com/changyisheng

Kristin Charles-Scaringi 43 (bottom l)
www.flickr.com/kpen

Angelo Chen 123
www.flickr.com/darkangel050

Jessie Chew 147 (top l)
www.flickr.com/freakish-jess

Samuele "Hum.as" Ciardelli 2
www.flickr.com/samuchappy

Victoria Clarkson 125
www.flickr.com/vikki-lea

William Clifford 45 (bottom)
www.flickr.com/williac

C1ssou 81
www.flickr.com/c1ssou

Claudia Cruz 7, 31
www.flickr.com/claudiapcruz

Elena Delgado Lemus 119 (bottom)
www.flickr.com/disorder-heaven

Alex Dixon 44
www.flickr.com/f_minus
www.arekkusu.net

Kevin Dooley 23 (t), 25 (l)
www.flickr.com/pagedooley

Thomas Edwards 73 (bottom)
www.flickr.com/photomonkey

Gigi Elmes 103 (l)
www.gigielmes.com

Mar Estragués 39 (r)
www.flickr.com/marestra

Vladimir Fedotov 145 (bottom l, r)
www.vladimirfedotov.ru
www.flickr.com/payalnic

Herval Freire 97 (top, 2nd top)
ww.flickr.com/herval

Chris Gatcum 5, 10, 11, 154 (r),
156–157, 158, 159, 161, 169–187
www.cgphoto.co.uk

Ian Gilbert 69, 85
www.flickr.com/acf_windy
www.wickerman.tumblr.com
www. windywandering.blogspot.
com

Ipek Gur 147 (bottom)
www.flickr.com/ipek_gur

Christian Hackfeld 74 (t)
www.flickr.com/chrishimself
www.chrishimself.com

Barbara Hanson 40 (top l), 41
(bottom)
www.flickr.com/baha1210
www.barbaralhansonphotos.tumblr.
com/

Johann Hansson 83 (t)
www.flickr.com/plastanka

Luis Hernandez Diaz 142 (l), 143 (l)
www.flickr.com/d2k6
www.d2k6.es

Naomi Ibuki 132
www.flickr.com/777
www.transrealspace.wordpress.com

Kimberley Jansen 149 (top l)
www.flickr.com/kimberlyjansen

Leah Johnson 22 (top r & back flap,
bottom r)
www.flickr.com/leahleaf

Erik Jorgensen 109 (l)
www.neonhobos.tumblr.com

Travis Juntara 95 (r)
www.flickr.com/61360523@N04

Gary Koh 149 (top r)
www.flickr.com/silvr

Lindsey Kone 89, 135 (top r)
www.flickr.com/lindseykone

Grisha Kravchenko 28 (both)
www.ihaveacamera.ru

Nestor Lacle 62, 65
www.lostaruban.com

Richard PJ Lambert 66–67, 79
(bottom l, bottom r)
www.flickr.com/auspices
www.richardpjlambert.com

Jeansman Lee 41 (top r)
www.flickr.com/jeansman
www.analoguelovetw.tumblr.com/

Daniel Littlewood 86
www.flickr.com/daniellittlewood

Rosario Lopez 117 (top r)
www.flickr.com/61360523@N04

Justin Lynham 21 & back cover, 99 (l)
www.flickr.com/sadmafioso

Tim Lucas 131 (top r)
www.toolmantim.com
www.flickr.com/toolmantim

Ksenia Makas 145 (top l)
www.flickr.com/polnostyuvse
www.polnostyuvse.livejournal.com

Yuri Markevich 27
www.flickr.com/kozlozay

Sean Mason 137
www.flickr.com/smason

Kent Mercurio 41 (top l)
www.kentmercurio.com

Kasi Metcalfe 101
www.flickr.com/kasimetcalfe
www.2fatfeet.blogspot.com

John Millar 151 (both)
www.flickr.com/hermes-

Ellen Munro 105 (bottom l, top r)
www.flickr.com/ellenmunro

Carlos Novillo Martín 107 (top l)
www.flickr.com/rustifari

Justin Ornellas 43 (t), 131 (top l),
139 (l)
www.justinornellas.com

Danielle Page 127
www.flickr.com/ofyourmind

Alexandru Paraschiv 77, 114
www.flickr.com/alexandru-paraschiv

Phillip Pessar 112, 131 (bottom)
www.flickr.com/southbeachcars

Gina Pina (spine)
www.ginapina.com

Sergey Podatelev 83 (bottom)
www.flickr.com/brightnesslevels

Nicolas Quaegebeur/Stéphanie Kac
139 (top r)/Nicole Beyeler
139 (bottom r)
www.flickr.com/ikhaan
www.ikhaan.com

Federico Racchi 110–111
www.flickr.com/moja2

Eric Reeve 119 (t)
www.flickr.com/jericho_is_unruly

Sol Robayo 43 (bottom r)
www.flickr.com/solrobayo

Jaume Salvà i Lara 107 (bottom)
www.jaumesalvailara.com

Giovanna Santinolli 153
www.flickr.com/govannasantinolli

Jelle Schokker 40 (top r, bottom l)
www.flickr.com/jelles

Robin Shields 168

Andrius Sidlauskas 17 & back
cover, 19
www.flickr.com/nefotografas

Jim Smith 91, 93 (l)
www.iwantapony.net

Steven Snodgrass 163 (top r)
www.flickr.com/stevensnodgrass

Jaclyn Sollars 126
www.flickr.com/jaci_sue
www.avalonstudio.net

Julia Stapinski 122
www.flickr.com/rearrange

Mimi Sun 115
www.flickr.com/mimisun

Holly Swick 121
www.flickr.com/hollylovesfilm

Tamaro 63 & front flap
www.tamirophotography.com
www.flickr.com/shang-lumpia

Mikael Tigerström 160 (bottom)
www.flickr.com/dirigentens

Angela Trevithick 141, 142 (r)
www.flickr.com/bigglesmith

Miguel Vaca 97 (third top)
www.flickr.com/miguelvaca

Giorgio Verdiani 154 (l)
www.flickr.com/giorgioverdiani

Erin Vermeulen 149 (bottom)
www.flickr.com/privateale

Tom Verre 93 (r & front flap), 99 (r)
www.syntheye.com

Nikolas Vigier 59 & front flap
www.flickr.com/boklm
www.boklm.eu

Mike Warren 74 (bottom) & front flap
www.flickr.com/mikewarren

Bill Weisner 117 (bottom r)
www.flickr.com/miguelvaca

Barbara Werth 107 (top r)
www.flickr.com/mcbricker

Darren Wickings 73 (t)
www.flickr.com/boccaccio1

Peter Wilbourne 23 (b)
flickr.com/photos/27760134@N03
www.peterwilbourne.4ormat.com

Mike Martin Wong 103 (r)
www.flickr.com/squeakymarmot

Kam Yip 117 (top l, bottom l)
www.flickr.com/kamyip

Katsuhiko Yokota 57
www.flickr.com/yo___ko

Paulo Zapella 22 (top l, bottom l),
163 (l)
www.flickr.com/paulozapella

Web **sites**

MANUFACTURERS

A-Power
Holgaroid backs
www.doctor-and.com

Fuji
Film and Instax Mini cameras
www.fujifilm.com

Holga
Cameras
www.holgainspire.com

Lensbaby
Effects lenses
www.lensbaby.com

Lomography
Cameras, film, and community
www.lomography.com

Poladroid
Software
www.poladroid.net

Revolog
Handmade 35mm film
www.revolog.net

Rollei Creative film
Blackbird, Crossbird, Redbird, and Nightbird film
(and pre-loaded single-use cameras)
www.macodirect.de

SuperHeadz
Cameras
www.superheadz.com

ToyCamera AnalogColor
Software
www.pentacom.jp

OTHER

Flickr
Photographic community with countless
plastic camera groups
www.flickr.com

Four Corners Dark
Image, interviews, and reviews
www.fourcornersdark.com

Four Corner Store
Plastic cameras, film, and more
www.fourcornerstore.com

HolgaRama
Plastic camera store
www.holgarama.com

The Holga Darkroom
Holga photos, tips, and more
www.holgajen.blogspot.co.uk

Holga Direct
Camera sales, reviews, and interviews
www.holgadirect.com

LOMO
Original Russian LOMO company
www.lomoplc.com

Squarefrog
All things Holga
www.squarefrog.co.uk

ToyCamera.com
Toy camera community
www.toycamera.com

Acknowledgments

Very few books are produced in isolation, and this one is no exception. First and foremost I've got to thank all of the photographers listed on the previous pages for taking the time to contribute to this project and for sharing their fantastic images. A visit to their collective web/Flickr pages is well worth the effort if you're looking to get some plastic camera inspiration!

I'd also like to thank Phil Bennett at HolgaRama (www.holgarama.com) for the loan of a few cameras and assorted accessories, and Gabriel Da Costa at Fujifilm UK for the Instax kit.

Big thanks also to the guys at Ammonite Press: Richard Wiles for giving me the chance to write this book in the first place (and then bearing with me as deadlines sailed by...), and Robin Shields for patiently piecing the pages together.

Finally, love to my girls: N, T, and GM x

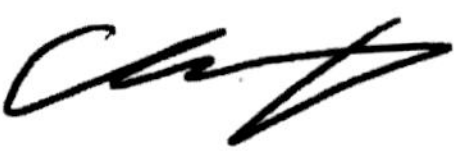

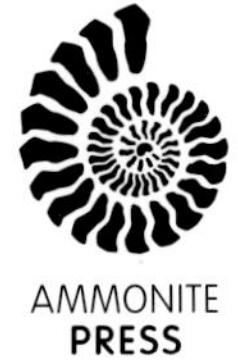

AMMONITE
PRESS